THE HISTORY OF
SUPERNATURAL

Art director: Keith Martin
Design manager: Bryan Dunn
Design: Louise Griffiths
Picture research: Helen Fickling
Publishing Director: Laura Bamford
Editors: Adam Ward and Trevor Davies
Production: Mark Walker

First published in Great Britain in 1997 by Hamlyn.
This edition published in 2000 by Chancellor Press,
an imprint of Bounty Books, a division of the
Octopus Publishing Group Ltd,
2–4 Heron Quays, London, E14 4JP

Copyright © 1997 Octopus Publishing Group Ltd

Reprinted in 2001

ISBN 0 75370 294 0

Produced by Toppan (HK) Ltd
Printed in China

THE HISTORY OF
SUPERNATURAL

Karen Farrington

CHANCELLOR
PRESS

CONT

ENTS

INTRODUCTION

Since the dawn of time man has sought to unravel the great mysteries of creation. To do so he has journeyed ever deeper into the shadowy realms of the supernatural. Yet still it appears he has only scratched the surface of a subject so broad that no one has defined its boundaries.

The ancient world contained ample evidence to prove the worth of the unworldly. Signs were perceived in the stars, in the weather and in the lie of the land. Cataclysmic natural events such as earthquakes, volcanoes – even rainbows – were accepted as the work of some all-powerful, unseen hand.

From these early studies of nature, local customs, superstitions and rituals evolved into major pre-Christian religions, the roots of which were firmly embedded in myth and magic.

As mankind grew intellectually sophisticated so the thirst for spiritual knowledge assumed greater importance. Princes and peasants alike still presumed themselves subject to an omnipotent power – a belief increasingly founded on intuition and a constant preoccupation with life after death.

World religions sought to provide the answers. So did philosophers, pseudo-scientists, magicians and even charlatans. The array of beliefs has become as diverse as it is fascinating. The thinkers of the present age are prone to influences. Hence the theory that poltergeists, long accepted as rogue spirits, are in fact manifestations of one person's hidden power and personality has come to the fore.

But for all the efforts made on its behalf the concept of a proven ultimate truth has remained tantalisingly elusive. The burden of proof has been too great to overcome and those convinced in the notion of unearthly or other-world influences at work in our everyday lives have become marginalised.

Science has perpetually scorned the attempts to validate the existence of supernatural forces. Consequently, there's still a natural reluctance among scientists and people to admit to a belief in, or an experience of, the paranormal for fear of being branded a lunatic. A century or more of fraudulent claims have further tarnished the business of psychical research. However, the barriers of rationalism and logic may yet be dismantled.

Inconclusive proof about the supernatural did not stop the late Hungarian-born writer Arthur Koestler and his wife Cynthia leaving their joint estate of £1.6 million for research into 'parapsychological phenomena' in 1983. It was sufficient to finance the Koestler Institute attached to Edinburgh University which has carried out some statistically fascinating research into Extra Sensory Perception. Institute staff work at enterprising ESP tests, avoiding sensationalism. According to latest results, it seems some people can receive telepathically sent messages from another person in a different room. The odds of this being a fluke result have been diminished to an insignificant 14 million to one chance. The problem remains that there is no foundation for knowledge without clear-cut evidence.

Yet even the most hardened sceptic must be troubled by strange instances which rear up beyond the boundaries of known truths. The nineties has seen resurgence in claims of the perplexing paranormal quest to sift through the evidence and weigh up the facts. The Koestler Institute reflects the modern desire to learn more about the unexplained. The supernatural has time and again shown itself unwilling to be minutely examined to everyone's satisfaction.

Little wonder that, despite technological advances beyond the comprehension of our forefathers, we are still absorbed by mysticism. Just as ancient mariners used a compass without understanding how it worked, so we may one day learn to accept supernatural phenomena as a simple fact of life, the last frontier of the mind.

RIGHT: *MEPHISTOPHELES AND MARGUERITE IN THE CATHEDRAL* – FRANK COWPER.

THE ANCIENT ARTS

Early man made the most of his resources –
fire, earth, air and water – but the elements
were not sufficient to fulfil all his needs. His
other concerns were food, fertility and death
– yet instinct was all he had to fall back on.
Against a background of uncertainty, magic
and mysticism emerged, playing increasingly
important roles. As life unfolded, ancient
civilisations searched for patterns which
could be interpreted to determine the most
successful way ahead.
The devil was also significant, an unseen
malevolent force which made itself felt
throughout everyday life.

CHAPTER ONE

MERLIN

Magician or madman, wily wizard or guardian of the good, Merlin is alive in the minds of schoolchildren today as mentor to the heroic King Arthur. But did he really live at all? The legend of Camelot's court magician has been scrutinised down the centuries, yet the facts are still few and hazy.

Much of today's perception of Merlin comes via Geoffrey of Monmouth, whose writings in the mid-12th century include *The Prophecies of Merlin* and *Vita Merlin,* a study of Celtic mysticism. Geoffrey had Merlin as the son of an earth mother coupled with an incubus, or devil. The angels of Hell proposed that the offspring of this union would be a force for evil on earth to counter-balance the good inspired by Jesus Christ. However, the baby was immediately baptised and embarked on a goodly life, but he retained the power of prophecy and miracle-making. Geoffrey describes Merlin as a talented engineer, a scholar and a mixer of drugs and mysterious potions.

ABOVE: IF MERLIN HAD LIVED, HE PROBABLY WOULD HAVE RESEMBLED THIS MAN IN SAXON GARB.

FIGHTING DRAGONS

A 6th century king of Britain, Vortigern, was trying to build a tower which persistently collapsed. His counsellors said that only the sacrifice of a boy born to a virgin would remedy this construction fault. The young Merlin was produced to Vortigern, his fate in the balance. But Merlin declared that a pool beneath the site of the tower was causing the tower to tumble. Furthermore, two dragons rested in the subterranean lake – a red one representing Wales and a white for the Saxons. Merlin explained how the dragons would emerge and fight until the Welsh red dragon was the victor, symbolising the day that the Welsh would finally overcome the might of the Saxons. Excavations soon proved Merlin right about the underground lake. And when Henry VII, a Welsh nobleman, took the throne in 1485 it was widely thought to be the fulfilment of Merlin's prophecy.

According to Geoffrey, Merlin went on to advise the next king of Britain, Ambrosius Aurelianus, on the subject of a suitable memorial for some treacherously slaughtered followers. Merlin described some mighty stones taken from Africa to Ireland by a vanished race of giants, which would be ideal if resited in Wiltshire, close to where the murders had been carried out by the villainous Hengist the Saxon. With the king's blessing, Merlin went to Ireland, purloined the stones known as the Giant's Dance, and flew with them over the Irish Sea to Salisbury Plain (perhaps with help from the Devil) where they were known thereafter as Stonehenge.

Henry VII.

Further portrayals of Merlin appear in Medieval French poetry and some Italian works, with each legend offering a fresh twist in the tale.

Christians have added a different emphasis. They depicted Merlin sporting the dark flowing robes of a monk when the pagan Druids were dressed in white; the sword in the stone appeared in a churchyard at Whitsuntide and Merlin was said to advise the Archbishop of Canterbury.

Much can be discarded – the ghost of Merlin said to haunt Merlin's Cave at Tintagel surely stems from the belief that the court of Camelot was sited there. Today we know that the castle at Tintagel was built in 1141 by Reginald of Cornwall, an illegitimate son of Henry I.

It now seems likely that Merlin was an ancient god linked to Britain. He was the 'evening star', while his twin sister Ganieda was the 'morning star'. A clue to this lies in an early name given to Britain, which translates as 'Merlin's Precinct'.

Modern writers identify Merlin as a Druid who acted as a shaman in Anglo-Saxon times, while over the years, Merlin has been variously characterised as a god and a magician.

Sir Thomas Malory introduced the 'sword in the stone' epic. Merlin, a wizard, raised the infant King Arthur, assisting him draw a sword apparently immovably lodged in a boulder.

THE BIRTH OF KING ARTHUR

When Ambrosius died and his brother Uther Pendragon came to the throne, Merlin contrived the birth of King Arthur by magically disguising Uther as heroine Igraine's husband. Following the birth of Arthur, Merlin faded out of Geoffrey's chronicles, having lived, impossibly, for well over two centuries.

Sir Thomas Malory published his book *Le Morte d'Arthur* in 1485, thus introducing the 'sword in the stone' epic. Merlin, a wizard, raised the boy Arthur, assisted him to the throne after inspiring him to draw a sword apparently immovably lodged in a boulder at Branstock. Malory's Merlin became infatuated by Nimue, also known as Viviane, who persuaded him to reveal his magic secrets. Some tales have him imprisoned forever by a spell cast by Nimue, under a stone, in a hawthorn tree or in a funnel of air. Others claim he went mad and spent his days living as a wild man in the woods.

THE TALE OF MERLIN AND ARTHUR WAS
MADE INTO *THE SWORD IN THE STONE* BY
THE DISNEY CORPORATION. NOW CHILDREN
IDENTIFY MERLIN AS THE KINDLY CARTOON
WIZARD WHO MAGICALLY TIDIES ROOMS.

Superstition is a form of layman's magic. In a bygone age beset by marauding devils and sorcery, people were constantly on the alert for possible harbingers of ill-fortune and looked to homespun remedies, such as crossing the fingers, to protect themselves and safeguard the future.

ANCIENT RITUALS

FRED⁺ SPURGIN

Nobel prize-winning zoologist Konrad Lorenz explains: 'For a living being lacking insight into the relation between causes and effects it must be extremely useful to cling to a behaviour pattern which has once or many times proved to achieve its aim, and to have done so without danger.'

CHIMNEY-SWEEPS, BLACKSMITHS AND LADDERS

Life among the superstitious is nothing if not complex. Take a popular folklore hero, the chimney sweep; seen as a bringer of good luck thanks to his connection with fire and hearth, a grimy-faced sweep is held to be an honoured wedding guest and a much-praised pedestrian who should be greeted with a bow. (Some say you should spit and make a wish when you see one.) Yet all this counts for nothing if the sweep is walking away from you when you happen across him. Then it's a sure sign that bad news will follow the encounter. A clean sweep, by the way, is disavowed of his lucky powers.

Blacksmiths are also believed to be lucky as they work with fire. Horses were once sacred beasts ridden by gods and symbolised fertility and virility, much of which has been conferred onto blacksmiths. Consequently, horseshoes – particularly those cast from the near hind-leg of a grey mare – are considered lucky. The best are those with four nails down one side and three down the other, seven being an auspicious number. Be sure to nail the horseshoe with its points upwards or the luck will pour out of it.

One of the most adhered to superstitions today is that of avoiding walking under a ladder. Ladders are sometimes seen as the route to heaven and those propped up over a path could be in use by any number of spirits. The ladder

The grimy chimney-sweep was a bringer of good luck, thanks to his connection with fire and hearth. He was an honoured wedding guest and a much-praised pedestrian who was to be greeted with a bow.

also forms a triangle, an ancient symbol of life and thought to represent the Father, the Son and the Holy Ghost. Anybody who breaks the triangle of this holy trinity does so at their peril! Those superstitious people who inadvertently walk under a ladder can remedy the situation by crossing their fingers, spitting over the left shoulder or staying completely silent until they see a four-legged animal.

THE THIRD LIGHT

The fear of the third light has numerous roots. Most likely is the possibility of offending the Holy Trinity. In the Russian Orthodox Church three candles were lit by the priest from one taper at funerals which helped to imbue the practice with ill fortune. During the First World War soldiers in the trenches who had a match alight for long enough to light three cigarettes were likely to be shot by an enemy sniper.

Knives have been held to have superstitious significance. In fact any metal object is said to have the potential to ward off witches. In olden

times a knife might be plunged into the front door of a home to protect the family from witches and fairies. Yet knives should never be crossed for an argument will follow. The giving of knives must also be accompanied by a coin to ensure that the friendship between the two parties remains intact.

Love and marriage are accompanied by volumes of superstitious lore. It's bad luck to have a lizard or a pig cross the path of a bride, to break something at the wedding feast or for the bride to see herself in a mirror while she's wearing her gown – this could prevent the marriage from taking place at all. The bride should leave her house right foot first, and hope that she does not encounter a funeral procession.

In England the bride may well be given an effigy of a black cat for luck, but in Belgium, Spain and America the black cat is seen as the symbol of very bad luck.

GODT NYTAAR!

As winter drew near, the superstitious Celts were gripped by fear. If the gods were angry the sun might never shine again. With the prolonged hours of darkness the spirits of the dead and assorted demons were free to roam the earth. Against this background of dread a special celebration evolved some 2,000 years ago to protect and nourish – Hallowe'en.

HALLOWE'EN

THE LORD OF THE DEAD

In Celtic Britain winter lasted from 1 November to 30 April and summer dawned on 1 May. The end of summer was officially on 31 October, a feast day dedicated to the lord of the dead, Samhain. Fires were lit which not only helped to rid communities of rubbish but also symbolised the renewal of the earth and lured the dead away from the homes of the living. Surplus livestock which could not be fed over the winter months were slaughtered, providing food for all. Sheep were mated to ensure next year's stock. At the height of the festival young boys would dip torches into the flames and run around the village to ward off evil spirits.

The most macabre element of the Samhain celebrations was the sacrifice of animals or even humans in a wicker cage. The Druids would divine the future by observing the victims' writhings as they were thrown into the fire.

In the autumn, the Romans had a festival called the Feralia, which honoured the recently deceased, and the feast of Pomonia, a tribute to the goddess of fruit, when apples and nuts were used in jocular games. During the Roman occupation of Britain the feast of Samhain was further coloured by these traditions.

AN EARLY 20TH CENTURY GREETING CARD IS EMBELLISHED WITH SYMBOLS OF HALLOWE'EN, INCLUDING THE JACK O'LANTERN.

Such powerful celebrations could not be ignored by the Church; the elders decided not to obliterate the centuries-old feast day. Instead they hijacked it. In A.D. 834 All Saints' Day was switched from 13 May to 1 November and so 31 October became All Hallows' Eve (Hallows being another word for saints).

ALL SOULS' DAY

In 988 the church instituted 2 November as All Souls' Day and pagans were urged to pray for the dead instead of to them. This meant that saints largely replaced the spectre of spirits. Despite this the habit of Hallowe'en still lingered on in Europe. Sir James Frazier, a 19th century writer on the occult, said about Hallowe'en: '...the time of year when the souls of the departed were supposed to revisit their old homes in order to warm themselves by the fire and to comfort themselves with the good cheer provided for them in the kitchen or the parlour by their affectionate kinfolk. It was, perhaps, a natural thought that the approach of winter should drive the poor, shivering, hungry ghosts from the bare fields and the leafless woodlands to the shelter of the cottage with its familiar fireside'.

This was the origin of the 'trick or treat' tradition which went to America with the Irish and Scottish immigrants. At the time the aim was to dress as a spirit in order to win the food left out for the dead.

WITH APPLES PLENTIFUL IN AUTUMN, GENERATIONS OF PEOPLE HAVE MIMICKED THE ROMANS BY PLAYING GAMES LIKE APPLE-BOBBING.

JACK O'LANTERN

The legend of Jack tells of a blacksmith, who made a deal with the Devil. For seven years Jack would be the best blacksmith in the world, but then he would have to give his soul to Satan. Before this date Jesus and St Peter visited the forge, offering Jack three wishes. To St Peter's horror, instead of a passage to Heaven, he asked for the power to keep someone in a nearby pear tree for seven years. His second and third wishes would have a victim confined to a chair and a purse for similar lengths of time.

When the Devil came to collect his soul, Jack had him climb the tree, sit in the chair and shrink into the purse until finally the evil spirit fled.

However, on Jack's death both St Peter and the Devil rejected him, so Jack was doomed to wander the earth, holding a turnip he had been eating containing a coal scooped up from Hell.

UNTIL THE FEN SWAMPLANDS WERE DRAINED AT THE START OF THE 20TH CENTURY, TRAVELLERS TOLD OF JACK O'LANTERN WHO HAUNTED THE MARSHES, DANCING AND CASTING SPELLS. IN FACT THE LIGHTS WERE PROBABLY MARSH GASES IGNITING, AN ENTIRELY NATURAL PHENOMENON.

As darkness fell, witches stole out of their houses to mount broomsticks, fire-rakes, cats or even hypnotised human beings, their destination was the sabbath or sabbat, the witches' orgy. The sabbath was a mixture of flames and feasting, with toads lurking in the undergrowth and owls dipping soundlessly overhead.

WITCHES' SABBATH

The food was, for the most part, stolen, although the centrepiece was a round, black, ceremonial cake. Sometimes there were black candles or alternatively an eerie funnel of flickering lights. To the sound of high-pitched chanting, witches danced, jerking in spasms of ecstasy as they evoked the devil.

Witches' sabbaths were special meetings unlike the weekly, low-key esbats. They were lurid, licentious and horribly frightening – it is likely that none ever took place.

A MYTH PRODUCED BY TORTURE

The descriptions of sabbaths came from the trials of witches accused in the 14th century. Under torture the victims used their wildest imaginings to satisfy the sadistic leanings of the inquisitors, who themselves further embellished the stories.

Like a snowball, tales about the sabbath picked up momentum. Before long, every interrogator was keen to know the details of how, when and where their victim marked the sabbath. As they brandished vile implements of torture, few were disappointed by the desperately involved descriptions of the 'witches'.

The inquisitors believed that dancing was evil because it could induce high emotion and even sexual excitement. This is undoubtedly how the folklore of a witches' ritual dance came into being; equally sex was frowned upon by the Church, which chose celibacy for its priests. The sexual element of sabbaths was intended to further demonise those involved. Years later psychoanalyst Sigmund Freud noted the enormous size of the penis in most depictions of the devil at a sabbath and observed that sexual repression certainly played a large part in the witch craze of the Middle Ages.

Of course, the brief of the inquisitors was to make their helpless prey appear as ferocious and

PAINTINGS LIKE THIS ONE BY GOYA IN 1797-98 GREATLY INFLUENCED THE PUBLIC'S CONCEPTION OF THE WITCHES' SABBATH. THE WITCHES SQUAT AROUND THE DEVIL WHICH APPEARS MORE ANTELOPE THAN GOAT.

evil as possible. It was essential to people that the fictional Sabbath had hags, demons, imps, familiars and, of course, Satan himself. In 1608, the writer Guazzo described a European sabbath in which the devil initiated an apprentice, accepted a posterior kiss from his followers and danced frenetically among them. Who could doubt the extreme and unsavoury measures taken against witches in the face of such evil? Furthermore, the procedure of the sabbath became a parody of the Catholic Holy Communion to arouse yet more dread among the population.

Accounts of frenzied witches sabbaths came from 14th century trials. Sadistic inquisitors extracted wild descriptions from their victims under torture.

There is another explanation for witches' sabbaths which was favoured in later years by the level-headed Lutherans and others. They thought that witches travelled to sabbaths only in spirit form, while their bodies remained at home apparently sleeping.

HORROR STORIES AND EXECUTIONS

In 1668 the people of Mora and Elfdale in Sweden were horrified to see their children fall into nightly trances. The whisper around the villages became a shout – the youngsters had become the tools of witches.

An investigation heard evidence from worried parents. But the most sensational tales came from the children themselves. One child after the other told of how they had been carried to a witches' sabbath at a place called Blakolla to the presence of a plump, jovial devil by the name of Locyta who gave them the ability to fly on broomsticks. The children were then initiated by Locyta and learned spells, feasted and danced. When they revealed their incredible stories to the stunned investigators it was in a deadpan and uniform way. One of the children accused, a young girl, explained how her spirit flew to the sabbath, while her body remained in bed.

CHILDREN WERE SACRIFICED TO THE DEVIL AT THE SABBATHS, ACCORDING TO THIS PRINT WHICH APPEARED IN THE 1896 EDITION OF JOHN ASHTON'S BOOK – *THE DEVIL IN BRITAIN AND AMERICA.*

As they were convinced that witches were at work, the judges were extremely harsh in their sentencing. Fifteen of the children aged between nine and 16 were executed. A further 60 of them were forced to endure a birching and a weekly caning for a year. Nowadays it seems likely that the children were the innocent victims of mass hypnosis, or may have taken a hallucinatory drug. The identity of this mystical 'Pied Piper' who was responsible for depriving the children of Mora and Elfdale of their minds was never revealed.

Reginald Scot, who was one of the first sceptics to throw doubt upon the very existence of witches in his book *Discoverie of Witchcraft* in 1583, certainly believed that the witches' sabbath was nothing more than a figment of festering minds, '. . . he is too much a fool and a blockhead, that supposeth those things to be done indeed, and corporally, which are by such persons fantastically imagined'.

INQUISITORS AND THE WITCH CRAZE

Catholic elders of the Middle Ages believed Europe was blighted by a witch epidemic. Their response was to send in the Inquisition. Already tried and tested against so-called heretics of previous centuries, the inquisitor monks had wide-ranging powers to seek out witches – and destroy them.

In 1484 Pope Innocent VIII issued a Papal Bull that stated that all '. . . (witches) do not shrink from committing and perpetrating the foulest abominations and filthiest excesses'. He subsequently urged all clergymen to assist inquisitors in nailing witches.

THE HAMMER OF WITCHES
His words were reinforced two years later by *Malleus Maleficarum* (Hammer of Witches), a book written by two discredited Dominican monks, Heinrich Kramer and Jakob Springer, who found themselves a niche as witch-hunters.

Malleus Maleficarum was the witch-hunter's Bible, giving advice on how to identify witches, the prosecution procedures, etc. So authoritative was the publication that folklore became fact and witchcraft was confused with devil worship. This meant that thousands of innocent women were burned at the stake.

ABOVE: GALILEO FELL FOUL OF THE VATICAN'S INQUISITION. IN 1632 HE HAD TO APPEAR BEFORE VENGEFUL ZEALOTS WHEN HIS SCIENTIFIC FINDINGS WERE IN OPPOSITION TO CHURCH LORE.

Witches were reputed to have an identifying mark shaped like a nipple. If the inquisitors failed to find a suitable mole or birthmark, they decided the mark was invisible. According to *Malleus Maleficarum* a pin or blade inserted into the mark caused no bleeding or pain to a witch. The inquisitors often used instruments with retractable points, so that the point seemed to pierce the skin without bleeding, when, in fact, it was pushed into the handle.

Giant scales were sometimes used in judging a witch. If the accused was heavier than the weights set against her then she was guilty. Sometimes the chosen weight was as light as a Bible.

Another method of judging witches was to tie the woman, naked and shivering, to a chair in a putrid cell and watch to see if a 'familiar' – a demon in animal form – approached. Given that the cells were generally infested with vermin the inquisitors were rarely disappointed. Witches were burned at the stake sometimes having been strangled prior to the fires being lit.

'THOU SHALT NOT SUFFER A WITCH TO LIVE'

For the Protestant witch-hunters one line of the Bible gave them the authority they desired. They interpreted literally Exodus xxii, v 18: 'Thou shalt not suffer a witch to live.'

While torture was never legalised in England, interrogators were happy to starve their victims into submission or deprive them of sleep for days. A convicted witch in England was hanged.

In Puritan England, witch finder Matthew Hopkins went to work as the self-styled 'Witch-finder General'. His stock in trade was brutally questioning elderly women until they confessed to being a witch and named their associates. Hopkins was welcomed as he travelled about in eastern England, rooting out 'witches' and receiving a fat fee for his services. He used all the tools of the inquisitor's trade, including the previously mentioned knives with retractable blades. About 400 people were sent to the gallows by Hopkins in just 14 months. His dubious methods were finally exposed and he retreated to his home town of Manningtree in Essex where he died in obscurity.

> *'Even if an attorney were allowed to the prisoner, the former would from the outset be suspected himself, as a patron and protector of witches, so that all mouths are shut and all pens are blunted.'*

In retrospect there seems little doubt that a mania overcame the populations of England and Europe, probably with insecurity in those changing times at its root. Those who spoke out publicly on behalf of convicted witches were themselves branded as devil worshippers and were put to death. Jesuit Friedrich Spee von Langenfield wrote in 1631 how he had prepared 200 people for death after they were convicted of witchcraft and heresy. All were innocent, he believed, and his hair had turned grey with stress.

'Even if an attorney were allowed to the prisoner, the former would from the outset be suspected himself, as a patron and protector of witches, so that all mouths are shut and all pens are blunted, and one can neither speak nor write.'

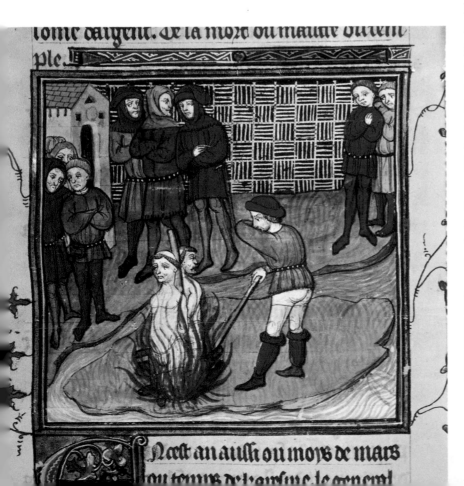

JACQUES DE MOLAY, LAST LEADER OF THE KNIGHTS TEMPLARS, WAS BURNED AT THE STAKE FOR DEVIL WORSHIP DESPITE THEIR SERVICE TO CHRISTIANITY.

In 1692 Salem was an unremarkable town in Massachusetts. In this Puritanical stronghold witch fever took hold and spread throughout the population; neighbour denounced neighbour and children accused well-respected townsfolk of hideous Satanic practices. Before the frenzy had evaporated it claimed the lives of 22 people. Two dogs were also executed for practising witchcraft.

SALEM WITCHES

ABOVE: COTTON MATHER THOUGHT SALEM WAS FILLED WITH WITCHES. BELOW: HALLOWE'EN-STYLE CAPERS, LIKE *SNAPP APPLE NIGHT* BY DANIEL MACLISE (1806-70), CONVINCED PURITANS EVIL WAS AFOOT.

The furore was sparked in the minds of impressionable children. A group of girls habitually met in the home of the local minister. Rev Samuel Parris had arrived in Salem from the West Indies and brought with him two slaves, John and Tituba. It seems Tituba, who was half-Carib and half-Negro, was still attached to the rituals of her ancestors and told the girls all about the magic of her people. They may have been genuinely affected by Tituba's words and actions. Or, given the strict Puritanical upbringing of the girls which even deemed dancing as evil, they may have felt guilt at witnessing un-Christian worship and believed they would get into serious trouble. What is certain is that nine-year-old Betty Parris, her cousin Abigail Williams, 11, and their friend Ann Putnam, 12, went hysterical.

GROANING, FLAILING AND WRITHING

Symptoms of groaning, flailing and writhing convinced their parents that the girls were bewitched. In February 1692 the girls named a trio of women who they claimed were responsible for casting spells upon them. They were Tituba, a beggar woman called Sarah Good and a widow by the name of Sarah Osburne. None of the three were church-goers and the ruling Puritans disapproved of them all. Tituba was obviously an outsider, Sarah Good was a pipe-smoking outcast and Sarah Osburne had offended many by living in sin before marrying her second husband.

Under interrogation Tituba furnished the Puritans with an imaginative confession, vivid with devil idolatry. The authorities took no further action against her as anyone who willingly confessed and implicated others walked free. It was those who refused to confess and maintained their innocence that were sent to the gallows.

The purge in Salem escalated rapidly, fanned by the words of men like Rev Cotton Mather of New England who had studied witchcraft and was convinced of its manifestation in the town. Over 400 people were arrested, among them five-year-old Dorcas Good, daughter of the doomed Sarah, who was chained up for more than seven months. Two people died in prison, including the sickly Sarah Osburne. Countless others fled.

THE TERRIBLE TOLL

Nineteen people were hanged, including Deputy Constable John Willard after he refused to make further arrests. Among the victims was former minister Rev George Burroughs, accused of seducing young girls into witchcraft and said to have bitten the girls he molested. Burroughs's body was dragged to a shallow grave and buried

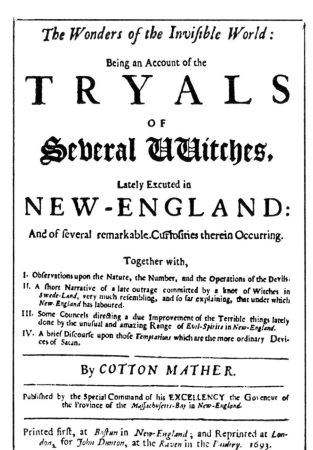

ABOVE: THE INGERSOLL TAVERN WAS THE SCENE OF THE INITIAL HEARINGS AT THE HEIGHT OF THE SALEM WITCH TRIALS.
BELOW: TITLE PAGE FROM A WITCH-HUNT PAMPHLET.

The Wonders of the Invisible World:

Being an Account of the

T R Y A L S

O F

Several Witches,

Lately Exuted in

NEW-ENGLAND:

And of feveral remarkable.Curfofities therein Occurring.

Together with,

I. Obfervations upon the Nature, the Number, and the Operations of the Devils.

II. A fhort Narrative of a late outrage committed by a knot of Witches in *Swede-Land,* very much refembling, and fo far explaining, that under which *New-England* has laboured.

III. Some Councels directing a due Improvement of the Terrible things lately done by the unufual and amazing Range of *Evil-Spirits* in *New-England.*

IV. A brief Difcourfe upon thofe *Temptations* which are the more ordinary Devices of Satan.

By COTTON MATHER.

Publifhed by the Special Command of his EXCELLENCY the Governeur of the Province of the *Maffachufetts-Bay* in *New-England.*

Printed firft, at *Bofton* in *New-England*; and Reprinted at *London,* for *John Dunton,* at the *Raven* in the *Poultry.* 1693.

with a hand, foot and his chin left exposed, as was the custom with witches. Burroughs had been the Rev Parris's predecessor and many of those accused were closely linked to the former parson.

Two women were hanged after numerous men in the town declared the pair transformed themselves into beasts and knocked on bedroom windows. The court proceedings were infected with hysteria. One court record tells how one of the accused 'fell down and tumbled about like a Hog'. When the courthouse roof collapsed one of the accused, Bridget Bishop, was thought to have put 'the evil eye' on it, forcing it to crumble with just one look.

Most disgraceful of all was the pressing to death of Giles Cory, who was in his eighties. When he refused to plead he was pinned down in an open field and rocks were piled high on his chest to make him plead guilty or not guilty so he could be tried. Cory died rather than dignify the ludicrous proceedings with a plea.

By October 1692 the people of Salem wearied of bloodshed and hysteria and the persecution stopped. A day of mourning was declared and judges and juries apologised to bereaved families.

CONCEP- TIO.

PRÆG- NATIO.

COLOR CŒLESTINUS.

COLOR CŒLESTINUS.
cum tua terra nigra.

WHITE MAGIC

White magic is, in many ways, at the heart of the 20th century revival in paganism and so-called New Age cultures. Rather than a specific art in itself, it is more a generic term in which the power of nature is deployed through ritual as a force for good, curing the ills of individuals or, indeed, whole communities. Perhaps green magic is a more accurate term. Some would claim that all magic is white and that it is perverted only by those who twist it for their own evil ends. Other sectors of society believe magic of any hue is sinful.

CHAPTER TWO

For centuries alchemy was akin to the quest for the Holy Grail. Once alchemists had cracked the code to the mysteries of life, they knew they would have the most precious and powerful abilities at their fingertips. Like the Grail the alchemists' dream remained elusive.

ALCHEMY

Alchemists were the avid pioneers of science, but worked from a different perspective from modern chemists. Theirs was an age of mysticism in which equal emphasis was placed on supernatural forces and on natural, earthly power. Here was an extraordinary crossbreed attempting to turn the physical into the metaphysical.

THE ELIXIR OF LIFE AND THE PHILOSOPHER'S STONE

The dream was to discover the elixir of life, ensuring immortality through wisdom. In addition there was the lure of turning base metals into gold using the sought-after philosopher's stone, an aim interpreted now as a metaphor for spiritual development. Some alchemists were devoted to finding a universal medicine that would cure the ills of mankind.

Among those who practised alchemy were the distinguished scholar and philosopher St Thomas Aquinas, who called it a 'true but difficult art'. Pope John XXII was devoted to it and many monasteries pursued the technique. King Charles II of England even had a laboratory built in his bedroom.

Alchemy has a double-pronged history developing simultaneously in 3 B.C. in the ancient cultures of both Egypt and China. The Egyptian strain, which was strongly influenced by the Greeks, became categorised as Western alchemy. Its founder was reputed to be Hermes Trismegistus, the mythical figure based on the gods Thoth and Hermes.

The Egyptian god Thoth was associated with mystical wisdom, magic and writing. When large numbers of Greeks moved to ancient Egypt, they discovered Thoth was almost identical to their own god Hermes and the two were conjoined. The myth of Hermes Trismegistus described how he ruled for 3,226 years as a wise king and wrote 36,525 books on the principles of nature. Although most of his works were lost in a great fire, the fragments that remained were buried in a secret place.

One of the legendary works, the *Emerald Tablet*, is believed to be inscribed with the secrets of the universe and it is this that alchemists held dear. Trismegistus declared, 'The wise man rules nature; not nature the wise man . . . The will of man extends over the depth of the sea and the height of the firmament.' It was clearly a very enticing thought.

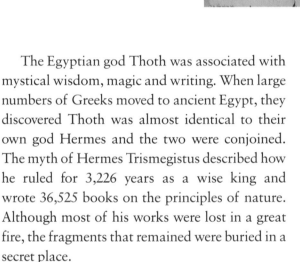

ABOVE: 16TH CENTURY IMPRESSION OF AN ALEMBIC, DISTILLING APPARATUS WITH THE COMPLEX FORMULAE BY WHICH IT WAS BELIEVED ALCHEMISTS PRODUCED THE PHILOSOPHER'S STONE.

The Egyptians devised the scientific process of joining opposites, involving the four 'elements' – fire, earth, air and water – as set out by Aristotle. To the Egyptians sulphur represented the soul, thought to be masculine, while mercury was the spirit, which was female. Centuries later, European alchemists added salt, symbolising the body, to the vital ingredients. The Egyptian tradition spread through the Roman and Arab cultures before arriving in Europe via Spain.

One can only speculate on the success of the alchemists. However, during railway construction in 1963 a wealth of artefacts were found. Among them was a copper cylinder and an iron rod, almost certainly an early electrical cell. It was dated from the Parthian period, about 200 B.C. An early triumph of the alchemists? Jewellery of that period was known to be gold or silver plated. It could be that alchemists stumbled on a voltage device while attempting to transform base metals.

ABOVE RIGHT: *THE ALCHEMIST*, BY TENIERS PERCE, GIVES US AN INSIGHT INTO THE LABORATORIES OF CENTURIES PAST. BELOW: ELIZABETHAN ASTROLOGER AND ALCHEMIST JOHN DEE, WITH PARTNER EDWARD KELLEY, ATTEMPTED TO RAISE THE DEAD IN A GRAVEYARD AT WALTON-LE-DALE, LANCASHIRE.

THE AGE OF REASON

It was only when Robert Boyle published his *Sceptical Chymist* in 1661 that the long accepted principles of alchemy were finally questioned. Transparent greed on behalf of the alchemists diminished their reputation. The age of reason prevailed and alchemy went out of fashion.

Alchemy also developed by word of mouth in China where it was mostly devoted to the pursuit of immortality by the repeated distillation of elixirs. It was closely linked to Taoism, China's only indigenous religion.

In India, too, alchemy flourished and the 'wisdom of life' medicine was sought from about 1000 B.C. Yoga played a vital role in both aspects of Eastern alchemy.

It was this deeply philosophical approach to alchemy which attracted the interest of Carl G. Jung and sparked a revival of the culture in the 20th century.

ALCHEMISTS RECORDED THEIR PROGRESS IN SYMBOLISM WHICH WAS, FOR THE MOST PART, INDECIPHERABLE. ONE ALCHEMIST MIGHT BE ABLE TO COMPREHEND THE EXPERIMENTS OF THE NEXT ONLY IF HE HAD A WIDE-RANGING UNDERSTANDING OF THE FELLOW'S PERSONAL PHILOSOPHY. QUALIFICATION AS AN ALCHEMIST INCLUDED AN EXEMPLARY CHARACTER – PURE IN THOUGHT AND DEED.

CHARMS AND TALISMEN

Sever the hand of a recently hanged man and you have a passport to riches and power. That was according to rogues of the 18th century who would dry the limb, pickle it and turn it into a candleholder. A light flickering from the macabre charm was said to bewitch all around, allowing thieves to pillage homes and shops at will.

There's no evidence that the gruesome procedure ever worked and there must have been many vagabonds left pondering what went wrong as they were marched off to the jail by furious homeowners.

Episodes like these appear bizarre but they do show the faith that people placed in charms, amulets and talismen. Even today there are those who cherish certain bracelets or a rabbit's foot.

'A MEANS OF DEFENCE'

An amulet can be an object, an inscription, a drawing or a symbol. The word probably comes from the old Latin term *amoletum*, which translates to 'means of defence'. Amulets are intended to deflect and protect against ill fortune and are usually worn close to the skin for maximum benefit. The article matters little. It is the belief that people place in them that is the key. If someone sets out for a long journey with a beloved amulet they feel reassured and enjoy a sense of wellbeing. Without it they feel exposed to nameless, faceless terrors and accordingly perform less well.

Most amulets are natural objects with special virtues, for example stones with holes, a four-leafed clover or a beautifully veined rock. The range extends to religious inscriptions written in Latin, Hebrew or Islamic script, animal and human parts or quirks of nature like oddly shaped vegetables. The power of the inscription would be particularly potent in days when few

ABOVE: THE EYE OF HORUS ON THE SIDE OF A BOAT IN ISTANBUL IS SAID TO PROTECT AGAINST EVIL AND THE POWERS OF THE UNDERWORLD.

people could read and, even today Muslims carry around with them passages from the Koran or a miniature volume, while the sign of the cross is one of the most popular amulets in the modern Western world.

The magic word abracadabra, known to even the smallest child, was long believed to have magical protective powers. In A.D. 2 the physician Quintus Serenus Sammonicus said that the word abracadabra inscribed on an amulet and worn around the neck would relieve the symptoms of fever. After nine days it had to be thrown over the shoulder into an east-flowing river.

Images of eyes have long held a mythological significance, particularly imitations of the eye of Horus. In ancient Egypt, Horus was the benign hawk-headed sky god who was in conflict with the evil Seth. Legend has it that after Horus castrated Seth, depriving him of his powers, Seth tore out the eye of Horus and buried it. This symbolic eye is supposed to ward off evil spirits.

Horse brasses, although now purely ornamental, were first made to repel evil spirits from vulnerable steeds.

The magic word 'abracadabra' was thought to have protective powers from as early as A.D. 2, particularly against fevers.

ELIZABETHAN INJUNCTIONS

Amulets are often confused with charms. Strictly speaking a charm involves an incantation – the word derives from the Latin *carmen*, meaning a song, such as 'Hiccough, hiccough go away, Come again another day'. Closely associated with witchcraft, charms were abolished in England in 1559 by the Elizabethan Injunctions which banned 'charms, sorcery, enchantments, invocations, circles, witchcraft, soothsaying or any such like crafts or imaginations invented by the devil'.

Today, charms are seen as lucky icons. A corn dolly, traditionally made from the last tuft of a harvest, is a symbol of good fortune. The lowly rabbit became something of a target after its foot was found to bring luck. Ironically, they were considered bad omens for seafarers, yet rabbits are associated with the powers of witchcraft, speed, fertility and the renewal of spring.

A talisman is another traditional name for an object, drawing or symbol of good luck, endowed with magic powers to bring about wealth, health, fertility, virility and even power. They are active rather than passive, like amulets. Magic swords, such as Excalibur, and magic lamps are talismen.

Holy relics with the power to heal are also considered talismen. The most notorious is the Holy Grail, often sought but never found. Traditionally, there are three ways talismen are given powers. The first is by nature, the second by God or the supernatural and the third is by magic.

EXCALIBUR, THE FAMOUS ARTHURIAN TALISMAN, IS RETURNED TO THE DEEP BY A SPIRIT HAND.

Bizarrely, after a knife-cut, it was the weapon that was given treatment, rather than the injury.

PLANTS AND HEALING

When the village wise women of old mixed a potion containing the plant woody nightshade to combat tumours, it was considered to be magic. However, when researchers at the University of Wisconsin in America discovered in 1966 that an extract of the very same plant helped in healing cancer in mice, it was celebrated as a triumph of modern science.

The Indians of Peru ground the bark of the cinchona tree and used the powder to soothe those who had a fever; the medical pioneers of the 17th century discovered quinine in the very same tree and successfully administered it to relieve sufferers of malaria. For years healers praised the qualities of the foxglove for those who were struck down with heart ailments. Much later the healing properties of the drug digitalis, also from the foxglove plant, was extolled by doctors.

Soldiers' wounds were treated with mouldy bread long before the discovery of penicillin.

CUTS CURED WITH A KNIFE

Without a doubt, the herbalists were on to something. But before abandoning the prescribed pills that are dispensed by pharmacies today, you should bear in mind the cow dung poultices made up for cancers and the chicken-dung-and-lard poultices for pneumonia. It seems comical today to consider that once upon a time, after someone was cut by a knife, it was the weapon that was given treatment rather than the injury. Sometimes the offending knife was plunged into the earth, sometimes it was cleaned until the wound healed. In extreme cases an ointment made up of bizarre ingredients such as boar's grease, powdered worms and the moss from a disinterred human skull was applied to the offending blade.

In addition to the folklore cures, there were remedies borne out of ritual. The plant St John's Wort was widely held to cure nervous disorders, but only when the plant was picked on Midsummer's Eve. The herb vervain, used to staunch

The left portion of the page contains an illustration from a medieval manuscript showing a mandrake plant in human form chained to a dog, surrounded by Latin manuscript text. The labels "Mandra gore" and "655" are visible within the illustration.

A 12TH CENTURY MEDICAL TREATISE SHOWING A MANDRAKE PLANT WITH FETID LANCE-SHAPED LEAVES AND A ROOT IN HUMAN FORM CHAINED TO A DOG.

piles of stones at crossroads to please their gods, while anyone who had recently eaten garlic was forbidden to enter certain temples. There is an Islamic legend which says, 'When Satan stepped out from the Garden of Eden after the fall of man, Garlick sprang up from the spot where he placed his left foot and Onion from that where his right foot touched.'

The corpse robbers at work during the plagues thought they could protect themselves from infection by drinking a mildly antiseptic, garlic-based potion. During the First World War the wounds of French soldiers were treated with garlic.

Today garlic is thought something of a wonder food. Scientists believe that, thanks to its sulphur content, garlic lowers blood pressure, reduces cholesterol production in the liver and raises levels of the beneficial lipoproteins in the blood. It can also be a decongestant if taken raw and has anti-viral and anti-bacterial properties. Its drawbacks, besides the odour, are its potential for causing headaches and skin complaints.

Various plants have had various superstitions attached, i.e. beans – the souls of the dead were thought to dwell in bean fields and those who slept in one overnight were likely to wake insane.

MANDRAKE AND DEMONS

The lengthy brown root of the mandrake was used as an anaesthetic in operations at around the time of Christ. It was also held as a cure for insanity and as an exorcising drug – demons being unable to tolerate its smell. Considered deadly to the gatherer because of its Satanic associations, dogs were used to haul it out of the ground.

Warts were once rubbed with a potato, which was then discarded. As the tuber rotted, so did the wart. This could be lifesaving as warts were interpreted as a witch's mark. When the humble spud came to England, it was marketed as an aphrodisiac and sold at over £250 per pound. Today it is known as a source of starch, fibre, potassium and Vitamin C – and the price has plummeted.

Linked to disaster or death, superstitious herbalists would try not to transplant parsley or give it away – in fact it is full of Vitamin C and iron. Rosemary is said to grow only in gardens where the woman rules the house; it soothes indigestion, headaches, neuralgia and colds.

the blood flow from wounds, was only ever used medicinally if it was picked at certain phases of the moon, whilst chanting a series of spells.

The accompanying rituals have little credibility today, yet in those days, patients were unable to tell whether it was the herb, the relevant moon phases or the incantations that induced healing.

GARLIC AND THE DEVIL

For years garlic was believed to have many healing qualities in various cultures. Perhaps deterred by the powerful odour, the ancient Greeks left it on

In the realms of the supernatural fur and feather have an exalted place. Animals were of key importance as familiars to witches, pets who were thought to be possessed by spirits, demons and imps. There were few witch-hunters who were unable to come up with evidence of a suspect's resident familiar, be it cat, dog, toad, mouse or fly.

ANIMALS

The cat became widely associated with witch-craft and feline familiars were reputedly fond of ghosts purring affectionately in the company of invisible spirits, while dogs and horses took fright. Witches were said to assume the appearance of cats, which led to people refusing to chat freely in the presence of their cats in case witches learned their innermost secrets.

Witches were said to transform themselves into a hare and steal the milk from cows. Isabel Gowdie recited to Scottish witch-finders of the spell which she used to turn herself into a hare. 'I shall go intill a hare, With sorrow and sych and meikle care; And I shall go in the Devil's name, Ay while I come home again.'

Allegedly, the only way to rid the countryside of a witch-hare was to shoot it with a silver bullet. Instead of a hare's body, you might find an old lady's corpse, or the witch may lay dead at home.

THE HOOT OF AN OWL

Another animal linked to witchcraft and considered to be an omen of ill fortune was the owl, a bearer of bad tidings. Its hoot was once said to precede news of a death. An owl which hooted near the home of a maiden was thought to be telling the world that she had lost her virginity. Who can say how many young girls were tormented by this random symbolism?

Whistling birds – like curlews, whimbrels or plovers – were thought to represent the tortured souls of unbaptised babies, or drowned seamen trying to warn former shipmates of danger.

A single magpie is widely known as an unlucky sight. To counter it people might raise their hats and greet the bird, cross themselves, or spit thrice over their right shoulder and once in

ABOVE: THE WITCH'S CAT WAS MORE THAN JUST A CUTE FELINE. IT WAS BELIEVED TO BE A DEMON IN A FUR COAT CAPABLE OF INCREDIBLE FEATS, INCLUDING SPYING ON NEIGHBOURS AND REPORTING BACK THEIR INNERMOST SECRETS.

the direction of the bird before saying, 'Devil, devil I defy thee'. Superstitious Somerset folk carried an onion to repel the evil brought by the bird.

Other animal activities that warned of death were said to be an adder on the doorstep; a bat flying three times around the house; a cow breaking into the garden, a butterfly at night; a plague of mice and a toad hopping over someone's foot.

Lucky animals include the cock who crows at dawn to disperse the night's evil spirits, thus their image was put upon weather vanes and steeples. A 19th century builder wishing to protect a church from evil buried a cock in the foundations.

Other sacred birds include robins – stained with blood trying to relieve Christ's suffering on the cross – swallows, wrens, ravens and doves. Shape-shifting witches were allegedly unable to transform into doves, while the sick were kept from death if they used a pillow of dove feathers.

TRAVEL TO THE LAND OF THE DEAD

Celts believed their souls travelled to the land of the dead on horseback and horses in the Middle Ages were imbued with clairvoyant powers. An indication of the powerful imagery attached to them is the 374-ft-long White Horse carved out of the chalk-bottomed turf at Uffington, Berkshire, the handiwork of an unknown Celtic tribe.

Much folklore attached to animals stems from the practice of augury, particularly potent in

The ancient Roman practice of augury has provided much of the folklore which surrounds animals and birds.

Roman times. An augur observed wildlife and predicted the future from their antics. Usually, an animal emerging from the right was lucky while any wandering from the left brought bad luck.

Although augury went out of fashion, there have been amazing incidents in which animal behaviour might have forewarned man. Animals fled from the island of Krakatoa in 1883, jumping into the sea and swimming for their lives, days before the volcano erupted. In October 1923 the residents of Tokyo were driven mad by the howling of dogs. As their pets fell silent a massive earthquake struck. If the Japanese had known that, just one year earlier, the cats of Copiapo in Chile had deserted the town before an earthquake the signs might have been better read.

Given the apparent inner powers of animals, it is hardly surprising that mankind has sought, like King Solomon, to communicate with them.

ABOVE: WOLVES WERE HATED, AS MARAUDERS AND SYMBOLS OF WITCHCRAFT. THEY WERE HANGED ALONGSIDE CRIMINALS.
LEFT: A MAGICAL STONE TO BE EXTRACTED FROM THE HEAD OF A TOAD FEATURED IN MANY MAGICAL FORMULAE.

Superficially, many of the world's tribes appear primitive. Only on closer inspection does the advanced spirituality displayed by the majority of the third world peoples give the Westerner food for thought.

TRIBAL MYSTICISM

In prehistoric times, hunters donned the skins and heads of animals in order to approach herds unseen or sought to achieve the powers of the given animal, for example, the strength of a horse or the speed of a deer. Many tribal dances still feature animal heads and skins. As the ancient tribesmen sought a greater control over their lives they turned evermore to magic.

Today we can only speculate on the meaning of the symbols and signs that survived from those times. The Totem Stones of Easter Island are a staggering example of ancient mysticism. Here are 593 statues carved out of volcanic rock, standing 10–50 ft high, their purpose presumably linked to funeral rites. Hieroglyphic tablets at the feet of the statues were burned by fearful missionaries of a previous century. Even now the culture of this Polynesian island is shrouded in mystery.

Cave drawings have also given clues to the spiritual development of tribes. French Neolithic cave paintings show the significance of masks, depicting men wearing them during ritual dances. From North America, across the Pacific Islands, to India, Europe and elsewhere, the mask was a sacred object and the wearer adopted its spirit.

FIREWALKING RITUALS

Firewalking is another amazingly mystic ritual. In 1637 the French Jesuit Father Paul Lejeune was attempting to convert the Huron Indians near Quebec to Christianity. To display their own powers they drew glowing coals from the fire, rubbed them against their bodies and even put hot stones into their mouths, apparently without ill effect.

Firewalking occurs around the world, with participants going barefoot across burning pits 30–60 ft in length without damage to their skins. To prepare themselves, firewalkers chant and meditate to reinforce their strong belief that they will not be harmed. The practice was recorded as long ago as A.D. 1, and it is familiar in many cultures, including those in India, Japan, the Pacific Islands, New Zealand and the Balkans.

Some claim that sweat and saliva act as a protective barrier to firewalkers. Others believe the brain secretes special substances that affect chemical changes in the body. US plasma physicist Dr Bernard Leikind reports that coals are variously hot. Just as you would not suffer serious burns from putting your hand in an oven (until you touched the oven shelf) nor would you from walking across hot coals. Sadly, there are those who have sustained severe injuries. Firewalkers contend that it shows the power of the mind over matter, that the hypnotic trance in which they place themselves gives them an immunity to pain.

THE DOGON TRIBE

There are still more mystifying aspects of tribal life. In the mid-1950s, French anthropologists Marcel Griaule and Germaine Dieterlen emerged from years of studying a central African tribe with an incredible story. The Dogon of the southern Sahara had revealed an amazing knowledge of astronomy. Their worship of the star Sirius – the brightest in the sky – was understandable, but their tributes to Sirius B were staggering. Sirius B, a star which revolves around Sirius, is invisible to the naked eye and was only discovered with a powerful telescope in 1862. It wasn't photographed until 1970. Tribesmen were aware that it takes 50 years for tiny Sirius B to orbit Sirius and that it's an elliptical orbit, not a circular one. The Dogon also knew Sirius B as 'the heaviest star' and indeed it possesses enormous density.

The Dogon tribe believe that many years ago fish-tailed aliens visited them to impart this specialised knowledge. While scientists are sceptical of the role of extraterrestrial missionaries, they are hard pushed to give another explanation.

The exact knowledge gained by a few isolated tribes with no sophisticated instruments at their disposal is intriguing. Perhaps ancient cultures which thrived around the Mediterranean were thousands of years ahead of Galileo in inventing the telescope and studying astronomy. Perhaps tribesmen heard these stories as they travelled the region. Or perhaps beings from the Sirius galaxy – whose likenesses coincide with ancient drawings of gods in Babylon, Egypt and Greece – visited earth before vanishing. Without further proof, the sceptical Westerner refuses to believe such a thing. The spiritually aloof Dogon, however, do not question the wisdom of ages.

ABOVE: AN AZTEC ENGRAVING REVEALS THE VIOLENT SACRIFICE OF A DEER.
BELOW: A NAMPUKI MASK FROM MALEKULA, MOULDED FROM TREE FERN AND EMBELLISHED WITH VEGETABLE FIBRES AND PIG TUSKS, WAS A KEY PART OF PIG SACRIFICES.

For years white men in North America had been eating into native American territories, trampling over sacred sites and annihilating ancient traditions. During the 1880s, according to the tribes of the west, the south-west and the plains, the white man was facing imminent destruction. Dead tribesmen would come alive again and native Americans would live side by side in harmony with nature.

TRIBAL RITES

THE GHOST DANCE

Native Americans were urged to take part in the Ghost Dance, a modification of an ancient dance intended to honour the dead. A mystic called Wowoka of the Paiute tribe described a vision of water and mud that was going to cover the earth and wipe out the whites. Native Americans would be saved through their circular dance.

Word of the Ghost Dance spread rapidly, with tribal dancers donning shirts rich with eagle feathers and painted with red symbols. White men were concerned at the way their impending doom was so warmly received, particularly among tribes like the Sioux, and in November 1890 the Ghost Dance was banned from all Sioux reservations. The dance continued illicitly and troops were called into the Rosebud and Pine Ridge reservations. There was a struggle and Chief Sitting Bull of the Hunkpapas was killed along with several of his men.

Big Foot, leader of the Miniconjou, was arrested and taken with his people to camp at Wounded Knee Creek. On 29 December 1890, after bungled intervention by cavalry soldiers,

about 300 defenceless native Americans were slaughtered there, a massacre which marked the end of the Ghost Dance fervour.

THE SUN DANCE

Another tribal rite popular with many American Indians was the Sun Dance. Its origins lay with the plains native Americans; its purpose was to promote health, fertility and plentiful food. Although the dance was deeply symbolic for the tribespeople who took part, it was abhorrent to white observers because of the self-abuse incorporated into it. Banned at the turn of the century, it wasn't until 1978 that the American Indians were lawfully allowed to hold a Sun Dance again.

Although details vary among tribes, the main element is a sweat lodge built of sticks and made steamy by sprinkling holy water onto burning

ABOVE: PRIESTS IN THE CARIBBEAN GATHERED THEIR COURAGE THROUGH MUSIC, TRANCE AND DANCE AS THIS PICTURE BY BERNARD PICART, PRODUCED AROUND 1700, SHOWS.

> *'As the drum beats, it establishes the heartbeat for the dancers, our tribe and all mankind. We feel this link in our hearts, we reach into our innermost centre.'*

coals. Those entering the lodge purify themselves among the elements of earth, fire, water and air.

Male dancers are painted with symbols, the flesh pierced, either on the breast or back, with wooden poles inserted into the bloodied holes. Ropes or thongs from the pegs extend to a central pole and are bound to it, representing the joining of the human spirits with that of the Great Spirit. Dancers, blowing whistles made of eagle bones, then dance frenziedly with their faces to the sun.

The dance lasts up to four days. Most dancers rip themselves free of the binding as they dance, while the others are cut free. Onlookers encourage the dancers to continue and tend their wounds. The suffering is a key to the ritual – flesh symbolises darkness and ignorance; ripping the flesh represents freeing the tribe of such burdens.

Thomas Yellowtail, Sun Dance chief of the Crow tribe, explains the mystic significance of the occasion: 'As the drum beats, it establishes the heartbeat for the dancers, our tribe and all mankind. We feel this link in our hearts, and when the drum gives its call and the dancers respond by blowing their eagle bone whistles, we reach into our innermost centre and blessings penetrate all those present the same time that our prayers rise up to all the universe.'

ABORIGINAL TRACKERS

Aborigines are also known for their psychic abilities. In April 1943, Jack Murray, superintendent of the aboriginal settlement of Delissaville, Darwin, set out by launch with expert tracker Mosic and another aborigine to search for a missing airman. As they motored along, Mosic suddenly pointed to a creek, much the same as any other. Murray turned down it and they continued until Mosic steered the boat to the bank. It was, said Mosic, identical to his dream the night before. While Murray was pondering this statement, the faint cries of a downed US airman reached them. Lieutenant Pete Johnson was not even the pilot that Murray had been sent to find. Johnson had bailed out of his blazing aircraft six days earlier and was already presumed dead. The rescue party arrived just as Johnson had decided to commit suicide, tormented by insects.

THE NATIVE PEOPLE OF NEW GUINEA ADOPT A VARIETY OF PERSONAS WHEN THEY DON A RITUAL MASK AND COSTUME.

PATH OF DARKNESS

People have always sought to lay the blame for the ills of the world at somebody's door. Who better to take the rap than the devil and his earthbound agents, witches?

The devil (a.k.a. Satan, Lucifer, Beelzebub, Belial, Exu and others) became the scapegoat for all the mishaps and evils that befell mankind, the universal impression of the devil was one of a blackened beast with horns, tail and cloven hooves.

Down the centuries, folklore, literature and art have helped to broaden the view, but the classic devil image is hard to shift.

CHAPTER THREE

SATANISM AND BLACK MAGIC

Satan is the linchpin of the black arts, yet there are several ways of paying homage to Old Scratch, just as there are different strands to Christianity. Most observers lump one kind of devil worship in with the next, and who can blame them?

The secrecy that characteristically surrounds devil worship and black magic makes it difficult to unravel. In the case of devil worship, it is impossible to come up with a national or international number of Satanists as few centres of their activities will voluntarily provide statistics. Few followers today believe that Satan is the rightful ruler of earth who was usurped by God. Most view Satanism as a route to material wealth and earthly power.

CHURCH OF SATAN

Satanism came out of the closet on 30 April 1966 when the flamboyant Dr Anton Szandor LaVey launched the Church of Satan in San Francisco, peppered with inverted crosses and elaborate rituals. This was during the Swinging Sixties and LaVey capitalised on the desire among many rebellious teenagers and young adults to have drugs and sex on demand.

Delighted with the response to his church, LaVey produced *The Satanist's Bible* in 1969, which detailed the philosophies and rituals he favoured. The book has sold 800,000 copies worldwide – the Swedish edition was launched in

ABOVE: IN MEXICO THE FEAST OF THE DEAD, 2 NOVEMBER, IS MARKED BY THE DISTRIBUTION OF SUGAR SKULLS EACH BEARING A NAME TO FAMILIARISE THE RECIPIENT WITH THE NOTION OF DEATH.

'The cult attracted them because it offered a simple explanation for their inadequacies: they were bewitched or under an unlucky star or not vibrating to the right rhythm.'

1996 – and LaVey's church has become the *modus operandi* for numerous other Satanic groups.

Public tolerance of the thriving Satanist sect was put to the test by the horrific killings of pregnant Sharon Tate, hairdresser Jay Sebring and three others by Charles Manson's 'Family', who appeared to be deeply embroiled in devil worship.

A former animal trainer and official police photographer, LaVey began seriously to doubt the virtue of God after seeing terrible scenes of death and destruction on the streets. He crystallised his view of the dark path. 'Satan is a symbol, nothing more. He's a symbol of man's carnal nature – his lust, greed, vengeance, but most of all, his ego. Satan signifies our love of the worldly and our rejection of the pallid, ineffectual image of Christ on the cross.'

On the back of philosophical Satanism came those with an interest in sadism and various forms of sexual deviancy. There is also increasing evidence that drug cartels have used devil worship in order to ensure loyalty among their workers.

American social scientist Dr Edward Moody joined the Church of Satan to see what motivated its congregation. He discovered that it was commonly made up of inadequate and marginalised members of society. 'The cult attracted them because it offered a simple explanation for their inadequacies: they were bewitched or under an unlucky star or not vibrating to the right rhythm. their failure was supernatural, the remedy was supernatural. The rites and medicines of the church promised the success that had so far eluded them.'

WORSHIP OF SETH

The Church of Satan split in the 1980s and those opposed to LaVey began the Temple of Set, led by Michael Aquino. The idol they put up for worship was Seth, the Egyptian associated with drought and starvation. Other Satanic groups include the Black Chalice in England and the Process Church, founded by Robert DeGrimston in London in 1964, which was widely thought to be Satanist. Confusion arose thanks to one of the church symbols, a goat's head in a pentagram. The Process Church, which has since abandoned the symbol, claims it accepts God and Satan as dual powers in the universe and believes 'as you give, so shall you receive'.

It remains difficult to distinguish between those Satanists who are moved by the movement and those who are seeking a life of cruelty, self-indulgence and self-aggrandisement.

However, Satanism is accepted as a semi-legitimate religion. In 1994 in Denver, Colorado, a US Federal Judge ruled that prisoner Robert Howard, who was serving ten years for kidnapping, was entitled to perform Satanic ritual in his cell in the same way that other inmates might choose to go to the chapel.

THE COVER OF A BOOK PRINTED IN 1643 ILLUSTRATES THE COMMON CONCEPTION OF A WITCH-HAG, WITH HOOK NOSE, WARTS AND RAVEN FAMILIARS.

A MOST
Certain, Strange, and true Discovery of a
VVITCH.
Being taken by some of the Parliament Forces, as she was standing on a small planck-board and sayling on it over the River of *Newbury*:

Together with the strange and true manner of her death, with the propheticall words and speeches she vsed at the same time.

sept 28
Printed by John Hammond, 1643.

The devil needs souls to thrive; witches need unearthly powers for sorcery – together they seem made for each other.

'The end product of black magic is to disturb reason and produce feverish excitement which emboldens to great sensuality and crime.'

BLACK MAGIC AND BLACK MASS

There is little to associate witchcraft with the devil, although historically the bonds between the two were forged long ago when people believed in the power of the devil, while his earth-bound agents were thought to be witches.

Centuries of paintings and engravings show the devil surrounded by servant witches – a by-product of the witch craze which dominated the politics of the Middle Ages. Given inquisition years, the hags in *Macbeth* and the pointed hats and broomsticks of Hallowe'en, it is hard to alter people's perceptions of witches and witchcraft.

There have been instances, too, which have thoroughly reinforced the stereotyping.

MARQUISE DE MONTESPAN

Marquise de Montespan was mistress to Louis XIV of France. She won the coveted position by praising his vanity – calling him 'Louis the Invincible' – and she was even seen as an unofficial queen, but she fell from grace dramatically.

Initially occasional and merely tragic, the number of deaths among healthy male members of the king's court began to escalate and it became clear that something was amiss. Louis XIV asked detective Gabriel de la Reynie, the lieutenant general of the police in Versailles, to investigate these mysterious fatalities.

The policeman tracked down a witch called la Voisin who had provided the poisons that were used in the string of killings. Disturbingly, she was also involved in illicit abortion services and allowed the tiny foetuses to be used in horrific Satanic rituals. The Marquise de Montespan's naked body was used as an altar during these black masses.

ABOVE: THE MARQUIS DE SADE, WHO LENT HIS NAME TO SADISM, WAS THOUGHT BY MANY TO BE DRIVEN BY DEVILS. IN 1814 HE WAS CONFINED TO A MENTAL ASYLUM IN CHARENTON.

in the middle of the 14th century at a time when the Church was corrupt and inept.

Black mass is usually performed in a clearing by a defrocked priest wearing a black cloak decorated with fir cones. Tradition dictates that one female assistants must be a prostitute, the other a virgin. Other elements integral to the ceremony are an altar (possibly a stone slab), black candles, sacrificial bowls and a criminal's skull, in addition to an inverted crucifix and a Bible bound in human skin. Participants who smear their faces with the blood of a goat which has been boiled with vinegar and crushed glass are convinced they will see the devil himself during proceedings!

Black masses also feature a full confession giving useful blackmail material against the initiate.

Today, from what we know, black magic appears to be male-dominated, urban, secretive and sexually excessive.

At la Voisin's trial, her daughter testified, 'At one of Madame de Montespan's masses, I saw my mother bring in an infant, obviously premature, and place it over a basin over which its throat was slit and its blood drained into the chalice.' This blood sacrifice was made in return for favours.

Today, there are still examples of witchcraft closely entwined with Satanism: desecration of churchyards and Satanic graffiti on Christian places of worship undoubtedly occur.

A. E. Waite, who has studied the occult, noted, 'The end product of black magic is to disturb reason and produce feverish excitement which emboldens to great sensuality and crime.'

However, the extent of black magic in Europe and America is in doubt. Some claim it is merely the meat of Hollywood horror stories, while others are convinced it is systematically organised and widespread among all elements of society.

HATE AND MURDEROUS INTENT

A black mass, the key celebration of black magic, is set up to be the polar opposite to the Catholic mass. The aim is to channel the collective thoughts of the assembly to gain increased power. While most of the manipulators of the black masses are interested in love and lust spells, there are processes to use for hate and murderous intent. The first black masses were held in Europe

The story is based on a real character, and possibly even two. Johann Faust was a wandering scholar who lived between approximately 1480 and 1539. Another man of a similar name and nature lived and died at around the same time. One or both of these Fausts were keen students of sorcery, prophecy, alchemy and astrology. The Faust that is preserved in legend travelled widely and earned himself a reputation for evil. It is likely that Faust was a charlatan, however. Martin Luther, who was alive at the same time and in the midst of denouncing the Catholic Church, certainly considered him to be a serious threat to society. Despite an obscure existence, Faust was remembered for a long time after his death for his occultism.

THE LEGEND OF FAUST

The tale of Faust is an enduring one. He's a man with an insatiable thirst for knowledge who is prepared to trade his soul to the devil so that he may learn all there is to know – with absolute knowledge comes absolute power. But the day of reckoning looms when Faust must keep his side of the bargain and submit to Satan.

An anonymous author first immortalised Faust in the work *Faustbuch* published in 1587. It was a motley collection of magical tales in which Faust was imbued with fantastic powers akin to those of Merlin. The devil was called Mephistopheles and, in addition to ponderous drama, there were comic moments, usually at the expense of the people on whom anti-hero Faust preyed.

THE TRAGICALL HISTORY OF D. FAUSTUS
It was the English dramatist and poet Christopher Marlowe who was the next author to seize upon the tale. In about 1592, he wrote the play *The Tragicall History of D. Faustus* after being inspired by a translation of the *Faustbuch*. In turn, his work was translated

back into German and became the basis for numerous other plays revolving around the Faust theme.

Compounding the public perception of Faust there began a healthy trade in books which told how to forge pacts with the devil, or how to break them. Most famous of them all was the *Magia Naturalis et Innaturalis*.

Next to take up the story was the German writer Gotthold Ephraim Lessing who developed a different slant on the story. He commended Faust's desire for knowledge and consequently ended the tale by reconciling him with God.

GOETHE'S ADAPTATION

This same approach was adopted by Johann Wolfgang von Goethe, whose adaptation of the legend was considered his finest work. Goethe was a statesman, poet, scholar and a student of Shakespeare. The first part of his poem 'Faust' appeared in 1808, with the aspirations of man being one of the key themes. The second part of the same work was written shortly before his death in 1832 and was published posthumously. This second epic was more philosophical than the first and reflected Goethe's passion for astrology and the occult. It ended with Faust eventually finding redemption.

It was the widely translated lyrical poetry of Goethe that became the basis of two operas, *The Damnation of Faust* by Hector Berlioz and *Faust* by Charles Gounod.

Although the story of Faust was continually being refashioned and adapted throughout the ensuing centuries, no one found a style which could match that of Goethe's. His version was the inspiration for German novelist Thomas Mann, whose 1947 version, *Doctor Faustus*, depicted the troubled times of a genius composer, and who, perhaps most successfully, rivalled Goethe in popularity and skill.

ABOVE LEFT: REMBRANDT WAS INTRIGUED BY THE FAUST LEGEND. THIS ETCHING SHOWS FAUST WITH AN AMULET AND MAGIC MIRROR. RIGHT: THE COVER OF A BOOK PUBLISHED IN 1624 RELATING THE TALE OF DR FAUSTUS.

The Faust that is preserved in legend travelled widely and earned himself a reputation for evil.

ROBERT JOHNSON AND JIMI HENDRIX

The legend of Faust would not die. During the 1930s a rumour swept America that blues star Robert Johnson had traded his soul with the devil in return for his extraordinary musical skills after a meeting at some remote country crossroads. Decades later much the same was said of guitarist Jimi Hendrix, who died in 1970 from a drugs overdose at the age of 28.

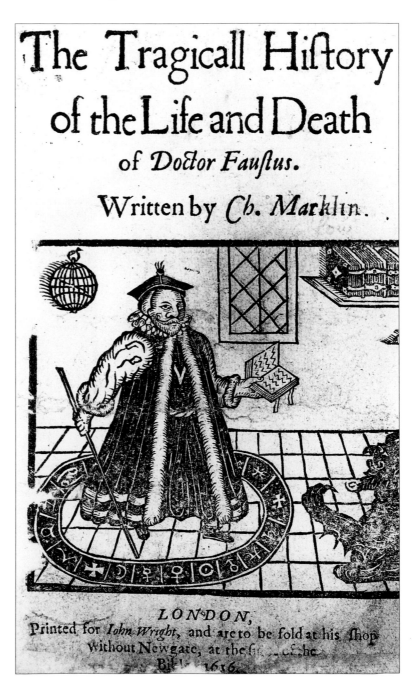

Possession – a word that strikes terror into the heart. There can be few more alarming scenarios than that of the body being taken over by an unseen, evil force. Traditionally, the invasive demon commandeers the very will of its victim, contorts the body and controls the mind. However, this is an alarmist view.

POSSESSION

There are three types of possession, the most infamous being that by the devil or one of his disciples. Today even those who believe in demonic possession freely admit it is not as straightforward as it once seemed.

WITCHES AND WIZARDS

For years churchmen believed the devil entered someone's body, either directly or through the intervention of witches and wizards. Acting as agents to the devil, the spellmongers whipped up an enchantment and administered it to the victims as food, apples being the most popular.

According to the Catholic Church, anyone showing signs of clairvoyance, greatly increased physical strength, voicing streams of blasphemy and capable of levitation was undoubtedly possessed by the devil. The only hope for the victim was an exorcism. This view was very much the medieval standpoint.

There is now another view, that someone might be possessed by a spirit as it attempts to leave the mortal world for the realms of the immortal. There may be nothing devilish in the spirit at all, although it causes its host headaches, mood swings, sleep difficulties and other traumas. The spirit which attaches itself to a living

human may be trying to give a warning or a message. On being asked to leave, most of these wayward spirits will go willingly.

In some societies, possession by troublesome demons is blamed for a whole host of personal dilemmas, including physical pain, miscarriage, infidelity and bereavements. The victim is most

ALTHOUGH CLERICAL REBEL MARTIN LUTHER FLEW IN THE FACE OF MANY CHURCH TEACHINGS HE WAS CONVINCED BY THE EXISTENCE OF THE DEVIL.

likely a woman from the lower orders of society, as it is considered that a female is weaker and therefore less able to protect herself from rampant devils. The intervention of an exorcist helps to raise her profile by increasing her respectability.

MENTAL ILLNESS

A further dimension of black possession is that of mental illness. Some therapists have concluded that conditions such as a multiple personality are caused by possession and can only improve through exorcism. Harvard University graduate M. Scott Peck, a practising psychiatrist, declared that two of his patients suffering from multiple personalities had been invaded by evil spirits which were duly exorcised. His book *The People of the Lie*, published in 1983, described the cases.

Californian psychiatrist Ralph Allinson went further and stated that many multiple personality cases showed signs of possession, benign and evil. The success of an ensuing exorcism depended, he said, on the measure of faith held by the victim.

Therapists remain largely on the fence over the issue. They might seek to diminish the 'voices' of demons heard by someone claiming to be possessed, whereas an exorcism will heighten them. However, few would rule out possession and exorcism completely.

In South American countries, where people believe afflictions like epilepsy and schizophrenia are the result of demonic possession, psychiatrists often act as spiritualists.

POSSESSION AND MEDIUMSHIP

When mediums hold seances, they are actively seeking possession by a spirit. The medium invites the spirit to take over his or her body on the assumption that it will leave as quickly as it arrived. Obsession might be a better description for this type of possession.

Similarly, in the Christian Church congregations may seek possession by the Holy Ghost in ecstatic worship. This is often manifested by the worshipper speaking in tongues, or glossolalia and recorded in the New Testament when, seven weeks after Passover, the apostles 'were all filled with the Holy Spirit and began to speak in other tongues, as the Spirit gave them utterance'.

The Catholic Church came to regard speaking in tongues as a mark of demonic possession and those who were affected were branded heretics. But in the 19th century, the gift of speaking in tongues was once again recognised as God-given.

IN MANY EASTERN CULTURES PEOPLE WHO EXHIBIT THE SYMPTOMS OF SPIRIT POSSESSION ARE THOUGHT TO HAVE BEEN FAVOURED BY A GOD, ALTHOUGH THEY MIGHT STRIVE TO ACHIEVE THAT STATE BY CHANTING, DANCE AND TRANCE. IN THIS ALTERED STATE, THE PERSON WILL NOT FEEL PAIN, WILL TALK AND ACT IN THE MANNER OF THE GOD AND MAY IMPART PREDICTIONS.

For centuries the notion of exorcising devils which inhabit humans has prevailed. Some scriptures insist that Jesus was an exorcist. According to Mark 1: 32–34, 'That evening, after sunset, they brought to him all who were sick and those who were possessed by devils. The whole town came crowding round the door and he cured many who were suffering from diseases of one kind or another; he also cast out many devils.'

EXORCISM

From 1614, the Roman Catholic Church had a formal exorcism rite, the *Rituale Romanum*. Those were the days when the church bell was used as a cup to administer a 'holy potion' of sherry, oil and herbs. The relic of a saint might be forced into the mouth of the 'possessed' – any struggle being taken as a further proof that there were devils within them.

19TH CENTURY ARTIST LUCAS Y. PADILLIA EUGENIO'S PICTURE *A SCENE OF EXORCISM*.

IMAGINARY DEMONS

Yet the process was not restricted to the Catholic Church alone. The Jewish faith and Protestant churches have a history of exorcisms, the new wave of charismatic churches and their associated 'deliverance' ministries particularly so. However, many of those people exorcised down the centuries were actually suffering from physical or psychological illnesses.

Nowadays, the authorities of both Catholic and Protestant churches are low-key about the devil and his ability to invade human beings. Over-zealous priests and ministers – and even lay exorcists – have wreaked havoc with the fragile minds of those that they diagnose as being possessed by the devil.

Each Catholic diocese has a priest who is responsible for exorcisms although they are notoriously secretive about exactly what it is they do. Pope John Paul II is known to have carried out an exorcism on a young woman on 27 March

The word 'exorcism' literally means 'binding oath'. Exorcists aim to place a binding oath on the demon to exit the body, whether it wants to or not.

1982, but the Vatican refuses to furnish the world with any further details. However, Father Gabriele Amorth, principal exorcist of Rome, insists, 'The Church has never had a doubt that the Devil exists. Our language may be more discreet today, but the idea remains the same.'

To put his role in proportion, Father Amorth revealed that of the 50,000 people who had come to see him, only 84 were genuine cases of possession. Legitimate Catholic exorcists claim to have seen their 'patients' levitate to the ceiling, vomit nails, glass shards and pieces of radio equipment, assume mighty strength and be paralysed. Other reported effects of exorcism include diarrhoea, spitting, vomiting and objects flying about.

Anglicans, too, have trained exorcists who have to work to strict guidelines laid down in 1975. The rules governing exorcists emerged in part because of the killing in 1974 of a woman by her husband following a midnight exorcism at a parish church in Yorkshire. At his trial the defence counsel said the man acted in a fit of madness prompted by the exorcism at which a Church of England vicar, a Methodist minister and their respective wives had officiated.

ABUSES AND BREAKDOWNS

The exorcism system has been open to abuse, however, and Canon Dominic Walker, chair of the Christian Deliverance study group – the Church's official exorcism monitor – admits that untrained exorcists are a major worry. Some allegedly possessed people were beaten as the exorcists tried to knock demons out of them. One unfortunate woman was forced into staying in a locked room against her will. 'They were trying to order the demons out of her. She was becoming increasingly frightened and hysterical – not because of the demons but with what they were trying to do to her.'

One 56-year-old woman from the Midlands was told by her local vicar that she was infested with more than 100 demons and eventually lost her job as a manager in an insurance company following a breakdown.

'He used to hold me down with others and scream at me, commanding the evil spirits to leave my body. I don't believe in demons any more. I have become agnostic. I shall never enter a church again. I felt emotionally raped.'

Another victim of a 'deliverance ministry' was a 50-year-old woman who was exorcised, with the approval of her local vicar, by lay people twice a week for nearly a year. 'I was completely brainwashed by them. I could only watch certain programmes on television, read certain books – otherwise they said I'd receive demons from them.' She had a breakdown and was in hospital for five weeks.

Following its creation in 1892, the Ouija board brought comfort to bereaved families who could 'talk' to the dead, especially popular in the aftermath of the First World War.

Today, few people reach adulthood without trying a Ouija board, usually using a roughly drawn circle of letters and an upturned glass. Although the makers insist it is simply an entertaining game, critics fear that dabbling with a Ouija board could damage a player's mental health.

The Ouija board was invented by American Elijah J. Bond, taking its name from the French and German words for yes, oui and ja. The board, now marketed by an American game company, Parker Brothers, includes letters of the alphabet, the numbers 0 to 9, the words yes and no and a heart-shaped pointer on three felted legs. The user asks a question, places his or her fingertips on the pointer, sometimes along with other players, and waits for the pointer to spell out a reply.

The concept of the Ouija has been around for years. In about 600 B.C. in China, a remarkably similar technique was used to communicate with

OUIJA

the dead. In 500 B.C. in Greece, a popular device was a table on wheels acting as a pointer. In the middle of the 19th century came the planchette, attributed to both a French Spiritualist of the same name and a German milkmaid. It also consisted of a three-legged platform, two of legs on wheels and the third a pencil point. As the user touched the platform pointer, a spirit was invited to write out a message or produce a drawing.

'A DANGEROUS TOY'

With both the Ouija and the planchette it is likely that the user moves the pointer rather than a visiting spirit. However, there have been many reports

DUD CORNER CEMETERY IN LENS, FRANCE – AFTER THE FIRST WORLD WAR MANY FAMILIES ATTEMPTED TO CONTACT THE DEAD.

of the pointers flying from the board and an apparent invasion of spirits, some of them hostile. Some people believe the board reveals hidden quarters of the mind, leading to problems in mental health. Others worry that it is a gateway to possession by negative or evil spirits. US psychic Edgar Cayce branded Ouija 'a dangerous toy'.

Advocates of the Ouija board see it differently. They claim that the board can be used innocently, for example to find lost objects and to gain precious insight into the spirit world. It can be used for automatic writing where the user takes down messages dictated by spirits on the other side.

PEARL CURRAN

In 1913 the Ouija board transformed the life of Pearl Curran from St Louis, who was idling away her time on the board with a friend when the pointer spelled out, 'Oh, why let sorrow steal thy heart? Thy bosom is but its foster-mother, the world its cradle and the loving home its grave.'

The poetry had a startling effect on Pearl, a high-school drop-out, and she continued using the Ouija to find out more. By the following month she learned the spirit or discarnate being talking to her was a Quaker woman, Patience Worth, who had lived in 17th century England before emigrating to the American colonies, dying in an Indian massacre.

Through Pearl she wrote a magnificent array of poems, plays and novels, numbering 4 million words in five years. The story of Pearl and Patience swept the world. Pearl eventually discarded the Ouija board and fluently recited Patience's words in automatic speech. Sceptics believed that Patience was another side of Pearl's own personality emerging after being unleashed by the Ouija board. For five years the pair worked prodigiously until in 1922 Pearl became pregnant. Contact between the two diminished; so did the public interest. Curran died in 1937 leaving the riddle of why the language used by Patience was so heavily weighted with Old English – in use centuries before she was supposed to have lived.

IN 1963 WRITER JANE ROBERTS USED A OUIJA BOARD TO COMMUNICATE WITH SETH, WHO DESCRIBED HIMSELF AS 'AN ENERGY PERSONALITY ESSENCE'. SHE ENCOUNTERED HER PSYCHIC ABILITIES FOR THE FIRST TIME AFTER SHE WENT INTO A TRANCE IN THE MIDST OF COMPOSING POETRY. EVENTUALLY SHE FOUND THAT THE BOARD WAS NO LONGER NEEDED. SINKING INTO A DEEP TRANCE SHE WOULD BE TAKEN OVER BY SETH WHO TOLD OF HOW THE PAST, PRESENT AND FUTURE OCCURRED SIMULTANEOUSLY AND SPOKE OF MULTIPLE REINCARNATION.

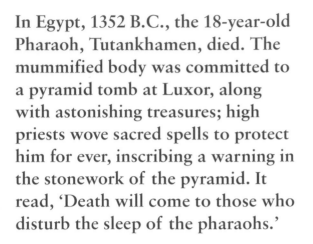

In Egypt, 1352 B.C., the 18-year-old Pharaoh, Tutankhamen, died. The mummified body was committed to a pyramid tomb at Luxor, along with astonishing treasures; high priests wove sacred spells to protect him for ever, inscribing a warning in the stonework of the pyramid. It read, 'Death will come to those who disturb the sleep of the pharaohs.'

PHARAOH'S CURSE

An archaeological expedition headed by archaeologist Howard Carter and Egyptologist Lord Carnarvon broke into the tomb in 1923. Both knew of the curse which had so effectively protected the tomb's gems and relics from grave robbers. Lord Carnarvon had gone as far as to consult a mystic and several mediums before he left Britain and each of them urged him not to open the pyramid.

THE DEATH OF LORD CARNARVON

Less than two months later Lord Carnarvon, aged 57, died, his face scarred by an infected mosquito bite. At the moment of his death in the Continental Hotel, Cairo, on 5 April 1923 the city's electricity failed. Simultaneously, at his home in England, a faithful hound began baying and then died.

Two days later, when examining Tutankhamen's body, a mark was found on his left cheek identical to Lord Carnarvon's.

It might all have been dismissed as coincidence except for a chain of mysterious deaths.

ABOVE: FOR CENTURIES THE HIGH PRIESTS' CURSE DETERRED MANY FROM PLUNDERING TUTANKHAMEN'S PYRAMID.

Archaeologist Arthur Mace, another member of the expedition, went into a coma at the Continental Hotel and died, although doctors were unable to pinpoint his illness.

George Gould, who was a close friend of Lord Carnarvon, went to Egypt, peered into the tomb and was dead within two days.

Radiologist Archibald Reid, who examined the body of the king, died soon after complaining of tiredness, as did Carnarvon's personal secretary, Richard Bethell. The list of casualties from both the expedition itself and all those connected with it increased alarmingly. By 1936 some 33 people had died suddenly, including Carnarvon's half-brother, who had committed suicide whilst temporarily insane.

Mohammed Ibrahim, Egypt's director of antiquities, was run over and killed in 1966 after the government agreed to send the tomb's treasures to Paris for an exhibition.

By 1969, Richard Adamson was the only surviving member of the 1923 foray (Howard Carter died of natural causes in 1939). He maintained the curse was nothing but mumbo-jumbo — although he changed his mind after his wife died within a day of him publicly denouncing the curse and their son broke his back soon after Adamson spoke out again.

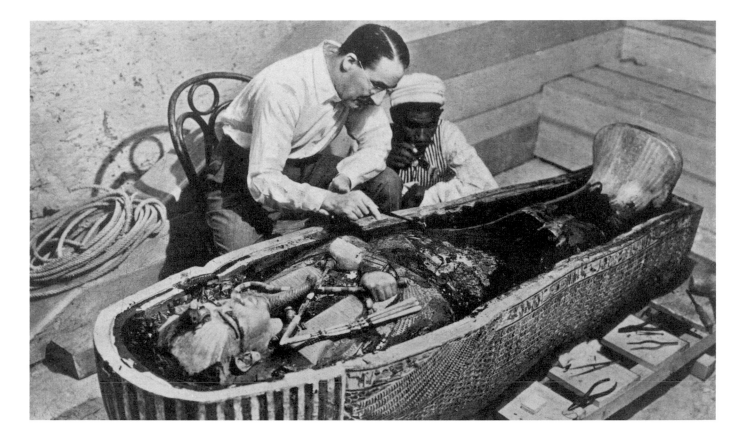

Ken Parkinson, the flight engineer, suffered a heart attack each year on the anniversary of the flight from Egypt until a fatal one in 1978. The flight lieutenant Rick Laurie died of heart failure two years earlier. Another of the flight's crew lost his home in a fire, a second suffered two heart attacks and a third left the RAF through illness.

As recently as 1992, a BBC documentary team filming inside the tomb were hit by a catalogue of disasters. Two nearly died when their hotel lift crashed 21 floors to the ground and lights fused during filming inside the pyramid, leaving the terrified crew in darkness. After they re-enacted a ritual which reputedly raised the dead, a sandstorm blew up leaving them with conjunctivitis.

A SCIENTIFIC EXPLANATION

In 1949, scientist Louis Bulgarini wrote, 'It is definitely possible that the ancient Egyptians used atomic radiation to protect their holy places. The floors of the tombs could have been covered with uranium. Or the graves could have been finished with radioactive rock. Rock containing both gold and uranium was mined in Egypt. Such radiation could kill a man today.'

His theory was backed up in 1991 by Egyptian scientist Sayeed Mohammed Thebat of Cairo University, who, by chance, visited mummies in a museum carrying a Geiger counter. He said, 'We may at last have uncovered the reason why so many people who entered unopened tombs later died of unexplained wasting diseases.'

ABOVE: HOWARD CARTER, WHO REMAINED UNTAINTED BY THE CURSE OF KING TUT, EXAMINES THE SARCOPHAGUS FROM THE TOMB.
LEFT: TUTANKHAMEN'S DEATH MASK, NOW ON DISPLAY IN CALIFORNIA.

Billed as the greatest vessel of the era, the steamship *Great Eastern*, designed and built by Isambard Kingdom Brunel, promised great riches and prestige for her owners. Instead she brought only misery and catastrophe.

CURSED SHIPS

Brunel was rightly proud of the ship and its design. It had a 211-metre-long hull that was double-skinned. The metal sheets were separated by compartments, so that if the ship were holed only one section would fill with water and she would stay afloat.

The construction of the *Great Eastern* took four years and did not go smoothly. The original owners ran out of money and sold the project on, but finally the paddle-steamer was launched on 31 January 1858. But Brunel never saw his ship in action. He suffered a stroke on the eve of its first sailing and died a week later.

MYSTERIOUS ACCIDENTS

Not long afterwards one of its funnels exploded when a valve was accidentally left shut, fatally scalding five men and destroying the Grand Salon. A sixth man later died in the paddle. Three months after this the captain, coxswain and the son of another crewman drowned near the ship while out in the small boat.

On its way to Britain the steamer ploughed into a smaller boat, drowning two of its crew. The boat was now crippled by costs and she was eventually sold for scrap.

As the hull was dismantled the skeletons of a man and a young lad were discovered. A riveter and his apprentice had disappeared during the construction of the vessel, but the ship-owners thought they had left to find work elsewhere. Who would be surprised if they had not sought revenge for their cruel death by cursing the ship that carried their corpses.

MARIE CELESTE

The most famously jinxed ship ever to sail the seas was the *Marie Celeste*. This two-masted, square-rigged brig was discovered meandering aimlessly in the Atlantic; her crew had mysteriously vanished, along with the ship's sextant, chronometer, navigation book and the emergency small raft.

The crew of the brig *Dei Gratia* happened across the *Marie Celeste* on 5 December 1872. They could not have known that the ship in their sights, launched in 1861 as the *Amazon*, had been blighted by a succession of catastrophes.

The condition of the sails indicated the ship had encountered a terrible storm. Yet inside, an uncorked bottle of cough medicine stood intact. A meal was prepared although not served. While the compass lay smashed on the deck, there were no obvious signs of a struggle. The last log entry was made on 25 November.

ABOVE: THE *GREAT EASTERN* WAS BESET BY DIFFICULTIES. DESIGNER BRUNEL NEVER SAW HER AT SEA. HE SUFFERED A STROKE A WEEK BEFORE HER MAIDEN VOYAGE.

The fate of those aboard the *Marie Celeste* was never discovered. During the next 11 years she had 17 different owners and the mishaps continued. Finally, she ran aground in Haiti in 1884 and was left to crumble on a coral reef.

MODERN-DAY DISASTERS

In more recent times, a similar strife-torn ship has been labelled a 'cursed' vessel – the Italian cruise ship *Achille Lauro*.

In 1971, seven years after the Italian shipping magnate Achille Lauro had bought her, she had a collision with a fishing boat, leaving one man dead. Ten years after this two people lost their lives when a fire broke out during a cruise of the Canary Islands.

In October 1985, Palestinian gunmen hijacked the ship off the coast of Egypt. Passengers and crew were held hostage while the terrorists demanded the release of 50 prisoners in Israeli jails.

Before the crisis was over an American, Leon Klinghoffer, was shot dead in his wheelchair.

On Wednesday 30 November 1991, off the coast of Somalia, a fire began in the engine room. The blaze eventually claimed the lives of two elderly people. After pitching at an angle of 30 degrees the *Achille Lauro* sank to the bottom of the Indian Ocean.

ONE WOMAN, MRS JOAN MURRAY, SURVIVED
THREE OF THE GREATEST SHIPPING DISASTERS
OF THE 20TH CENTURY. SHE WAS RESCUED
FROM THE *TITANIC*, WHICH SANK IN APRIL
1912 OFF NEWFOUNDLAND, WITH THE LOSS
OF 1,513 LIVES. IN MAY 1915 MRS MURRAY
FOUND HERSELF SCRAMBLING TO THE SAFETY
OF THE LIFEBOATS ONCE AGAIN WHEN THE
UNARMED LINER *LUSITANIA* WAS SUNK OFF
THE IRISH COAST BY A GERMAN U-BOAT. THE
DEATH TOLL OF THIS DISASTER WAS 1,195.
AND SHE WAS FORTUNATE FOR A THIRD TIME
IN 1927, ESCAPING DEATH IN THE ATLANTIC
WHEN TWO SHIPS, THE *CELTIC* AND THE
ANACONDA, COLLIDED.

Can the wearer of a jewel plundered from an Indian temple really provoke the wrath of a god? The catastrophes which plagued the various owners of the Hope diamond demonstrate that it may be possible.

CURSED GEMS

The fate of the person who gouged the diamond from its original site at the temple of a powerful and vengeful god Rama Sitra in Mandala, Burma, is unknown. However, the French trader, Jean-Baptiste Tavernier, who brought the 44.5 carat diamond home from the East is known to have met a grisly end. He had disappeared whilst on a trading trip to Russia and his remains were discovered in Siberia, where dogs had been gnawing at his bones.

CHANGING HANDS AND BAD LUCK
In 1668, Tavernier had sold the gem to Louis XIV, King of France, who had it fashioned into the shape of a heart for his mistress, Mme de Montespan. She was disgraced in a black magic scandal and the jewel was returned to take its place in the collection of crown jewels.

After Marie Antoinette, the wife of Louis XVI, wore it and was subsequently beheaded during the French Revolution in 1793, it surfaced again in 1830 in Amsterdam, where a Dutch diamond cutter Wilhelm Fals made the diamond into its present shape. Fals's own son Hendrick was besotted by the stone, so much so that he took it for himself and fled to London. Once there his conscience got the better of him and he hanged himself in a fit of remorse.

KING LOUIS XIV HAD THE FATED HOPE DIAMOND FASHIONED INTO A HEART FOR HIS MISTRESS, MME DE MONTESPAN, BEFORE SHE FELL FROM GRACE IN A BLACK MAGIC SCANDAL.

The diamond was returned to Wilhelm, who sold it a few years afterwards to Anglo-Irish banker Henry Philip Hope. Henry gave the stone its name and felt no ill-effects from it before presenting it to his cousin, Lord Francis Hope. The curse was once again activated when the peer's marriage collapsed. His wife May declared the diamond was to blame and with some accuracy predicted misfortune for all its future owners.

MURDER AND MADNESS
In 1904 the diamond was purchased by French broker Jacques Colot who later lost his mind and committed suicide in an asylum. But not before he sold it to Russian nobleman Prince Kanilovsky. The prince presented it to his lover, Mademoiselle Ladue, an actress at the Folies-Bergères in Paris. He later shot and killed her – although no one knows why – and soon afterwards he was stabbed to death in the street.

Merchant Habib Bey was hoping for a tidy profit when he sold on the gem, but unfortunately

he drowned before receiving any of the cash due to him. The next owner of the fateful jewel was the Greek dealer Simon Montharides. Not long after he had sold the diamond, his horse and carriage plunged off a cliff, killing himself, his wife and their child.

Soon after Abdul Hamid III, Sultan of Turkey, bought the Hope an uprising in Turkey in 1909 abolished the sultanate. Pierre Cartier, of the renowned jewellery family, bought the gem and sold it without incident to Evalyn Walsh McLean, the daughter of a mining tycoon and wife of publisher Ned McLean. The diamond had cost her $40,000 in 1917 and its purchase heralded a calamitous period which made her miserable for the rest of her days.

A year after buying the diamond, Evalyn's eight-year-old son Vinson was killed by a car in a freak accident. Unhinged by the tragedy, Ned McLean took to drinking and finally died in an asylum. The couple's daughter died of an overdose of sleeping pills in 1946.

On her death in 1947, Evalyn left the fated gem to her six grandchildren. A dealer bought it two years afterwards and presented it to the Smithsonian Institution in Washington. Nevertheless when a granddaughter of Evalyn McLean was found dead at her home in Texas in December 1967 after taking a cocktail of drink and drugs, the gem was once again under suspicion.

ABOVE: MARIE ANTOINETTE WORE THE HOPE DIAMOND. SHE WAS LATER GUILLOTINED IN THE FRENCH REVOLUTION. RIGHT: THE HOPE DIAMOND, BEAUTY OR BEAST?

Could the sharp business practices of two of the world's most memorable patriarchs have been the subject of curses which have blighted their families ever since?

CURSED FAMILIES

The Kennedy and Onassis dynasties have dominated the headlines for decades and exerted an enormous influence on world events. Yet few families have been so famously ravaged by bad luck. Each personal disaster has come under close public scrutiny and observers can only wonder at the appalling string of tragedies. Little do they know that the heads of both families were guilty of shameful wheeler-dealing.

UNSAVOURY BUSINESS DEALINGS

Dealing in booze during America's Prohibition made Joe Kennedy a millionaire before he was 30

years old and paved his way to political power – he was ambassador to Britain during the Second World War. However, his business activities were hideously unsavoury.

When Kennedy was thwarted in his attempts to buy a cinema chain in 1928 he ruined the man, Alexander Pantages, who was standing in his path. A young actress called Eunice Pringle accused Pantages of rape and he was jailed for 50 years. Although the verdict was later overturned, Pantages was finished and Kennedy got the cinemas he desired. Pringle, who died in mysterious circumstances shortly afterwards, apparently made a deathbed confession that she was paid by Kennedy to frame Pantages.

After they broke up, Kennedy's long-standing mistress, the actress Gloria Swanson, discovered he had hi-jacked her tax losses to reduce his own federal bill. Further, a fur coat he had given her was actually paid for by her own cash.

KENNEDY'S ASSASSINATION

A father of nine, Kennedy was determined to see one of his sons President of the United States. The eldest, naval airman Joe Jnr, died in 1944, aged 29, flying a plane laden with explosives. Daughter Kathleen also died in a plane crash in 1948. The aspirations of Kennedy were centred on John and all went according to plan. His tenure as President of the United States was tragically ended on 22 November 1963 when he was assassinated in Dallas, Texas, aged 46. His father, who had suffered a stroke in 1961 which rendered him speechless, endured the agony in silence.

It fell to Robert, the third brother, to take the family mantle into the political arena. However, his destiny mirrored his brother's when he was shot campaigning for presidency in 1968, aged 42.

Kennedy senior died in 1969, but not before his youngest son Edward became embroiled in a scandal which effectively ended his political career. Ted left a party held at Chappaquiddick with campaign worker Mary Jo Kopechne in his

EDWARD KENNEDY'S CHANCE TO FURTHER THE FAMILY'S POLITICAL AMBITIONS WERE KILLED OFF BY A SCANDAL AT CHAPPAQUIDDICK.

car. The vehicle plunged from an 85 ft bridge into fast-running water, killing 29-year-old Mary Jo. After crawling to the water's edge Teddy returned to the party and urged his friends to keep quiet. In the morning he gave himself up to the police.

THE KENNEDY PATRIARCH SURROUNDED BY HIS WIFE AND HIS NINE CHILDREN BEFORE A STRING OF TRAGEDIES BLIGHTED THE FAMILY.

The family curse continued with Robert's son David dying of a drugs overdose in 1984, aged 28. Teddy Junior was struck down with cancer and had a leg amputated.

ARISTOTLE ONASSIS

Both Joe Kennedy and Aristotle Onassis had a reputation for underhand business tactics. Both their families suffered greatly. Like Kennedy, Greek-born Aristotle Onassis was a ruthless self-made millionaire. And like Kennedy he used dubious business practices to carve his niche.

He married shipping heiress Athina Livanos and they had two children, Alexander and Christina. Onassis was frequently unfaithful, but the marriage remained unchallenged until he encountered opera diva Maria Callas. He and Callas were besotted with each other. Athina sought a divorce and Callas's cuckolded husband,

Giovanni Battista Meneghini, put a curse on the pair. Meneghini warned Callas that the millionaire would never marry her – and he didn't. Jackie Kennedy, widow of the American president, was wooed and won by Onassis, leaving Callas hurt and confused on the sidelines.

Alexander died in 1973 after his plane crashed after taking off from Athens airport. Then came the suicide of his mother. Athina's body was found in Paris in October 1974. Onassis, miserable in his marriage to Kennedy, returned to Callas although he was suffering from a wasting disease. He died in agony on 15 March 1975 and the faithful Callas was dead 30 months later.

After a string of unhappy liaisons, in 1988 on a trip to Buenos Aires, drug-dependent Christina was found dead of natural causes, aged 37, leaving behind a daughter.

BRUCE LEE AND THE DRAGON CURSE

Another man who was convinced he was cursed was Kung Fu star Bruce Lee. The star of cult classics like *Enter the Dragon* and *Fists of Fury*, Lee was born in San Francisco in November 1940, but moved to Hong Kong, the home of his family, when he was a toddler. As a teenager, Lee scrapped much like any other lad. Then he discovered Kung Fu, the martial art which had him high-kicking and hard-punching his way to success.

Along with the physical skills he mastered there was the spiritual side of Kung Fu. Lee learned to fear invisible demons which would one day confront him in a do-or-die battle. He was reluctant to father children in case the demons he was cursed with were passed on. The one he dreaded most was called the Dragon.

Lee found fame first in Hong Kong and later in America. But in May 1973 the symptoms of his impending fate were showing. He collapsed, apparently with a convulsion, on a film set. Two months later he was dead, aged 32 years. The post

BRANDON LEE INHERITED HIS LOVE OF KUNG FU AND AN ASSOCIATED TERROR OF DEMONS FROM HIS FATHER BRUCE.

mortem revealed a massive brain haemorrhage although rumours soon circulated about the role of jealous Hong Kong gangsters in the death.

BRANDON LEE

To his son, Brandon, Bruce Lee handed down his love of Kung Fu and the same gnawing terror of evil spirits. Unwilling to evoke any of the demons which he believed claimed his father, Brandon refused the lead role in a blockbusting film about his dad. Brandon was so morbidly obsessed that he even drove a hearse.

In March 1993 he was set for stardom in a film called *The Crow* which told the tale of a murdered rock musician returning from the dead. A stunt went mysteriously wrong when Lee was shot by a gun that should have contained blanks.

Brandon Lee inherited his father's morbid fear of demons, and died in a mysterious accident while filming The Crow.

He died at 27, two weeks before he was due to wed production worker Eliza Hutton. Robert Lee, Bruce's brother and Brandon's uncle, said, 'I don't know if our family is cursed but I am seriously starting to think about it. It seems like a never-ending story.'

THE CRAVEN FAMILY CURSE

A philandering 17th century nobleman thought nothing about ditching the servant girl he made pregnant in an 'upstairs-downstairs' love affair. As he exiled her from his estate, William Craven was unmoved by her bitter pleas.

Little did he know that the scorned mother-to-be was of Romany stock. Using age-old spells she issued a vengeful curse, that Craven and his heirs would never die a natural death. For 200 years the terrible oath has held good and the Craven family has been blighted.

The fate of William Craven is unknown. However, since one of his descendants was made an earl in 1801, the family history has made depressing reading and the curse has become a legend. None of the first four earls lived beyond the age of 57. The fifth earl drowned during a drunken party in 1932, aged 35. His son, the sixth earl, died of leukaemia in 1965, when he was just 47 years old.

SUICIDE AND TRAGEDY

Then the title passed to his young son Thomas, who grew to be obsessed by the curse and his forthcoming doom. Coupled with a run-in with the police, Thomas Craven found the burden too hard to bear. In 1983, when he was just 26 years old, he shot himself.

The earldom was in turn inherited by Simon, Thomas's brother, who laughed at the idea of an ancient curse controlling his destiny. However, in August 1990 he died at the wheel of his Mini car when it collided with two parked cars in Eastbourne, Sussex. Craven was driving back from his job as a student nurse at Eastbourne District Hospital when the accident occurred. The burden of the title was then passed on to his 16-month-old son Benjamin.

A neighbour commented: 'It's awful to think that the curse of the Cravens has claimed another victim. What's going to happen to the baby?'

The curse has gained so much credence that it is believed to have tainted the Craven estates. Villagers quoted the curse following the suicide of Dr Robert Reid, a former science editor at the BBC. He bought Morewood House in Hamstead Marshall, Berkshire, from Thomas Craven who was struggling to pay off £3 million in death duties. Shortly before Simon Craven's death, Reid was found gassed in his Range Rover. His 25-year-old marriage had recently broken up.

Bruce Lee was a cult martial-arts hero before his untimely death at the age of 32 following a brain haemorrhage.

The endearing appearance of thatched cottages and medieval façades of Coggeshall in Essex belies a macabre mystery which has put this pleasant place at the centre of a psychic crime wave. At the root of the trouble, it's claimed, is a powerful curse.

CURSED PLACES

It was in Coggeshall that witchfinder-general Matthew Hopkins carried out his work, interrogating and hanging men, women and children on the pretext that they were sorcerers. Market Hill, Coggeshall, was allegedly the site of witch executions and the village is also at a junction of ley lines, thought to be paths of mystic energy.

During the 1980s, when residents were more concerned about property prices than the paranormal, the first in a series of bizarre events occurred – the disappearance of a doctor's wife, 35-year-old Diane Jones.

She went missing after drinking in the local pub. Her battered body was discovered three months later in a wood in Brightwell, 35 miles from her 16th century home at Coggeshall. Forensic scientists concluded she was two months pregnant and had died on the night she vanished. Her killer has never been found.

SUSPICION AND INTERROGATION

Her husband, Dr Robert Jones, was questioned by police for more than 60 hours. He admitted that had not alerted police for nine days after Diane, his third wife, went missing. He believed she had walked out.

ABOVE: WITCH-FINDER GENERAL MATTHEW HOPKINS WHO TERRORISED COGGESHALL. LEFT: THE PICTURESQUE TOWN AT THE CENTRE OF STRANGE HAPPENINGS.

Less than two years after the killing of Diane Jones, Coggeshall was again stunned by a brutal murder. The victim was Patsy Bull, wife of a millionaire antique dealer, and her murderer was her husband, Wilfred.

After her body – shot at point-blank range – was discovered in the antiques warehouse owned by the family, police suspected she was the victim of ruthless raiders. However, her husband was soon arrested and charged.

The court heard how Bull and his wife had become wealthy dealers in antiquities. Bull was cowed by his wife and for six years had an affair with a widow, Carol Scotchford-Hughes. It was a row over his infidelity which led to Patsy's death. Found guilty of murder, Bull was jailed for life.

MORE BRUTAL MURDERS

In 1985 five bodies were discovered at a farmhouse at Tolleshunt D'Arcy, some two miles from Coggeshall. The victims were Neville Bamber and his wife June, their adopted daughter Sheila and her six-year-old twins, Daniel and Nicholas. Police were alerted by Sheila's brother Jeremy who told of a frantic phone call from his father. 'Your sister's gone crazy and she's got the gun.'

Armed officers stormed the house and found the dead bodies. Neville Bamber had been shot nine times and clubbed with a rifle butt. June had been shot between the eyes, Sheila suffered two bullet wounds, one of which severed the jugular vein, and the boys had five and three shots to the head respectively.

Jeremy Bamber told police that his sister, who worked as a model and was known as 'Bambi', was mentally unstable and had a knowledge of guns. At the time police believed that she had gone beserk, slaughtering the family then turning the gun on herself.

Her friends were not convinced. In a search of the house, Bambi's cousins Anne Eaton and David Boutflour discovered a gun silencer in a cupboard. Missed by police, the silencer had a hair and specks of Bambi's blood on it. Clearly she did not put it in the cupboard herself.

Then Bamber's girlfriend Julie Mugford came forward two weeks after the funerals. She told them the free-spending Bamber was responsible for the killings in order to inherit the family wealth and that he sought to commit the perfect crime. Although Bamber maintained his innocence, he was found guilty.

In 1986 champion clay pigeon shooter Jimmy Bell shot his wife and himself in Coggeshall. In 1988 restaurateur Peter Langan died at nearby Alphamstone in a fire he started himself in a bid to stop his wife Susan from leaving him.

Other sinister incidents include the shooting and wounding of the Vicar of Nayland in 1989 whilst he was mowing his lawn. Susan Whybrow plotted with a lover to kill her husband.

THE CURSE OF THE PALACE

On the Grand Canal in Venice, the Ca'Dario Palace sits like a honeymooner's dream. A fondant of medieval design, its ornate façade rising up from the waterfront is unmistakably Venetian, faded now, yet still redolent of a former glory.

But knowing its melancholy history, few would choose to linger. According to locals the grand building is cursed and the bad luck which accompanies the ownership of this prize property shows little sign of abating.

The palace was commissioned by diplomat Giovanni Dario in 1488. An overseas troubleshooter, Dario was apparently not resident long enough to feel the full force of the curse. But his unfortunate son-in-law Vincenzo Barbaro was publicly disgraced and stripped of his civic office after insulting a city dignitary. He was later murdered while his wife Marietta, Dario's daughter, died of shame.

A STREAM OF OWNERS

There came a stream of owners, many of their fates now lost in the mists of time. But the Armenian diamond merchant who went bank-

rupt is still remembered, as is Englishman Rawdon Lubbock Brown who bought the palace in 1839. He lavished money on it before he too went bankrupt and apparently killed himself.

Afterwards the building was made into flats and French poet Henri de Regner was one of the residents. He died there of malaria.

In the 1950s, eccentric American Charles Briggs owned the palace until he was deported from Italy on account of his predilection for the country's young soldiers. By 1968 Count Filippo delle Lanze of Turin had moved in. Within two years he had been savagely murdered by his butler and lover, Raul Blasich.

High-living Kit Lambert, manager of the rock group The Who, then took up residence. He died at the age of 45 from a brain tumour. Next in the line of blighted owners was Fabrizzio Ferrari, a wealthy financier whose sister was later killed in a car crash, shortly before he lost his fortune.

Raul Gardini, an Italian tycoon, yearned to have the palace to present to his daughter as a fabulous wedding gift. He bought the company that owned the palace in the 1980s in order to secure it. But for all his money he could not beat the curse which apparently haunted the place. The marriage of his daughter failed and, in July 1993, Gardini shot himself to avoid a major corruption investigation.

CURSED SOUVENIRS

Tourists flock to Ayers Rock in the Australian national park to witness its magnificence at sundown. The rock, which stands at 335 metres (1,100 ft) above the arid plains south of Alice Springs, is transformed in the dying sunlight when it becomes spectacularly flushed with pink and then blood red. Carried away with the awesome natural magic of the place, some holiday-makers are tempted to pluck a pebble from the rock as a keepsake.

It is just such mementoes which have been returned by the hundred to the park rangers, dispatched by people who believe the chipping has brought them bad luck.

One letter from Arizona accompanying a returned piece of rock read: 'Please return it to its place of rest as I have suffered a lot of sickness since I removed it.'

An Australian woman claims she has developed diabetes since taking some rock and that her baby was stillborn. 'I just hope that by returning this rock whatever evils I may have unleashed on myself may subside a little,' she wrote.

ABORIGINES HAVE LONG HELD AYERS ROCK TO BE SACRED AND THEY CALL IT ULURU. BUT TO THEM THE PREVAILING SPIRITS ARE FRIENDLY. PERHAPS THE KEY TO THE CURSE LIES IN THE TOURISTS, OF WHOM FIVE HAVE FALLEN TO THEIR DEATHS FROM AYERS ROCK IN THE PAST 15 YEARS.

When rock and roll arrived, there were mutterings from Christian fundamentalists about it being the sound of Satan. Different it may have been, but devilish it was not, with its roots firmly planted in gospel music.

BLACK METAL

But in the half century since rock began, the assertions of evil lurking behind the lyrics of songs should not be dismissed. Satanists and pseudo-Satanists have sought to air their credo to music. The result is the somewhat ominous emergence of black metal, an offspring of heavy metal.

SENSATIONALISM AND HYPE

Plenty of groups publicly embraced Satanism, cashing in on the shock value of black antics. Stories of Ozzy Osborne and Alice Cooper biting off the heads of live animals on stage held teenagers in thrall. (The animals were, of course, imitation.) Names of groups like Black Sabbath and ACDC – reputed to stand for Anti-Christ, Devil's Child – were calculated to excite rebellious youths. There were reports of Satanic messages incorporated into heavy metal and only revealed when the music was played backwards. It was a coup for record company publicity people who could not resist fostering 'evil' images.

When a couple of youths killed themselves after listening to the band Judas Priest, their families sought damages from the group and the record company, claiming the lyrics had subliminally compelled the youngsters to turn guns on

JIMMY PAGE OF THE BAND LED ZEPPELIN WAS A STUDENT OF THE WORKS OF 'THE BEAST' ALEISTER CROWLEY.

themselves. The legal manoeuvres on behalf of the families failed on the grounds that listeners responded to dark lyrics only if they were pre-disposed towards violence – but not before dangerous Satanic symbols had been found dotted all over the group's albums.

Jimmy Page of Led Zeppelin was absorbed by the works of Aleister Crowley, while Marc Bolan spent two years living with a black magician in Paris. He believed the spells he learned in his youth were partly responsible for his success. In an interview with *Rolling Stone* magazine in 1972, Bolan said, 'A successful rock and roll record is a spell . . . There are words, there are spells and rites and masses to conjure up or call down elemental forces and beings and even gods.'

RIVALRY AND MURDER

However, the home of die-hard Satanic rockers seems to be Norway where fans seized on Black Metal and made it their own. Luridly named bands, including Morbid Angel, Dark-throne and Impaled, flourished. The Black Metal scene in Scandinavia was uncovered following the murder of Oystein Aarseth, known as Euronymous, lead singer of the band Mayhem. He was stabbed 23 times on 10 August 1993 by Varg Vikernes, alias Count Grishnackh, the leader of rival band Burzum, and contender for the headship of Norway's flourishing Black Metal movement that was held by Aarseth. Vikernes reputedly wore a necklace made from splinters of the skull of Dead, the Mayhem lead singer who put a bullet through his head in 1991. Before his arrest Vikernes outlined his beliefs to the music magazine *Kerrang!*

'All Norwegians are sons of Satan by nature. I consider it blasphemous to build churches on Odin's soil. Norway is Odin's soil. The ones building the churches are the criminals.'

Police believed he was planning to dynamite a Norwegian church during mass. Church-burning in Norway had already become something of a national pastime. In 1994 four members of a British band called Necropolis were jailed for causing £100,000 worth of damage to Kent churches. During their attacks they painted their faces black and white in the style of the Norwegian Black Metal devotees and carried ceremonial weapons, including swords and scythes.

OZZY OSBORNE INCLUDED MACABRE ANTICS IN HIS STAGE ACT. FANS WERE COMPELLED BY HIS EXTREME BEHAVIOUR WHICH INVOLVED THE KILLING OF 'LIVE' ANIMALS.

TO MOST THE BEATLES SONGS WERE CLEVERLY WRITTEN, EXPERTLY PERFORMED AND AN ENJOYABLE DIVERSION. ONE MAN FOUND THEM AN INSPIRATION FOR EVIL. CHARLES MANSON, AN ADVOCATE OF BLACK MAGIC AND SATANISM, WAS THE SELF-STYLED LEADER OF 'THE FAMILY', A DUBIOUS HIPPY COMMUNE. HE TOLD HIS FOLLOWERS THAT THE BEATLES AND HIMSELF WERE MENTALLY ATTUNED. FROM THE WORDS OF VARIOUS RECORDS, SPECIFICALLY ON 'THE WHITE ALBUM', HE DEDUCED THAT THE SUPERGROUP WERE CALLING ON HIM PERSONALLY TO START A VIOLENT REVOLUTION. HE BELIEVED THE SONG HELTER SKELTER REFERRED TO 'THE FAMILY' EMERGING AS WORLD LEADERS, LITTLE REALISING THAT TO THE BEATLES IT WAS THE NAME OF AN AMUSEMENT PARK SLIDE. MANSON AND HIS FOLLOWERS WERE RESPONSIBLE FOR AT LEAST 35 DEATHS, MOST FAMOUSLY THOSE OF HEAVILY PREGNANT ACTRESS SHARON TATE AT THE HOLLYWOOD HOME SHE SHARED WITH HUSBAND, FILM DIRECTOR ROMAN POLANSKI, AND THREE FRIENDS.

It was 2 am and pitch dark as a nightwatchman patrolled the boundaries of a waterworks at Keresley, near Coventry, in 1949. Suddenly, the man started as the beam of his lamp illuminated a terrible sight. In the middle of a meadow in front of him was sitting a huge, black dog. 'It was bigger than me and I'm 5'10",' he said. The eyes of this mammoth canine appeared to be flickering with fire – or was it the reflection of his light?

The terrified fellow didn't wait to find out – he dashed back to the security of the pumping station and locked himself in.

Next morning he nervously told a colleague what he had seen. Instead of mocking him, his workmate admitted seeing just such a beast on two occasions, but had kept quiet. A neighbouring householder then showed them a paw print found in his garden 'as large as a dinner plate'.

TERRIFYING SIGHTINGS

Spectral black dogs have long been a feature of the English countryside and have lent their names to pubs, roads and parks. Coventry has a Black Dog Inn, Dog Lane and areas known as Dogland, Black Pad and Hounds Hill. It was this same hound that appeared to a man returning from the pub on horseback. When the man lashed out with his riding crop the black dog exploded. The horserider was discovered afterwards in a ditch with scorch marks on his tattered clothes.

The traditional black dog is large, about the size of a calf, has a shaggy coat and burning, saucer-shaped eyes – one of the many forms allegedly adopted by the devil. It may be phantom

BLACK DOG

ABOVE LEFT: WITCHES WERE BELIEVED TO MOUNT SUPERNATURAL BLACK DOGS AND RIDE THEM TO THE SABBAT CELEBRATIONS AS THIS 1926 BOOK ILLUSTRATION SHOWS.

The traditional black dog is large, standing over five feet tall, and has burning, saucer-shaped eyes. Its face can appear human.

or fairy, an omen, a guardian or a witch's familiar. Another name for it is the bargest or padfoot.

Newgate Prison has its own black dog which is believed to be the ghost of a prison inmate. Some hold it to be executed highwayman Luke Hutton, while others favour a 13th century learned man gaoled on charges of witchcraft who was killed and eaten by other starving inmates. Newgate's black dog was said to appear the night before an execution and travel with the condemned as they made their way to the gallows at Tyburn.

A WALL OF SILENCE

The role of a mythical black dog baffled Detective Superintendent Robert Fabian as he investigated the gruesome murder in Lower Quinton, Warwickshire, of farm worker Charles Walton, who was found impaled on his own pitchfork. Across the chest and throat of the 74-year-old victim was scratched the sign of the cross, carved with his own hedge-trimming hook. Walton claimed he could converse with birds and animals and was regarded as something of an eccentric.

Police found themselves confronted by a wall of silence. None of the 450 villagers would confide in them about possible theories or suspects.

One evening he saw a large black dog go by and asked an approaching boy whether the dog was his. Terrified, the lad fled, leaving Fabian mystified. During the investigation Fabian discovered the body of a black dog hanging from a tree. That night he visited a local pub, the Gay Dog, and attempted conversation with the locals.

At the mention of the black dog, one man told how back in 1885 a ploughboy had come across the dog nine times on successive days. On the last occasion the dog turned into a headless woman before his astonished eyes. She glided past him, close enough for him to hear the rustle of her silk dress. The next day the boy's seemingly healthy sister died. The ploughboy was Charles Walton.

Later Fabian wrote, 'When Albert Webb and I walked into the village pubs silence fell like a physical blow. Cottage doors were shut in our faces and even the most innocent witnesses seemed unable to meet our eyes.' There were undertones of witchcraft and black magic but not an iota of evidence.

Finally Fabian pulled out of Lower Quinton, having taken a staggering 4,000 statements. He suspected a local farmer who owed money to Walton, but could not prove it. The strange case of Charles Walton remained unsolved.

THIS 1865 PAINTING, *LADY GODIVA'S PRAYER* BY SIR EDWIN LANDSEER, SHOWS THE BLACK DOG THAT WAS SAID TO ACCOMPANY LADY GODIVA ON HER NAKED RIDE THROUGH COVENTRY.

To hard-headed scientists the explosion which crippled the Apollo 13 space mission was an unforeseen disaster which was masterfully retrieved. There were plenty of untrained observers who, with the benefit of hindsight, found the drama entirely unsurprising. The fault lay, they claimed, with those who decided to burden the moon-bound expedition with the unlucky number 13.

OMENS AND UNLUCKY 13

More than that, the rocket had taken off at 13.13 local time from Pad 39, three times 13, on 11 April 1970. Add the numbers of the date (11, 4, 70) to get 85 and then add those two numbers together to find, guess what, another 13. These couch experts barely raised an eyebrow when the explosion occurred on 13 April.

TRISKAIDEKAPHOBIA

People possessed of this morbid fear of the number 13 are called triskaidekaphobics. They are known to live in fear of Friday the 13th which crops up on the calendar about every seven months. But why is 13 feared?

Most point to the Last Supper which Jesus attended with 12 others. In fact the threat of 13 is older still, featuring in Norse mythology. There were 12 gods gathered at a feast when the troublesome spirit of Loki entered and began a row which ended in the death of Balder, a popular god. The Romans saw 13 as a sign of impending disaster. Down the centuries 13 continued its unlucky associations with the number of witches in a coven believed to be that number.

In the hotel industry the figure 13 features largely. Many large hotels do not have a room numbered 13 or a 13th floor, skipping from 12 to 14. If 13 people turn up for dinner, there's a saying which claims one will die within the year. To calm the fears of superstitious diners London's Savoy Hotel keeps a lucky black cat model which can be placed on a chair as diner number 14.

Some people genuinely believe they will sidestep the bad luck which will surely come to them if they live in a house numbered 13 by changing it to twelve and a half. There are state lotteries in Spain and Italy which omit the number 13 because it is so alien to good fortune.

OMENS OF DOOM

In the same way, omens can be bad for your health. It is reputed that any man who sees a star

ABOVE: THE NUMBER 13 WAS BELIEVED TO BE UNLUCKY BY MANY FOLLOWING THE LAST SUPPER ATTENDED BY JESUS AND HIS 12 DISCIPLES.

fall or a flower that is blooming out of season knows that he is about to die. If his conviction is strong enough, the omen may well come true. It has nothing at all to do with the quirks of nature that he has just witnessed and everything to do with his blind faith.

Other death omens include a black beetle scuttling over a shoe; a butterfly at night; a rooster crowing at midnight; a cow lowing three times in your face; hearing the first call of the cuckoo when looking at the ground.

The superstitious who deal with the dead are in grave danger. Anyone seeing their own reflection in a hearse or the reflection of a corpse in a mirror is, by lore, doomed.

Homemakers, beware! The happy trio which sets about making a bed will soon be reduced to a duo for one of them will surely die. Likewise, if all three are reflected in a mirror, the days of one are numbered. The seemingly innocent act of planting lily of the valley in the garden is also fraught with danger. While in the garden, never burn elder wood, the Christmas holly decoration which remains green or the old blackened stump of a tree struck by lightning unless you are ready to meet your maker.

The careless among us can cause the death of others, by singing at the table; sweeping the house on Good Friday; washing blankets in May; or decorating the house with flowering blackthorn, white lilies or hawthorn. The list is seemingly endless and the case for fatalism immense.

IN IRELAND THE BANSHEE — OR BANSIDHE — IS A SPIRIT WHO GIVES A BLOOD-CURDLING YELL AS AN OMEN OF DEATH. COMMENTATOR SHEILA ST CLAIR BELIEVES THE BANSHEE YELL 'IS PART OF AN INHERITED MEMORY . . . STAMPED ON OUR RACIAL CONSCIOUSNESS' RELEASED BY A MIND WITH DISASTER IN ITS SIGHTS AS A 'FOUR MINUTE WARNING'.

GHOSTS, GHOULS AND FABLED CREATURES

Ghosts may be those who are living, on the point of death or long dead. Some are malevolent, some benign; some are message-bearers, some are mute. They may be known to the person who sees them, or a complete stranger.

Do those floaty figures or disembodied voices arise from hallucinations? Could they be spirits trapped on earth? Are they proof of life after death? Do significant events leave a hallmark in the atmosphere which people occasionally glimpse? Those who claim to have seen them lend credence to all of the above theories.

CHAPTER FOUR

HAUNTED HOMES

The ancestral home of Princess Diana was exorcised to rid it of the ghost of her grandfather. Her stepmother Raine Spencer was convinced the spirit contributed to the illness of her husband Earl Spencer after he suffered a stroke. The earl had feuded with his father for years.

ABOVE: JUDGE JEFFREYS, 'THE HANGING JUDGE', RETURNED 300 YEARS AFTER HIS DEATH TO HAUNT YORK CROWN COURT, BEING SEEN CLEARLY BY THE PRESIDING RECORDER.

She arranged for a local vicar to visit the stately home in 1978. After it was blessed, the spirit did apparently disappear and the Earl made a recovery. The ceremony was revealed by Charles Spencer, younger brother of Diana, who became the ninth earl on the eventual death of his father in 1992.

'The exorcism was to get rid of my grandfather,' he explained. 'His ghost was seen as a negative force which might have something to do with my father's illness.'

The ghost of the seventh earl who died in June 1975 aged 83 was seen by staff and guests at the house as well as residents.

'One of them was the old housekeeper. She is a very steady person who worked here for years. He was also seen walking up and down the corridor by one of my first cousins,' said the present earl. 'People who've seen it say it makes the hair stand up on the back of their necks.'

FEUD ENDS IN DUEL

Another grand old house which has its own resident ghost is to be found in Lafayette Square, Washington DC, once the home of the distinguished naval officer Stephen Decatur and his wife Susan.

A feud between himself and another officer, Commodore James Barron, was to be settled by duel on the morning of 14 March 1820 in the grounds of the house. Decatur was a crack shot, and yet still he felt the chill wind of foreboding. Guests at the house on the night before the duel saw him staring moodily from his first floor bedroom window.

At dawn he left with a box of pistols under his arm to settle the issue. Barron fell first, wounded in the hip. But almost immediately after, Decatur fell from a wound in his right side. He was carried back to the house to die.

A year later the mournful figure of Decatur was spotted at the bedroom window. After the window was walled up, his ghost was frequently seen around the house, sometimes slipping out of the back door in the early morning, just as Decatur had done on the day he died. The sounds of weeping heard around the house are said to be his distraught wife. Decatur House is now a museum.

ROYAL GHOSTS — AND WHERE TO FIND THEM

The screams of Edward II, the homosexual king, who died after being tortured by a red hot poker in 1327, can still be heard around Berkeley Castle in Gloucestershire.

Anne Boleyn, mother of Queen Elizabeth I and second wife of Henry VIII, has been seen at the Tower of London where she was held before her execution in 1536.

Jane Seymour, third wife of Henry VIII, can be seen gliding along Clock Court, Hampton Court, bearing a lighted candle.

The horrific screams of Catherine Howard, Henry VIII's fourth wife, can be heard in the Haunted Gallery at Hampton Court on the anniversary of her arrest for adultery in 1542. She had escaped her guards and attempted to reach her husband to plead for her life before being dragged away.

Queen Elizabeth I (1533–1603) has been seen wandering at Windsor Castle, most frequently in the library. Among those who have seen Good Queen Bess is Princess Margaret the sister of Queen Elizabeth II.

Also in the library at Windsor Castle, the ghost of King Charles I, who was beheaded in 1649, has been spotted standing next to an antique table.

King George II (1683–1760) has been seen on the roof of Kensington Palace staring at the weather vane and asking, in his markedly German accent: 'Why don't they come?' He died at the palace in 1760 awaiting news from his native Hanover.

The ghost of Prince Philip's mother, Princess Andrew of Greece, was heard by nuns weeping at the White Russian Church of St Magdalene in Jerusalem after her remains were moved from England in 1988, 18 years after her death in 1969 aged 84.

CHARLES DICKENS HAD SCROOGE, HERO OF *A CHRISTMAS CAROL*, HAUNTED BY FOUR GHOSTS. IN 1862 DICKENS FOUNDED THE LONDON GHOST CLUB WHICH STILL EXISTS TODAY.

ANNE BOLEYN AND THE GHOSTS OF THE MURDERED PRINCES ARE OFTEN SEEN AT THE TOWER OF LONDON, WHILE THE SCREAMS OF TORTURED GUY FAWKES AND THE BLUDGEONED COUNTESS OF SALISBURY SOMETIMES SPLIT THE NIGHT.

Two doctors were only too keen to help the man who flagged their car down in the darkness on a deserted English country road. Although it was the early hours of the morning, the MacPhersons could see the fellow had been hurt in a road crash.

'Crashed my car. Need help,' he gasped. From the back seat of their car the man directed them to the scene of the accident. His car was wrapped around a tree. Inside the driver was dead, but his wife and child were still alive.

As he tended the child, Dr Malcolm Macpherson suddenly realised the man who had waved them down was missing. Then he looked at the body of the dead driver as it was being stretchered to an ambulance. Both he and his wife recognised it as being the man who had alerted them, not only by his face but from the distinctive cut on his hand.

At the inquest into his death, it was revealed that the man had died instantly. It was also clear that his wife and child would have died if they had lain undiscovered for the rest of the night.

GHOST OF SAVAGED KENNEL KEEPER

The ghost of a former kennel keeper is said to haunt Dog Kennel House at Stormont, Northern Ireland. He was supposed to have temporarily

FRIENDLY GHOSTS

abandoned the dogs in his care. When he returned the starving pack devoured him, leaving only his boots. Those boots are now regularly heard clumping about the place which is home to Peggy Leith. 'It is certainly a friendly ghost, like most Irish ones,' claimed Peggy. 'We are quite happy to live with it.'

The benefits of having a residence full of ghosts are not immediately obvious to all. Jeffrey Stambovsky was horrified when he discovered that the dream house overlooking the Hudson River which he was hoping to buy had a small population of ghosts.

Three ghosts had been identified at the house at Nyack, some 30 miles from New York City. One was a sailor in a powdered wig, another an

THE GHOST OF SARAH WHITEHEAD HAUNTS THE BANK OF ENGLAND. SHE IS SEEN FRANTICALLY SEARCHING FOR HER BROTHER PHILIP, AN EMPLOYEE WHO WAS HANGED FOR FORGERY IN 1811.

WHEN 'THE MAN IN GREY' WITH HIS POWDERED WIG AND TRICORN HAT IS SPOTTED IN THE DRESS CIRCLE OF THE THEATRE ROYAL IN LONDON IT BODES WELL FOR A SHOW.

The spirits were 'gracious, thoughtful and only occasionally frightening. They have been a delight to us'.

Stambovsky was not convinced. He pulled out of the sale, even losing the $20,000 deposit he had put on the $400,000 home after a judge ruled that vendors had no duty to reveal the existence of supernatural inhabitants.

NOT A GHOST IN SIGHT

The opposite problem had Canadian Professor Trevor Kirkham and his wife Judy resorting to law. They had bought Cringle Hall at Goosnargh in Lancashire in the belief that it housed a clutch of ghosts, including that of Catholic martyr John Wall. When the ghosts – and ghost-hunters – did not turn up they regretted their investment and subsequently claimed the property had been misrepresented to them.

MARINE MYSTERY

A sailor in the North Atlantic was startled to see a stranger scrawling in the log book. Although the fellow disappeared his message remained: 'Steer to the north east'. The Captain did so – and discovered a ship on the point of sinking. Among the survivors taken aboard was the man spotted by the sailor.

A DEVOTED DAUGHTER

After a hard day's work Dr S. Weir Mitchell was dozing in a chair when he was woken by a frantic knocking. When he went to the door he found a young girl pleading with him to visit her mother. Together they went immediately to her house and the sick woman was duly treated. Praising her daughter, the doctor was suddenly silenced when the woman said: 'My daughter died a month ago.'

SENTRY AT YPRES

An ambulance driver at Ypres was taking an injured soldier to safety during the First World War when he spotted a sentry standing in the road ahead. He braked hard but the guard had disappeared. In his place was a deadly crater into which the ambulance would have toppled had it continued its journey.

elderly gentleman in a blue suit with knee breeches and silver buckled shoes. The third was a young woman in a hooded cape.

Vendor Helen Ackley, who had lived in the house for 24 years, insisted the spirits were 'gracious, thoughtful and only occasionally frightening.' They had been alarming only once years before when they had woken her three children by shaking their beds violently, insisted Mrs Ackley. After that episode she maintained, 'They have been a delight to us.'

She was even prepared to welcome them to the house she was planning to move to in Orlando, Florida, although she could not guarantee they would come.

After former circus midget Fanchon Moncare was jailed as a gem smuggler, her eyes searched the public gallery until she homed in on the woman who had betrayed her.

KILLER GHOSTS

'I'll kill you,' shrieked tiny Moncare before being led away. Magda Hamilton leered back. With Moncare out of the way she was free to pursue handsome gambler Dartney Crawley. The bizarre rivalry between the two women had led Hamilton to turn police informer.

Moncare and her associate, Ada Danforth, had repeatedly pulled off a brazen scam. The pair travelled between France and New York with Danforth posing as guardian to Moncare, who played the part of a pretty young orphan heiress.

Passengers on the liner ships which plied the route in the 1870s were charmed by her girlish affectations. Little did they know the china doll she clung to was full of stolen jewellery which would be fenced in New York shortly after Moncare sauntered through customs.

Only after prompting by Hamilton did customs finally inspect the doll. Danforth was jailed for 20 years while Moncare, with a string of previous convictions, got life.

THE FACE OF A WITHERED HAG

Hamilton went on to make her way into café society. By now divorced, she woke up one morning some years later to find Moncare at the foot of her bed. Still dressed as a child, the midget bore the face of a withered hag. Hamilton escaped her by darting into the bathroom and locking herself in for the rest of the night.

Only when she reported the matter to police the next morning did she discover that Moncare

ABOVE: LORD LYTTLETON IS AWOKEN BY A GHOST, FROM *THE ASTROLOGER* 1825.
LEFT: KILLER GHOSTS SPAWNED MANY MOVIES INCLUDING *THE AMITYVILLE HORROR*, 1979.

had hanged herself in jail. That afternoon Hamilton booked herself a cabin on a liner heading for Europe which would leave the very next day.

However, on the morning of the trip, servants found her dead on her bed, her eyes bulging and blood congealed at the corners of her mouth. A medical examiner decided she had drowned in her own blood after a heavy object was rammed into her mouth. The murder weapon was never found. Yet investigators were mystified by the presence in Hamilton's mouth of several hairs from the head of a child's china doll.

Although it's rare, ghosts can be deadly. A malevolent spirit haunted 50 Berkeley Square in London and claimed several victims. Successive owners and neighbours were alarmed at the bangs and crashes perpetuated by the ghost which began after the death of one-time owner, British Prime Minister George Canning, in 1827.

Aristocrat Sir Robert Warboys pledged to spend a night in the most haunted room of the house, an upstairs bedroom. It was a cause célèbre among his friends who gathered in the house that night. Armed with a pistol and a bell pull to call for help, he retired to bed at 11.45 pm quipping: 'My dear fellows, I am here to disprove the bunkum of a ghost, so your little alarm will be of no use. I bid you goodnight.'

The ghost of 50 Berkeley Square claimed the lives of three people, all of whom died terror-stricken.

SHOTS IN THE NIGHT

Just 15 minutes later the bell rang wildly. Before anyone could reach him a shot rang out. The assembled gentlemen burst in to find Warboys dead on the bed, his face a picture of terror. He had fired the gun at whatever confronted him in the darkness – but to no avail.

In 1878 another nobleman decided to sleep in that same disturbing room. Lord Lyttleton took with him two guns, one of which was loaded with silver sixpenny pieces which were considered a charm against evil. When a spectre approached, he fired the silver coins and it vanished. The incident prompted him to investigate the history of the troubled house and he discovered that, as well

as Warboys, at least two other people had died there apparently following visits from the ghost.

The final fatality came in 1887. Two sailors, Edward Blunden and Robert Martin, from HMS *Penelope* found themselves in foggy London on Christmas Eve with nowhere to stay. A 'to let' sign indicated that 50 Berkeley Square was vacant, so they went inside. By chance they happened on the very bedroom where Warboys died. Martin slept, but Blunden became increasingly nervous. He nudged Martin back to consciousness just in time to see a dark apparition enter the room. When Blunden tried to grab a weapon, the ghost made a bee-line for him, enabling Martin to escape. The sailor ran until he found a policeman. When the pair returned to the property they discovered the body of Blunden at the foot of the basement stairs, his neck broken and his eyes wide open.

GEORGE CANNING (1770–1827), OF 50 BERKELEY SQUARE, WAS BRITISH FOREIGN SECRETARY FOR FIVE YEARS BUT DIED SOON AFTER BECOMING THE TORY PRIME MINISTER.

It still meant a long drive along isolated country roads in darkness to reach the station in Exeter in time for the train. With Marian at the wheel, Dennis dozed

Suddenly, she was blinded through her rear view mirror by the flashing lights of a car behind. 'Who is that idiot and why is he flashing me?' Marian asked her husband. He confessed he had not noticed any lights.

'Then the lights vanished. They swung to the side and there was a tremendous crashing sound like metal hitting iron railings. The noise was loud enough to wake Dennis,' explained Marian.

GHOSTS ON THE MOVE

When they arrived at their holiday hotel in north Devon in August 1977, disastrous news awaited Marian and Dennis Steafel. Her father had died back in London after a long illness. After talking to her mother, Marian and Dennis decided to return for the funeral, taking the overnight train from south Devon and leaving their three children to be cared for at the hotel.

'We stopped and got out of the car, but we couldn't see anything at all. We had to drive on so that we didn't miss the train but when I got to London, I telephoned the local police. I explained that I thought I had heard an accident but didn't see anything.'

A THREE-YEAR-OLD ACCIDENT
'"That's all right, my love," he told me. "The accident happened three years ago and you are the sixth person to have seen it since."'

ABOVE: LAWRENCE OF ARABIA IS SAID TO HAUNT HIS OLD HOME, CLOUDS HILL IN DORCHESTER.

A car had crashed at the very spot Marian saw the lights swerve, killing its occupants. The policeman felt the lights appeared as a warning to drivers in a highly charged emotional state.

A ghostly bus was reported dozens of times after it raced down the middle of a London street in the early hours, with no driver or passengers. The Number 7, running long after normal services were finished, was always spotted on the same dangerous bend in Ladbroke Grove. Once the sight of the bus even caused a fatal accident.

An inquest heard 'Suddenly this bus appeared, ablaze with light. The car swerved and smashed into the wall. The bus immediately vanished'.

Afterwards the council made the stretch of road safer and the ghost bus was never seen again.

BUMPS IN THE DARK

Train drivers were spooked as they roared through Bincombe Tunnel on the Weymouth to Dorchester line after a series of inexplicable bumps heard on the outside of the cab. In 1991 they claimed the noises were only heard between 8 pm and 9 pm on a Friday night. It was a popular spot for suicides in former days. But rail staff link the death of a passenger in 1987 to events on the 'ghost train'. Thinking he had missed the train the passenger had set off to walk through the tunnel – only to discover that the service was late. When it bore down on him in the darkness, he had no way of escape. One driver even believes he has seen a figure walking calmly by the track.

Goodwood House in Sussex was reputedly haunted by a phantom coach and horses although the last reliable sighting was more than 50 years ago. It may be that the dynamics of the ghostly carriage have fizzled over the years.

A COACH PULLED BY FOUR HEADLESS HORSES CONTINUES TO TAKE DAME ALICIA LISLE FROM ELLINGHAM CHURCHYARD, HAMPSHIRE, WHERE SHE WAS BURIED IN 1685. SHE WAS BEHEADED FOR ASSISTING REBELS DURING MONMOUTH'S REBELLION.

Yet when the photograph was pinned up at the base there was a collective gasp. There in the back row, behind the man four from left, was Jackson.

The incident was recorded in a book called *Flight Towards Reality* by Air Marshal Sir Victor Goddard, one of the founders of the RAF.

Sir Victor wrote: 'There he was, and no mistake, although a little fainter than the rest. Indeed, he looked as though he was not altogether there; not really with that group, for he alone was capless, smiling; all the rest were serious and set, and wearing service caps.'

GHOSTS IN THE FRAME

The official photo of the servicemen and women of the transport yard at HMS *Daedalus* taken in the summer of 1919 was a poker-faced affair. In full uniform the men and women of the base in Cranwell, Lincolnshire, stood erect and unsmiling – one of their number, air mechanic Freddy Jackson, had died just days beforehand on the very tarmac strip where they now posed, after stumbling into a whirring propeller.

UNTOUCHED NEGATIVES
'What is somewhat unusual, to say the least, is that this was an official photograph . . . also the certainty that there had been no hanky-panky in the dark-room.

'The negative was scrutinised for faking and was found to be untouched.' One of the women at the base was Bobbie Capel, a Wren driver who

ABOVE LEFT: THE GHOST OF DOROTHY WALPOLE, THE BROWN LADY, ASCENDS THE STAIRS AT RAYNHAM HALL IN NORFOLK.

regularly saw Freddy Jackson as she drove to and from the *Daedalus* vehicle maintenance yard.

The photograph perplexed her so much that she revived the mystery by publishing the photo in 1996 when she was aged 97.

Mrs Capel said: 'I cannot entertain the idea that this was a deliberate fake. For one thing the photographer came from outside the base. He didn't know any of us and, once he'd taken his picture, he left immediately. He just would not have known about the accident.

'Neither can I understand how the face could have appeared by some mishap. I have thought and puzzled over it for years but I can think of no explanation other than that it is the picture of a ghost.'

Mrs Capel, who joined the Wrens in 1917 as an 18-year-old driver, was one of 20 women stationed at HMS *Daedalus*. The base was responsible for training sea-plane pilots and was home to around 700 personnel.

'I am 97 and my memory is not always good. But I know there was only this one fatal accident among our group in the 18 months I was there. It affected us deeply.

'When we lined up for that photograph to commemorate the disbanding of the transport yard, we all knew one familiar face would not be with us. Only later did we discover that, actually, he was.'

CHEATS AND PSYCHIC PHOTOGRAPHY
Ghosts have been framed for about 150 years, with the first published example appearing in 1861 when Boston jeweller William Mumler took a self-portrait, only to find the image of a dead person next to his own. The new faces which appeared became known as 'extras'. Psychic photographer William Hope claimed that he snapped more than 2,500 pictures peopled with extras during 20 years.

The credibility of ghost photos has been severely dented, however, with numerous frauds. Yet there are a number which cannot be explained away as a double exposure or negative tampering.

Among the ghosts allegedly found on film is the Brown Lady of Raynham Hall, Norfolk. She was Dorothy Walpole, who wears a brown bro-cade dress. She is said to have no eyes. A tall, monk-like figure with a cowl hiding his face was photographed attending a formal dinner at St Mary's Guildhall, Coventry, in 1985. A shrouded figure has been snapped climbing the Tulip staircase at the Queen's House in Greenwich.

These are the photographic accidents which end up causing a sensation. Yet some psychics claim they can imprint images on film inside a camera without even using the lens and shutter. The technique was discovered in the early 1900s by Tomokichi Fukarai, president of the Psychical Institute of Japan. He tested clairvoyant Mrs Nagao by placing a camera in a bag. Later the film plate in the camera was shown to have registered the psychic activity. Fukarai coined the nomenclature 'thoughtography'. Believers of this phenomena think it could be thoughtography – the channelled thoughts of the subjects in the picture – that cause the images seen in spirit photography.

A PHOTOGRAPH CAPTURES THE SHADOWY FIGURE OF LORD COMBERMERE IN HIS LIBRARY. IT WAS TAKEN AS THE OLD MAN WAS BEING BURIED.

In 1990 in Oklahoma a family seeking refuge from the heady heat of a June evening retreated from their stuffy home to the yard, hoping to catch the breath of a breeze. The night was shattered when they became the targets of a phantom stone-thrower.

POLTERGEISTS

Assuming pranksters were to blame, Bill and Maxine McWethey, their 18-year-old daughter Twyla, and her little girl Desiree, went back inside, furious at the unprovoked attack. But their anger turned to dismay and then to fear when the stones kept coming. The house was under siege for 24 hours, with windows being broken.

The family lived at Centrahoma and the nearest sheriff was some seven miles away at Coalgate. Rather than contact the police, the McWetheys endured the torment. As Bill McWethey scoured the neighbourhood he could see no signs of whoever was responsible.

Attacks continued sporadically throughout June and July and still the perpetrator was unknown. One night about 50 curious people gathered during the hailstorm. One astonished witness suggested marking the stones with nail varnish and throwing them back. Amazingly, the stones were returned moments later. Another enterprising person plopped a marked stone in the pond. That, too, was hurled back.

SIR OLIVER CROMWELL'S ROUNDHEAD SOLDIERS STATIONED IN NORTHAMPTONSHIRE FOUND THEIR BELONGINGS STREWN EVERYWHERE BY A POLTERGEIST WITH ROYALIST SYMPATHIES.

The police were called for the first time in August. A deputy came to visit the scene, but was under fire even before he left his patrol car. He braved the barrage to look for those responsible, but found nothing. Alarmed, he leapt back into his car and drove off.

A BARRAGE OF COINS, SCREWS AND NAILS

The ammunition switched from stones to coins and later screws, nails and bric-a-brac. When winter came the activity continued inside the house. Two reporters visited the McWetheys and witnessed a volley of stones being fired, with Twyla as the prime target. They needed no further persuasion that a poltergeist was at work.

Soon the poltergeist began to make high-pitched noises. Through a muddle of metallic sound, he seemed to introduce himself as Michael Dale Sutherland. His unpredictable behaviour plagued the family. He dyed the pet parakeets using food colouring, ripped sheets from the bed, daubed symbols on mirrors using lipstick. He told the haunted Twyla that he was an alien left behind after a mission from Saturn. But according to Mrs McWethey, 'He lies a lot'.

A poltergeist is a boisterous, mischievous ghost particularly associated with people instead of places. It can be nasty. The word poltergeist is taken from two German words, 'poltern' meaning knock and 'geist' meaning spirit.

A LIKING FOR TELEPHONES AND ELECTRICITY

For centuries there have been reports of poltergeist activity – stone throwing, moving objects, throwing objects, strange knocking, pouring water, eerie lights, vile smells and even physical and sexual assaults. In modern times poltergeists have discovered there's fun to be had with electric lightbulbs and telephones.

One family in St David's, Wales, were paying £750 a quarter for power which they weren't using. Bill and Liz Rich and their three children found the consumption of electricity at their 14th century home rocketed when they were away on holiday. Although the house was eventually re-wired and installed with four test meters, the local electricity board could find no relevant fluctuations. Bill taped down the light switches so they could not be switched on at night.

In March 1994, medium Eddie Burks visited the household and declared that a profoundly evil force within it was feeding from the electricity. Burks went into a trance, luring the evil out of the house and into his body. The next month electricity costs fell by more than half.

Between December 1716 and January 1717, John Wesley, founder of the Methodist Church, was troubled by a poltergeist at his home of Epworth Parsonage in Lincolnshire. He and other family members heard rapping sounds, a soft footfall on the stairs, the rustle of a gown and the creak of a rocking cradle when none was there. His father, Samuel Wesley, challenged the spirit, affectionately known as Old Jeffrey by the family, to meet him face to face in the study. When he tried to open the study door a mighty force prevented him. Old Jeffrey eventually left, although no one is sure what prompted his departure.

Although some poltergeist incidents can be explained away as wicked horseplay there are others which, disturbingly, defy explanation.

STEVEN SPIELBERG'S 1982 FILM *POLTERGEIST* GAVE A TERRIFYING DEPICTION OF EVIL SPIRITS AT WORK.

SUPERNATURAL OFFICE

At a deserted lawyer's office in Rosenheim, Germany, pictures swung violently on the wall as if pushed by an unseen hand. Hanging lamps went into a spin and furniture moved around the room, seemingly of its own accord. Light bulbs blew, power points fused and the telephone repeatedly called up the speaking clock. The bizarre scene was captured on film in 1967 and had all the hallmarks of a poltergeist presence. But was there anything supernatural there at all?

Some theorists believe that a human not a spirit is at the root of poltergeist activity. The term used is recurrent spontaneous psychokinesis – which means mind waves controlling matter – emanating from somebody at or near the chaos. Certainly there is usually a human focus for a poltergeist, commonly an adolescent and frequently a girl.

FURNITURE WAS FLUNG ABOUT AT A HOUSE IN DODLESTEN, CHESTER, IN 1985. AT THE SAME TIME MYSTERIOUS COMPUTER MESSAGES WERE RECEIVED, APPARENTLY FROM A 16TH CENTURY MAN.

At the Bavarian law office the focus appeared to be a 19-year-old called Anna S. Whenever she walked down the hall, light fittings would swing behind her and the bulbs would explode.

MIND OVER MATTER?

Researcher Nandor Fodor was the first to debunk the notion of poltergeist haunting in the 1930s. He was certain that pent-up mental energy was more powerful than anyone had ever dreamed. Repressed anger, hostility or sexual tension unknowingly released by an unhappy subject wreak havoc.

Thirty years later his findings were endorsed by William Roll, project director of the Psychical Research Foundation in Durham, North Carolina. Roll said that teenagers found psychokinesis is an ideal outlet for aggression without fear of their being punished. He observed that those at the focus of poltergeist outbreaks may well be secretly satisfied with the results, even if they cause the energy explosions unwittingly.

Tragically, that could not be said of young Maria José Ferreira of Brazil, who became the target of a stone-throwing demon in 1965. Neighbour Joao Volpe took the 11-year-old into his home in Sao Paulo, Brazil, to study her case

closely. He witnessed stones flying around the room – the largest weighing 4.7 kg (10 lb) – as well as vegetables, eggs, even sweets. Without warning, the poltergeist turned nasty and began smacking Maria on her face and bottom. Needles began appearing in her feet, even when she wore shoes. On one occasion no fewer than 55 needles had to be extracted.

Volpe visited a medium to discover who or what was tormenting little Maria. A spirit allegedly told him that she had been a witch in a former life and was now being punished for her wicked spells. Maria was so tortured by the poltergeist that, aged 13, she killed herself.

PSYCHIC INVESTIGATIONS

It is true that, in some cases, psychotherapy has banished poltergeist activity. Yet it seems inconceivable that the needle assaults which afflicted Maria José Ferreira could be deemed the result of psychokinesis. In any event, the 'mind over matter' theory is not universally endorsed. Some investigators believe that only a proportion of poltergeists can be explained away in this fashion, among them parapsychologists Alan Gauld and A. D. Cornell.

Together Gauld and Cornell researched some 500 cases dating from 1800 to the 1970s and drew some intriguing conclusions. Nearly 75 per cent of poltergeist hauntings featured the movement of small objects, and only 36 per cent involved the displacement of large items. Just 16 per cent of poltergeists communicated directly with people, yet nearly 50 per cent made themselves known through raps and knocking. Less than 25 per cent of hauntings lasted longer than a year.

Other causes have been probed over the years, including the presence of death watch beetle, the effects of shrinking timber, the noises and vibrations of an underground stream and even subsidence. None have proved satisfactory.

THIS 19TH CENTURY PAINTING SHOWS A COUPLE AND THEIR MAID PROTECTING A CHILD ASLEEP IN ITS CRADLE FROM OBJECTS LAUNCHED MYSTERIOUSLY INTO FLIGHT AROUND THE ROOM.

IT IS AN APPARENTLY EVIL INTENT THAT MAKES POLTERGEISTS SO ALARMING. IN 1878, 18-YEAR-OLD ESTHER COX, LIVING ON A HOMESTEAD IN NOVA SCOTIA, BECAME THE FOCUS OF A POLTERGEIST. THE HAUNTING BEGAN AFTER ESTHER WAS THE VICTIM OF AN ATTEMPTED RAPE. THEREAFTER THERE WERE ASSORTED FIRES, BANGING AND CRASHING SOUNDS, WHILE ESTHER HERSELF WAS STABBED BY A PENKNIFE AND A FORK AND HIT ON THE HEAD WITH A BROOM. HER BODY SWELLED OMINOUSLY; TO THE HORROR OF ASSEMBLED MEMBERS OF HER FAMILY THE WORDS 'ESTHER, YOU ARE MINE TO KILL' APPEARED ON THE WALL ABOVE HER BED.

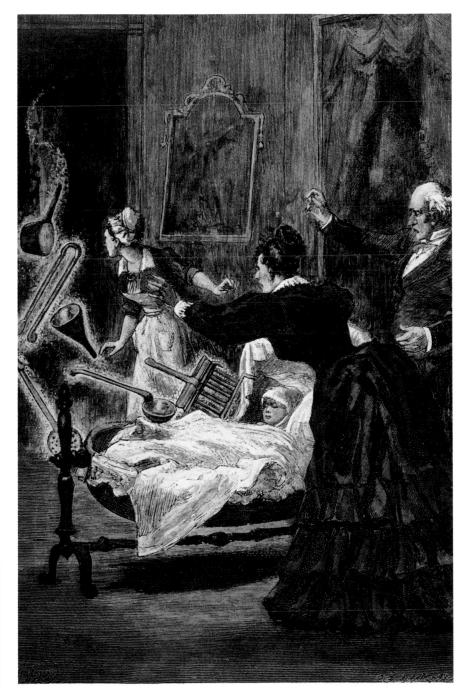

In 1727 a young Serbian soldier, Arnold Paole, came home from a campaign in Greece. He had seen some terrible things during war, none worse than the sight of a blood-sucking vampire, the living dead who feed on the blood of their victims. There was no cause for concern, he comforted the girl he hoped to marry. He had found the grave of the vampire and destroyed it.

VAMPIRES

Soon after Arnold had returned to his home village of Meduegna near Belgrade, he died in a fall. Yet following his death, there were reported sightings of him, too numerous to be ignored. Some of the people who had spotted him died themselves soon afterwards.

STAKE THROUGH THE HEART

Concerned villagers opened Arnold's grave 40 days after he was interred to find the body perfectly preserved – with fresh, dried blood around the mouth. Observer Johannes Flickinger, a military doctor, reported, 'They found that he was quite complete and undecayed, and that fresh blood had flowed from his eyes, nose, mouth and ears; that the old nails on his hands and feet, along with the skin, had fallen off, and that new ones had grown; and since they saw from this that he was a true vampire, they drove a stake through his heart, according to their custom, whereby he gave an audible groan and bled copiously.'

The body was burned, along with four people whose deaths were linked with him. The vampire of Meduegna was destroyed – or so they thought.

Flickinger and two other surgeons from Belgrade, Isaac Seidel and Johann Baumgartner, visited the village in 1732 to scour the local cemetery once more. They found 15 vampires, mostly women, all with suspiciously ruddy cheeks and a healthy glow. Paole had spread his favours more widely than at first thought.

VLAD THE IMPALER, BRAM STOKER'S INSPIRATION FOR DRACULA, LIVED AT THE CASTLE OF BRAN IN TRANSYLVANIA.

This was supposed to have happened in 1874, 23 years before the appearance of Bram Stoker's 'Dracula'. Yet the supernatural blood sucker had already appeared in fiction at least twice, in *Carmilla* by J. S. LeFanu and T. P. Prest's opus *Varney the Vampire*. And *Varney the Vampire* opens with the beast unpicking the lead from a diamond-shaped pane of glass – obviously, supernatural vampires became something of a myth!

Vampires have featured in cultures the world over, from ancient China in about 600 B.C. to the Babylonians, Persians, Greeks, Romans, Indians, Polynesians, Aztecs and even the Eskimos.

The fear of vampires was enormous; suicides were thought to be likely candidates – until 1824, they were buried at crossroads with a stake through their heart, the classic method by which vampires were slaughtered.

> *The 18th century saw widespread fear of vampires. Accordingly, some corpses were buried at crossroads with a stake through the heart.*

FICTIONAL DRACULA

Today's image of the vampire is largely the work of Irishman Bram Stoker, who created 'Dracula' in his cult novel of the same name. He put the inspiration down to the combination of Vlad the Impaler, a sadistic 15th century ruler of Transylvania, and a nightmare which had followed an indulgent supper of dressed crab.

In the late sixties, a hideous entity was seen prowling Highgate cemetery by night, and several dead, bloodless animals were found. Sean Manchester, head of the UK-based Vampire Research Society, investigated and branded them paranormal deaths. In March 1970, he was permitted to perform a ritual in a vault which contained three empty coffins. Three years later, he found what he thought was the body of the Highgate vampire in a casket beneath a derelict house.

The incident started a vampire panic that was fuelled in 1730 when a serving soldier, Count de Cadreras, declared at Freiburg University that, in a small village on the Austro-Hungarian border, he had exhumed the corpse of a farmer, who had died a decade previously, only to find it apparently blooming.

PANIC SPREADS TO ENGLAND

Rumours spread to England. The tale of a woman haunted by a vampire at Croglin in Cumberland became common currency. The thing picked out the lead holding a diamond-shaped pane of glass to reach her before fleeing back to its coffin in the church crypt. One of her brothers later shot the vampire in the leg. When they broke into the vault at the church the next morning, the family found it lying in a coffin with a fresh bullet wound. The vampire was duly burned and the haunting stopped.

Werewolves were men by day, fang and fur by night – with a taste for human flesh. A full moon was the traditional catalyst for the change. Some men could not escape their fate as a four-legged fiend. They suffered from a condition known as lycanothropy, which was either inherited or passed on through a werewolf's bite. Others sought to transform themselves into werewolves with the help of charms and spells. These were sorcerers whose astral body would roam in wolf form while the human body slept. Such men were thought to have a two-sided skin – human on the outside and furry on the inside.

The hunt for werewolves matched the ferocity of Europe's witch craze in the Middle Ages. In France during the 16th century there were 30,000 cases reported in just 100 years. Yet no one has ever proved conclusively that one existed. Believers claim that's because werewolves return to their human form when they are injured or killed.

TORTURE AND SUFFERING

In France, Henry Boguet, Supreme Judge of the St Claude district of Burgundy, was the author of the witch-hunters' guide *Discours des Sorciers* and his speciality was werewolves. To extract a confession he used all manner of torture.

Convinced that werewolves were unable to cry, Boguet would measure the tears that flowed from his prisoners as they were subjected to hideous agonies. Those who did not manage copious tears

WEREWOLVES

Many werewolf stories come from lycanthropics, those who believe they are turning into a werewolf.

were deemed to be werewolves or sorcerers. The sentence for both was death at the stake.

Among those put to death in France at the time was the Werewolf of Chalons. Otherwise known as the demon tailor, he was arrested in Paris in December 1598 after barrels of bones were found at his home. He was believed to have killed dozens of people after luring them into his tailor's shop, slitting their throats and then eating the corpses. He was burned alive at the stake and details of his identity and the court proceedings were destroyed to purge the horror of the case.

The case occurred just nine years before Peter Stump was tortured and killed on the wheel as a convicted werewolf. He was apparently caught in the act of removing 'the devil's girdle' by which he changed from man to werewolf at will. According to publicity at the time Stump had sold his soul to the devil in return for the ability to change himself into a werewolf. The account read, 'He took such pleasure and delight in the shedding of blood that he would night and day walk the fields

and perform extreme cruelties.' Stump, of Bedburg, was so depraved he even ate his own child.

Allegedly you can tell a werewolf in its human form by its sunken, staring eyes, eyebrows which meet in the middle, hair growing on the palms of the hands, a long third finger, low-hung ears or oval finger nails tinged with brown. Most cases can be explained by rabies which causes bouts of aggression. There are also those who suffer from lycanthropy, a mental illness in which people believe they are turning into a werewolf.

SOME CONVINCING EVIDENCE

Yet a case which occurred at the end of the 19th century still intrigues even today. An Oxford don, his wife and a friend took a summerhouse in a remote Welsh woodland by a lake. One day the professor happened across a large skull which he believed belonged to a dog. He took it back to the house for a closer inspection.

While the professor and his friend were out, the wife heard the sound of scratching outside. From the window she saw a monster, part man and part beast. In his story of the event, *The Werewolf*, author Montague Summers describes the events. 'The cruel, panting jaws were gaping wide and showed keen white teeth; the great furry paws clasped the sill like hands; the red eyes gleamed hideously. Half fainting with fear she ran through to the front door and shot the bolt.

'A moment later she heard heavy breathing from outside and the latch rattled menacingly. The minutes that followed were full of the acutest suspense and now and again a low snarl would be heard at the door or window and a sound as though the creature was endeavouring to force its entrance.'

On the return of the two men she fainted. They spent the night waiting for the creature's return. Suddenly, the face of a wolf with the eyes of a man appeared outside. They pursued it with sticks and a gun, but it escaped towards the lake.

The next day the professor took the skull he had found and cast it into the water. After that the beast never bothered them again.

ABOVE: MICHAEL LANDON IN THE 1957 FILM
I WAS A TEENAGE WEREWOLF.
LEFT: A MAN SUFFERING FROM WOLF-MANIA
OR LYCANTHROPY CARRIES OFF A CHILD.

FAIRIES

Among the Christmas magazines at the start of December in 1920, one cover line leapt off the page: 'An Epoch-making Event – Fairies Photographed'. Within three days, *Strand Magazine* was sold out, snapped up by an astonished public eager to learn more.

Readers found photographs of Elsie Wright, 13, and her 10-year-old cousin Frances Griffiths in a Yorkshire glen in the company of numerous fairies.

PHOTOGRAPHIC EVIDENCE

The pictures had been taken in 1917 after Elsie's parents – weary of her tales about fairies at the bottom of the garden – packed her off with a Midg quarter-plate camera to provide proof. As Elsie sat in the cupboard used by her father as a dark room, she crowed in triumph as the photograph apparently proved the existence of her fairy friends. Another photo was taken and developed. Yet the Wrights were still convinced their daughter was fooling. The telling negatives were thrust into a drawer where they remained for three years – until Elsie's mother attended a lecture which touched on the subject of fairies.

Soon afterward the photos and negatives were sent to Edward Gardner, an acknowledged expert in the field. Sceptical at first, he took the negative plates to various photographers. The first, H. Snelling of Wealdstone in Middlesex, testified that, 'These two negatives are entirely genuine, unfaked photographs of single exposure, open-air work, show movement in all the fairy figures and there is no trace whatever of studio work involving card or paper models, dark backgrounds, painted figures, etc.'

Photographers at Kodak's London headquarters were less forthcoming. Although they did not brand them as fakes, neither did they certify them as genuine. Gardner visited the Wrights at their home in Cottingley, Yorkshire. While they agreed to the photos being published, they refused to be identified and would not accept cash. So the motives for fraud – fame and fortune – were eliminated. Further, both girls showed signs of being psychic, which explained why they alone could see the little people.

Gardner teamed up with Sir Arthur Conan Doyle, creator of Sherlock Holmes and fervent believer in the supernatural, to produce the *Strand Magazine* feature. Conan Doyle went on to pen 'The Coming of the Fairies' which was published in 1922. Soon afterwards experts cast fresh doubts on the authenticity of the pictures,

© Walt Disney Company

leaving Conan Doyle open to ridicule. Elsie did
not confess to the hoax for six decades.

FAKES AND FURTHER SIGHTINGS

Yet even if the Cottingley photos were faked,
there was a flood of letters at the time from
people claiming they too had seen fairies.

From the Isle of Man the Rev Arnold J.
Holmes wrote: '. . . my horse suddenly stopped
dead, and looking ahead I saw amid the obscure
light and misty moonbeams what appeared to be
a small army of indistinct figures – very small,
clad in gossamer garments.'

A Mrs Hardy from New Zealand told how she
was pegging out washing at dusk when she heard
a galloping sound. 'I looked round to see that I
was surrounded by eight or ten tiny figures on
tiny ponies like dwarf Shetlands. . . . The faces
were quite brown, also the ponies were brown. If
they wore clothes, they were close fitting like a
child's jersey suit. They were like tiny dwarfs or
children of about two years old.'

THE CHANGELING

Fairies have peopled folklore since time began.
The word is derived from the Latin 'fata', the

IN 1895 MICHAEL CLEARY, A COOPER FROM COUNTY
TIPPERARY, BURNED HIS WIFE BRIDGET TO DEATH
BECAUSE HE THOUGHT SHE WAS A CHANGELING. HE
WAS ARRESTED AS HE WAITED AT A FAIRY FORT – THE
LOCAL NAME FOR AN IRON AGE BURIAL SITE – FOR HIS
TRUE WIFE TO RETURN.

name of the supernatural women who visited the
cradles of newborns to determine their fate.
Theories about their beginnings abound. Today
they are widely thought to be either the souls of
unbaptised children, the ghosts of ancestors
fallen angels compelled to remain on earth,
nature spirits, or small humans.

Fairies were certainly accused of stealing
mortal babies and replacing them with ugly
changelings, and the only way to rid the family of
a changeling was to ill-treat it.

Children's author Rev Samuel Chadwick com-
pounded the controversy when he declared, 'Eyes
that cannot see fairies cannot see anything.'

MAGICK, CULTS AND MODERN WITCHCRAFT

When Margaret Murray published *The Witch-Cult* in Western Europe in 1921, she waxed lyrical about a highly organised and subversive pagan group in conflict with Christianity which systematically undermined society in the Middle Ages.
Her theories were criticized by historians who knew witches of the era to be localised and solitary. Still, her words sounded a chord which signalled a revival of witchcraft, although it would take several decades to materialise.

CHAPTER FIVE

VOODOO

Through a lingering haze which clings to the verdant hillsides of Haiti at nightfall comes a thudding drum beat calling the faithful to worship.

And they come in their droves to the sacred site in a forest clearing, where black bodies clad in white robes dance ecstatically to the rhythmic music and voices become hoarse with chanting. So potent is the atmosphere that devotees fall into a trance. Before them an unwilling animal is dragged for ritual sacrifice, its terrified squeals silenced abruptly by the lunge of a knife. The lips which have uttered ancient and evocative prayers are soon stained red with animal blood.

These are the rites of Rada voodoo. Its sheer intensity is sufficient to alienate observers and there are few today who do not view the cult as innately evil.

50 MILLION FOLLOWERS
Voodoo, like witchcraft, is perceived as being entirely Satanic when in fact its dark side is only one facet of a long-established religion followed by 50 million people worldwide. It has like-minded sister religions, macumba and santeria, as well as different strands.

Derived from the word 'vodu' meaning 'spirit' in French West Africa, voodoo (or vodoun, voudou or hoodoo) is a cross-breed, born out of Catholicism and the native beliefs of the Africans who were transported to the Caribbean with the slave trade.

Slaves who were threatened with death by their masters if they practised their native rites incorporated much of the liturgy of Roman Catholicism into familiar rituals until the fine lines between the two faiths became blurred. Accordingly voodoo temples, or 'hounfours', have altars, or pes, smothered with candles, food offerings, beads and other paraphernalia, just as any Catholic church would. Those seen as saints from the Catholic perspective have become gods, or loas, to the voodooists. The

ABOVE: IN CUBA VOODOOISTS TAKE PART IN A RITUAL. OBSERVERS THINK THAT IT IS SATANIC, BUT FOLLOWERS ARE DEVOUT AND FREQUENTLY CHRISTIAN.

Voodoo is derived from the word 'vodu' meaning 'spirit' in French West African. It is a cross-breed, born out of Catholicism and the beliefs of African slaves.

voodooists, who dance in a frenzy and drink down the blood of sacrificed animals, think of themselves as being good Christians carrying out their religious duty.

A BLURRING OF BELIEFS

The most important voodoo celebrations in Haiti occur in July every year. The first of these occurs at a sacred waterfall called Sant d'Eau near Ville Bonheur on the 16th. It was here in 1843 that a man called Fortune, who was searching for his missing horse, saw a vision of the Virgin Mary. A similar apparition occurred in 1881, and local Catholic authorities devoted a chapel and shrine to the Virgin Mary at the site. If they hoped to curb local voodooists, they were sorely mistaken for the Haitians believed the vision was actually of Erzulie Freda, a goddess of beauty and love. So the waterfall became holy to both religions.

On 25 July Catholics celebrate the feast of St James the Greater, whom the voodooists believe to be the god of armour and warfare Ogou Fer. To win the favours of this explosive god, worshippers bathe in the muddy flats of Plaine du Nord and the festival culminates with the sacrifice of a bull.

Voodoo priests and priestesses are called houngan and mambo respectively.

While voodoo is practised in France, Spain, America, Brazil and Africa, it is commonly associated with Haiti where it remains most in evidence despite attempts as recently as the 1940s to suppress it. Two priests, one French and one Haitian, operating in the Marbial Valley caused havoc when they crusaded vehemently and sometimes violently against followers of voodoo. They ransacked houses in search of voodoo icons to smash and cut down trees, thought by Haitians to be the home of the voodoo gods.

The savage actions galvanised a shocked pop-ulation. Distraught villagers became 'possessed' by fleeing spirits and were exorcised by the priests. Stubborn spirits who refused to be driven out of human bodies by the Christian entreaties issued curses and predicted calamities. The following year, the Marbial Valley was paralysed by a terrible drought.

Against this background of division, a doctor with political aspirations working in the countryside began to consolidate support among his countrymen. Francois Duvalier became President in 1957, becoming an all-powerful ruler, and began an anti-Catholic campaign that cleared the path for voodoo – and its darker sides – to come to the fore.

BELOW: BRUTAL ATTEMPTS TO ERADICATE VOODOOISM IN HAITI HELPED PAVE THE WAY TO POWER FOR WITCH-DOCTOR FRANCOIS DUVALIER.

In 1962, Clairvius Narcisse, aged about 40, was taken to Haiti's Albert Schweitzer Hospital with all the symptoms of high fever. Within 48 hours he was certified dead and buried the following day.

ZOMBIES

Clairvius introduced himself to his sister 18 years after this event. She listened in horror as he told how he had been zombified on the orders of their brothers after he had refused to agree to the selling of family land. He couldn't remember how long he had lain in his coffin, but he was eventually restored to life by a voodoo witch doctor. He was then taken to work the fields with a gang of other zombies.

Two years later his master died and Clairvius managed to escape. He had wandered the country for 16 years as a beggar and casual labourer and only dared to reveal his true identity once he was sure the brother who had led the plot to zombify him was dead.

Many of Clairvius's claims were confirmed by official records. His empty grave was dug up. He bore a scar on his cheek caused by a nail driven through his coffin.

THE THREAT OF ZOMBIISM
Under the orders of Papa Doc, Haitians were enslaved by voodoo. The witch-doctors could be as ambitious and cruel as the white colonials that they had replaced. The greatest threat that a witch-doctor could possibly yield was that of zombiism. Transgressors could be killed and then raised from the dead to work as mindless slaves, just like the plot of a Hollywood 'B' movie.

In 1980 anthropologist Dr E. Wade Davis insisted, 'Zombiism actually exists. There are Haitians who have been raised from their graves and returned to life.' Dr Davis had been given the task of studying the zombie mystery by the head of the Port au Prince Psychiatric Centre, Dr Lamarque Douyon. Together they carried out exhaustive examinations of Narcisse. As the first authenticated and fully recovered zombie, he was priceless research material to Douyon and Davis.

FELICIA MENTOR DIED AND WAS BURIED IN 1907. BUT THIRTY YEARS AFTERWARDS ANTHROPOLOGIST ZORA HURSTON TOOK THIS PHOTO. FELICIA HAD SPENT THE INTERVENING YEARS AS A ZOMBIE SLAVE, DEPRIVED OF HER FREE WILL BY AN UNKNOWN POTION.

> *'Zombiism actually exists. There are Haitians who have been raised from their graves and returned to life.'*

After studying Narcisse and other similar cases, Dr Davis was convinced that witch-doctors used little-known poisons to induce a stupor. The victim looked dead and was buried. Some time later the victim was resurrected by administration of an antidote. Brain damage was possible, but that was of little concern to the witch-doctors.

Further evidence for his theory emerged when Davis paid US $2,400 for eight different samples of 'zombie powder' used by certain Haitian sorcerers, which proved to contain bits of human corpse, nettle, toad and puffer fish. Eaten as a delicacy in Japan, puffer fish causes anything from mild numbing to full-scale paralysis. Davis noted that two Japanese victims had been certified dead by doctors but had recovered before funeral services could be arranged.

The poison theory had first been advanced by anthropologist Zora Hurston in the thirties and had been ridiculed. But Davis remained convinced of his findings.

He remarked upon the fact that: 'Zombies are a Haitian phenomenon which can be explained logically. The active ingredients in the poison are extracts from the skin of the toad *Bufo marinus* and one or more species of puffer fish. The skin of the toad is a natural chemical factory producing hallucinogens, powerful anaesthetics and chemicals which affect the heart and nervous system. The puffer fish contains a deadly nerve poison called tetrodotoxin.'

JUST THE RIGHT DOSE

He went on to explain that: 'A witch-doctor in Haiti is very skilled in administering just the right dose of poison. Too much poison will kill the victim completely and resuscitation will not be possible. Too little and the victim will not be a convincing corpse.'

Davis also concluded that administering zombifying potions, though at the root of the whole voodoo religion, was not the only skill of the witch-doctors. So-called 'magical' powers have some vital role to play in reviving a zombie from the grave, over and above the antidotes

ABOVE: A ZOMBIE EMERGES. THE SIGHT OF SOMEONE RAISED FROM THE DEAD SENT ICY SHIVERS OF FEAR DOWN THE SPINES OF ON-LOOKERS.

themselves. There is also an art to mixing further, stupefying drugs which effectively turn the victim into a walking vegetable.

Other Western writers have debated zombiism. Alfred Metraux's fascinating study *Voodoo in Haiti*, first published in 1959, advised, 'There are few, even among the educated, who do not give some credence to these macabre stories.'

SHAMANS

At the core of tribal culture throughout the world is the shaman. He is a miracle worker, mystic, psychic, spiritualist, exorcist, fortune-teller, story-teller and weatherman, he is the beating heart of his community who feeds the souls of his people.

Shamanism began way back in the dark recesses of time and was once described as 'the world's oldest profession'. Archaeologists have found evidence of shamanic practices that date back to 20,000 years ago.

There were or are shamanic societies in North and South America, Alaska and Siberia, Asia, Australia, Africa and even Europe. Although the rituals and ceremonies vary, the essence of each strand of shamanism remains broadly the same.

A COSMIC LINK

The shaman is the link between this world and the cosmos. To be selected as one is prestigious – but there's no place for fakers. A shaman takes up his duties because he is the son of a shaman and has inherited powers, or after being selected by the spirits who literally call him to his vocation. Some men (for it is male dominated) are reluctant to respond to the supernatural beckoning. But the spirits' messages, which might come in dreams or visions or during serious illness, are compelling.

There's a training programme organised by an elder shaman which involves prolonged isolation, as well as tuition from a guiding spirit. Further qualifications are an iron discipline and unshakeable faith. One flaw in the method of being summoned is the possibility of those suffering from mental illness being welcomed to the ranks of the shamans, as their symptoms match those of people communicating with the spirits.

To be initiated, the candidate goes into a trance and endures a symbolic death and dismemberment followed by rebirth. There are tribes which, following this rite, treat the fellow thereafter as a ghost.

JOURNEY TO THE UNDERWORLD

A shaman must make spiritual journeys to the heavens or the underworld to receive his special knowledge. To do so he goes into a trance to the sound of beating drums, chanting or rhythmic dancing. Some reach the necessary altered state of consciousness by entering a traditional sweat lodge, an outdoor sauna, for prayer and meditation. Others fast, while there are some tribes who have a tradition of taking hallucinatory drugs. The Huichol Indians of Mexico, for example, eat the tops of the potent peyote cactus to achieve the necessary state of mind.

The shaman's body is inert, but now his spirit is free to fly magically to its destination. When food is scarce the Eskimos, steeped in the shamanic tradition, expect their shamans to travel to the bottom of the sea to consult with the Mother of Seals. Once there the shaman might discover that certain taboos have been broken and then have to decide on how best to make amends.

The task of a shaman might be to redeem a soul lost through illness or black magic, or to help a soul of the dead reach its destination in the sky.

When healing, a shaman will extract illness, either by sucking out 'bad' blood or by opening up the body of his patient. Unlike Western doctors, his aim is not always to cure. Sometimes he divines that the patient is ready to die and will attend to him accordingly.

Shamans appear to achieve a remarkable bond with nature, understanding the language and needs of animals and plants.

Moving in a world inhabited by numerous spirits, shamans must decide which are friendly, helpful and good - and which are mischievous or downright malevolent.

A POWERFUL PRACTICE

Arthur Versluis in his book *The Elements of Native American Traditions* said: 'To be a shaman is not merely a weekend of entertainment, at least not in any traditional culture. Rather, it is a very powerful and dangerous practice to which one is called, at times even against one's own desires, in order to work on behalf of one's tribe.'

Recently the shaman's art has enjoyed a revival. But there are many tribal elders who frown on the way ancient traditions, age-old wisdom and hard-won spiritual enlightenment are so freely shared.

ABOVE, LEFT: A TLINGIT SHAMAN'S MASK MADE IN THE EARLY 19TH CENTURY.
RIGHT: A SIBERIAN SHAMAN IN TRADITIONAL REGALIA. PAINTING BY GORDON WAIN.

MEDICINE MEN

They say the Canadian Mounties always get their man. With this in mind, Sir Cecil Denny, an ex-officer in the force, went into a local tepee seance, normally the reserve of the tribe's medicine man. Sir Cecil was a level-headed man and he was certain that he would spot a few tricks of the trade and expose the tribesman as a fraud. However, his account of the seance in 1879 makes for incredible reading.

'Presently the tepee began to rock, even lifting itself off the ground a foot or more behind me. When it is remembered that a large Indian tent consists of dozens of long poles crossed at the top and covered with buffalo hides, it will seem that it is nearly impossible to lift one side – for no wind can blow them over.'

Denny even slipped out of the swaying tepee, hoping to catch some assistant in action. There was no one around and, when the tepee rocked once more, the sides lifted from the ground to

ABOVE: AN AFRICAN MEDICINE MAN PERFORMS A RITUAL TO THE RHYTHM OF DRUMS. MEDICINE MEN (*WITCH–DOCTOR* IS INACCURATE AND DEROGATORY) ARE RESPECTED BY MYSTIFIED WESTERNERS.

reveal that there was nobody hoisting it up. The medicine man, in a trance, did not stir. Denny returned to his camp 'thoroughly mystified'.

THE INTOLERANCE OF THE MISSIONARIES

The art of the shamans and their brothers, the medicine men, has long perplexed Westerners. Missionaries who first came across the magic arts

of the tribes were not only supreme rationalists, but firmly believed in God. It was simple for them to rule out any display from the medicine men as the work of the devil. Much of the medicine men's paraphernalia was destroyed at the insistence of missionaries who could not tolerate a rival belief to their own.

But as more and more Westerners visited the remoter parts of the world the tales of magic and mystery grew. In the 1920s, botanist William Brigham touched a heavy wooden stick that had apparently been imbued with magic during a ritual in Hawaii. He was knocked backwards by a shock comparable to putting his fingers in an electric socket.

Conjuror Harry Kellar was staggered by the feats of magic achieved by a Zulu medicine man in the 1870s. First he caused a warrior's stick-like weapon – called a knobkerrie – to explode. Then, as the warrior lay on the ground apparently unconscious, the medicine man made him levitate to a height of 3 ft in the air simply by waving burning grasses over him.

FROM GENERATION TO GENERATION

Just as shamanic ceremonies are passed down through generations so a medicine man's bag is bequeathed through families. The medicine bundle was a bag made of leather or an animal pelt which contained everything the native American healer would need for his work. Apart from herbs and potions, there was likely to be fetishes, or objects deemed to have supernatural powers, charms, feathers, claws, symbols and much more. The contents of each medicine bundle were dictated by the spirits through shamanic practice.

BELOW: A SORCERESS RAIDS GRAVES FOR INGREDIENTS TO GO IN MAGIC SPELLS AND IS ARRESTED BY POLICE IN MARRAKESH, MOROCCO. THE STORY MADE FRONT PAGE OF THIS FRENCH JOURNAL, OUTRAGED BY THE AUDACITY OF THE COFFIN ROBBER.

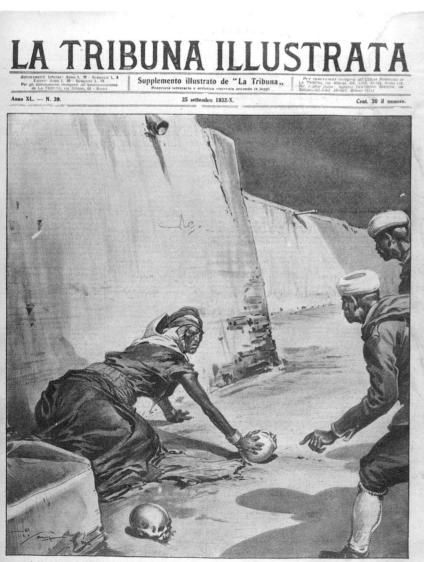

A Marrakesc (Marocco), la polizia locale ha arrestato una fattucchiera mentre, dopo aver aperte alcune tombe, stava per allontanarsi portando seco dei teschi. La donna ha confessato che il macabro bottino le avrebbe servito, come già altre volte, per preparare dei filtri magici.
(Disegno di VITTORIO PISANI).

IN ASIA THE DOMAIN OF MAGIC IS RULED BY THE FAKIRS. UNLIKE OTHER CULTS, THE FAKIRS FREQUENTLY PERFORM WITH THE AID OF CONJURING TRICKS AND ARE NOT ABOVE SUBSTITUTION OR SLEIGHT OF HAND.

HOWEVER, THE FAMOUS INDIAN ROPE TRICK IN WHICH THE FAKIR SHINS UP A ROPE SUSPENDED IN MID-AIR IS STILL BREATHTAKING. THIS AND OTHER APPARENTLY SUPERNATURAL ABILITIES DISPLAYED BY THE FAKIRS IS PUT DOWN TO YOGA TRAINING INVOLVING BREATHING CONTROL AND MEDITATION.

Man's passion for magic and his eternal quest to investigate the supernatural has instigated the creation of societies with an active interest in the occult.

The Druids were an ancient Celtic priestly caste which worshipped gods of nature and fully believed in reincarnation. Their role was divination, proclamation and spiritual guidance. They are probably best remembered for sacrificing people and animals in enormous wicker cages. The Druids were eliminated by the invading Romans who considered them savages. Druidry survived in Ireland until the arrival of Christianity in the 5th century.

No one knows the fate of the Druids. Perhaps they went underground to survive centuries of oblivion. The traditions were oral and so were likely to have been lost. Certainly the modern Druids claim no lineage from their ancient counterparts, but the movement was resurrected.

DRUIDS

ELIZABETHAN HEROES

Druids were hailed as heroes in the Elizabethan age, but it wasn't until the 17th century antiquarian John Aubrey suggested that Druids were the builders of Stonehenge that the cult came to the forefront of society's attention. Unfortunately they weren't, but he focused once more the minds and hearts of philosophers on their existence.

It was the ageing Aubrey who inspired John Toland in 1694, a prolific and controversial writer who was elected the first chief of the modern Druids. In Wales Druidry was fostered by the Glamorgan stonemason Edward Williams who went under the more exotic title Iolo Morganwg. Although later generations maintain this strand of Druidry is exclusively Welsh and the only genuine variety, it was in fact proclaimed on Primrose Hill in London.

Druidry continued to flourish and it attracted such luminaries as Winston Churchill, who was initiated into the Albion Lodge of the Ancient and Archaeological Order of Druids in 1908. In 1964 the movement was split into two, the Ancient Druid Order and the Order of Bards, Ovates and Druids, referring to the special Druid classes and functions.

The Ancient Druid Order is the most photographed group, being the one to publicly celebrate the summer solstice. Once their celebration took place at Stonehenge, but difficulties in crowd control led the police to ban the ritual.

Larger and more encompassing is the Order of Bards, Ovates and Druids which has a teaching programme, debates environmental and artistic principles and promotes sexual equality. It runs correspondence courses, workshops and has retreats for its members.

The Bards of Cornwall, who are organised with help from the Welsh Druids, have revived the Cornish language and carry out ceremonies in dark blue robes in some of the county's important stone circles.

LEFT: MODERN DRUIDS IN THEIR ROBES CELEBRATE THE SOLSTICE AT STONEHENGE BEFORE A BAN WAS IMPOSED ON THE RITUAL BY POLICE.

The lure of the Druids is in mystical promise – the search for greater understanding of the world and the inner self.

decade the religion had spread across seven states. The groups included the elaborately named Zen Druids of Olympia, the Hassidic Druids of St Louis and the Norse Druids of San Diego.

The lure is in its mystical promise, the search for greater understanding and for a communion with the inner self.

ABOVE: THE POPULAR VIEW OF A DRUID PAINTED BY GORDON WAIN IN THE EARLY 19TH CENTURY.
RIGHT: THIS ILLUSTRATION FROM A 1915 BOOK OF MYTHS HAS EVA USING A DRUID WAND TO BEWITCH THE CHILDREN OF LIR.

There is a strong Druid tradition in Brittany, France, as well where the legend of Arthur is also very pertinent.

DRUIDS IN AMERICA

In America, Druids came into being in 1963 as part of a tongue-in-cheek protest. The Reformed Druids of North America came together when Carleton College compelled all students to attend chapel services and the only exceptions to this ruling were those who were members of a minority religion. So students formed for themselves just such a religion. And even when the college's rules were relaxed merely a year later the members of the RDNA were sufficiently committed to the cause to continue. Within just a

Mystic monk, Siberian sage, faith healer –
or fraud? The truth about Rasputin, the peasant
who became confidant to the rulers of Russia,
has tantalised historians for decades.

RASPUTIN
(1871-1916)

Born in the Siberian outpost of Pokrovskoie in 1871, his appetite for sex and his rise to power in the Romanov court are not in dispute. It is his mystic powers that are the controversial issue.

Born Grigory Efimovich, Rasputin was the son of a drunken horse thief and his adolescent wife. As a child Rasputin was forced to work the land to scrape a living. Education was an afterthought, and Grigory took refuge in sex. Legend says he lost his virginity to a Russian general's wife, Danilova Kubasova, who, with six handmaidens, seduced him at her grand home near his village. Even then Rasputin looked unsavoury, with matted beard, filthy hands and a woeful

neglect of personal hygiene. Nevertheless, he proved a stallion to women. The name 'Rasputin' is Russian slang for a debauched woman-chaser.

A RELIGIOUS CALLING

He was allegedly overcome with a religious fervour whilst bathing in a village pond with three young women. This newly-found calling took him away from his long-suffering wife Praskovia

RASPUTIN AMONG HIS DEVOTEES, MOST OF THEM WOMEN.
CURIOUSLY, NONE WERE REPULSED BY HIS SHABBY APPEARANCE.

Feodorovna and three children and into the arms of the Khlisty sect.

A dubious religious group, also known as the Flagellants, the sect had 120,000 members. Its preachings were based on free love and meetings involved chanting, dancing and prayers by the light of flaming torches. Anyone who fell behind in the frenzy of worship was soundly whipped. At the end men and women fell hungrily upon each other. Rasputin learned a convincing line which he preached for the rest of his days.

'So long as you bear sin secretly and within you, and fearfully cover it up with fasting, prayer and eternal discussion of the Scriptures, so long will you remain hypocrites and good for nothings. It is necessary for you to sin. Only then can you know true holiness.' With this argument, he managed to sleep with many men's wives.

HOLY MAN AND MIRACLE-WORKER

Parallel with his reputation as lover came that of holy man and miracle worker. In 1904 he met eminent cleric Father John of Kronstadt, who declared that Rasputin was marked out by God.

In 1906, Prime Minister Stolypin's daughter was badly injured by a revolutionary bomb. Only after Rasputin prayed at the end of her bed did she show signs of improvement.

Soon his reputation spread to the Winter Palace in St Petersburg, home of Czar Nicholas II and his wife Alexandra. The couple were anxious about the fate of their only son Alexander. He suffered from haemophilia, an inherited condition which meant he bled uncontrollably from every scratch or bruise. The four-year-old Czarevich was bleeding profusely from an injury and Rasputin managed to stem the blood.

ACCURATE PROPHECIES

There are instances of his chillingly accurate prophecies. In a letter to the Czar in 1914 as Russia teetered on the brink of war Rasputin wrote, 'Again I say a terrible storm cloud hangs over Russia. Disaster, grief, murky darkness and

no light. A whole ocean of tears, there is no counting them, and so much blood . . . The disaster is great, the misery infinite.'

Still the Czar went ahead with the war against his cousin Kaiser Wilhelm of Germany. The cost to Russia was immense. Not only was the human toll distressingly large, but also the revolutionaries who had for years been gaining momentum now made capital out of the nation's catastrophe.

On 30 December 1916, Rasputin was lured to a palace in St Petersburg where four plotters killed him. When cyanide failed they shot him, then clubbed him. Rasputin was still alive when he was tossed into a freezing river where he was found two days later, his arm stiffly at right angles as if making the sign of a cross.

His followers were devastated, the Czarina among them. Still convinced of his powers, they recalled how he had told his close friends that he would not see the new year. One year later they saw another prophecy, the fall of the Romanovs.

In every age, history has recorded a remarkable thinker, philosopher, inventor and intellectual, their talents boundless, their contributions to mankind outstanding.

ST GERMAIN

What if all of them were the same man, returned in different times and various guises? That's the belief of some Theosophical and Rosicrucian followers and 'I Am' religious activity. He belonged to a Great Brotherhood in the Himalayas. A cycle of reincarnations gave him wisdom about natural and supernatural truth. His name is St Germain.

MANY MANIFESTATIONS

St Germain is said to have first appeared on earth 50,000 years ago. He was high priest of the Violet Flame Temple and preached the great destiny of his people. When they fell to temptation, he withdrew from the society which lapsed into obscurity.

He was thought to have returned to earth as the Old Testament prophet Samuel, as well as Joseph, mortal father of the infant Jesus.

His next manifestation was as St Alban, a martyr who was beheaded by the Romans in 303 and then, in the following century, as Proclus, chief of Plato's Academy in Athens.

In the 5th century he was known as Merlin, magician and adviser to King Arthur. He returned in 1214 as Roger Bacon, a monk and illustrious thinker who was years ahead of his time. Yet his work caused suspicion amongst his fellow Franciscan friars and his works were condemned in 1278. Bacon was then imprisoned as a heretic for 14 years, being released only shortly before his death.

St Germain sailed the seas as explorer Christopher Columbus before returning as eminent lawyer and philosopher Sir Francis Bacon. He was an alchemist, scientist, occultist and literary genius. He has even been accredited with some of the works of Shakespeare. He reputedly died on 9 April 1626.

Some students believe that reports of his death were bogus, that he lived on in obscurity. Did

ABOVE: SIR FRANCIS BACON, SCIENTIST AND OCCULTIST, WAS SUSPECTED OF FAKING HIS DEATH IN ORDER TO STUDY PHILOSOPHY IN ISOLATION.

Bacon join other Ascended Masters, his time on earth at a close? Or did he return as the Comte de St Germain, who first came to notice in 1740 in the upper echelons of Viennese society?

It was not only St Germain's charm, wit, wisdom and healing hands which drew attention – he admitted to being 150 years old.

ARREST IN ENGLAND

The mysterious Count travelled to Paris where, in 1743, he met King Louis XV and his mistress, Madame de Pompadour. The king was so beguiled with the Count's tales, that he employed him for secret missions abroad. In England, the Count was arrested and held until he could convince the authorities that he had been set-up.

After 1747 he paid two visits to India where he claimed to have satisfied his alchemical ambitions, but his special relationship with Louis XV was ruined when he made an enemy of the powerful Duc de Choiseul. However, he was welcomed with warmth into the Russian court of Catherine the Great. He became chief of her troops in the 1768 war against Turkey, upon which he called himself 'General Welldone'.

The Count eventually came to reside under the patronage of Prince Charles of Hesse-Cassel in Schleswig, Germany. He died here in 1784 at an unknown age. His tombstone in Eckenforde read, 'He who called himself the Comte de St Germain and Welldone, of whome there is no other information, has been buried in this church.'

Yet sightings of him continued until 1820. His detractors believed he was a clever fake, born of an Italian tax collector or a Bohemian occultist. However, his supporters point to his incredible talents: he was fluent in six languages, an accomplished scientist and seasoned traveller. Could all this be fitted into one short life?

Emperor Louis Napoleon III commissioned an investigation into the Count. The results were destroyed in a fire in 1871, a blaze sparked by the Count himself, his advocates have declared.

> AN ENCOUNTER WITH ST GERMAIN SHORTLY
> BEFORE HIS DEATH AT SCHLESWIG-HOLSTEIN
> LEFT A LASTING IMPRESSION ON CAGLIOSTRO.

> ST GERMAIN'S AUTHENTICITY WAS VOUCHSAFED BY 19TH CENTURY MYSTIC MADAME HELENA PETROVNA BLAVATSKY, CO-FOUNDER OF THE THEOSOPHICAL SOCIETY. BEFORE HER DEATH IN 1891, BLAVATSKY WAS BRANDED A PHONEY BY THE SOCIETY FOR PSYCHICAL RESEARCH IN LONDON. HOWEVER, IN 1986 AN ARTICLE IN THE SPR JOURNAL ADMITTED THE INVESTIGATION OF HER WAS FLAWED AND OFFERED AN APOLOGY.

Jung's work led him to collaborate with the other eminent psychiatrist of the day, Sigmund Freud. There was a mutual respect, but equally an innate strain existed in their relationship from the outset.

CARL G. JUNG (1875-1961)

ABOVE: CARL GUSTAV JUNG (1875–1961) WAS A PSYCHIATRIST BY PROFESSION BUT A PSYCHIC BY NATURE.

With many clergymen in his family, Carl Gustav Jung was expected to enter a ministry. Instead he studied medicine and became a psychiatrist.

Yet, despite his scientific training, he could not resist the allure of another family tradition, that of the psychical. Both his mother and grandmother had been noted for their ability to communicate with ghosts. Jung's grandmother, Augusta Preiswerk, had once fallen into a three-day trance, during which she channelled messages from the dead and revealed prophecies.

As he grew older, Jung found the study of the supernatural increasingly compelling.

PREMONITIONS AND PSYCHOKINESIS

Jung was born on 26 July 1875 in Kesswill, Switzerland. When he was small, he experienced powerful dreams, a field of study that would fascinate him in adulthood. He saw himself as having two distinct personalities, one being a wise old man who was something of a life-long guardian that he christened Philemon. Even when he was at school, Jung was subject to premonitions, clairvoyance, psychokinesis and the appearance of ghosts.

He put much of this behind him when, after becoming fascinated with philosophy as a teenager, he went off to university. He attended the University of Basle between 1895 and 1900 and then went on to Zurich University to win a Masters degree. At first he worked in the Burgholzli Asylum at the University of Zurich where he made a study of word associations.

also wary of Jung, having witnessed his use of psychokinesis to make books crash down. And perhaps Freud was right to be concerned. In his dreams, Jung killed Freud.

Jung's achievements went on to be significant and widely received. He identified the two basic psychological types of extrovert and introvert, with the determining factors thinking, feeling, sensation and intuition.

COLLECTIVE UNCONSCIOUSNESS

But perhaps he is best remembered for his theory about the collective unconsciousness. Deeper even than the unconscious layer of the mind, the collective unconsciousness is instilled before we are born and it is from here that instinct emanates. It would, for example, explain why distinct cultures living years ago and miles apart shared many of the same symbols and even worshipped the same gods. Another way of putting it is 'universal consciousness'. His contentions have neither been proved, nor disproved.

Jung's obsession with mythology, symbols – particularly those relating to alchemy – and unconscious images escalated.

In 1944 Jung hovered close to death following a heart attack. Later he told how he floated over the earth before arriving at a temple. His earthly feelings disappeared and he longed to enter the temple where he knew he would discover the meaning of life. However, his doctor appeared to him and reluctantly Jung returned to his body.

Jung began to build a castle of stone at Bollingen, Switzerland, representing the extension of consciousness he felt old age brought. His interest turned to synchronicity, the study of meaningful coincidence. Through I Ching, the ancient Chinese wisdom based largely on instinct and chance, Jung developed his favourite themes.

Three days before he died Jung had a dream which indicated his imminent death. On his death in Zurich on 6 June 1961, a storm tore across Lake Geneva and lightning struck his favourite tree.

His work led him to collaborate with that other eminent psychiatrist of the day, Sigmund Freud. The pair first met in 1907 in Vienna. There was a mutual respect, but equally an innate strain existed in their relationship from the first. Just as Jung could not accept Freud's theory that human behaviour was mostly linked to repressed sexuality, so Freud could not bring himself to publicly endorse psychic investigation. This gulf between the two was never bridged, even though Freud once admitted that, if he lived his life again, he might 'possibly choose just this field of research in spite of all the difficulties.'

When the two fell out in 1913, Jung suffered a breakdown which lasted six years. He gave the psychic side of his character free rein while, at the same time, keeping a scientific observation of the phenomena which occurred. Because Freud fainted twice in Jung's presence, he accused Jung of having a death wish against him. Freud was

RITUAL MAGICK

Chants, incense and incantations were the preserve of Eastern magicians, whilst European spellmakers went for folklore and fauna.

The ritual magic which practitioners such as Aleister Crowley took up years afterwards were inspired by two sources, the Hermetic Books and the Cabalah, the code of Jewish mysticism.

HERMETIC MANUSCRIPTS

The Hermetic manuscripts were allegedly the wise words of Hermes Trismegistus, a mythical figure who lived for hundreds of years, during which time he divined great truths. Hermes advised his son Tat on how to achieve the fluid consciousness needed to understand Hermetica.

'Withdraw into thyself and it will come; will and it comes to pass; throw out of work the body's senses, and thy Divinity shall come to birth; purge for thyself the brutish torments – things of matter.'

Tat did as he was asked and discovered he now had vision that extended far beyond that of his eyes. 'In heaven am I, in earth, in water, air; I am in animals, in plants, I'm in the womb, before the womb, after the womb, I'm everywhere.'

Many cabbalistic traditions were passed down by word of mouth before being committed to the written word. It was only during the 12th century, as these translations from Arabic first filtered through to the West, that they excited the alchemists, for here were magicians by another name. It was vital to maintain the ennobling title of alchemist, or they would risk accusations of witchcraft and all the terrors that would entail.

John Dee was among the first in England to experiment with ritual magic. A brilliant scholar and astrologer to Queen Elizabeth I, he was fascinated first by the stars and later by magic and the occult. Predictions made from the horoscopes he cast included the childlessness of Queen Mary and the coming of the Spanish Armada.

LEFT: ILLUSTRATION OF HERMETIC PHILOSOPHY FROM THE 13TH CENTURY BY SPANISH THEOLOGIAN AND MYSTIC ROMAN LULL.
RIGHT: FREEMASONS ASSEMBLE FOR THE INITIATION OF A MASTER IN THE EARLY 18TH CENTURY.

Among the first to experiment with ritual magic in England was John Dee, astrologer to Queen Elizabeth I. A brilliant scholar, he was fascinated first by the stars and later by magic and the occult.

JOHN DEE

With the patronage of Queen Elizabeth, Dee travelled overseas in his quest for the truth of the supernatural. When he returned to England he embarked on a new method of divination, scrying, and employed assistant Edward Kelley on a salary of £20 a year. Through Kelley, Dee contacted 'angels' who communicated in a cypher which was later christened the Enochian language. It bore no resemblance to any known language, although laborious translation by Dee proved it was workable.

Among the less savoury antics in which Dee and Kelley allegedly indulged was the exhumation in Walton-le-Dale, Lancashire, of a corpse which was forced to speak by use of magick. From 1583, rumours abounded about the evil sorcery carried out by the pair which incited fearful locals to break into Dee's empty home in Mortlake, Surrey, and ransack the library, destroying many of his valuable records.

Kelley suggested that the angels wanted Dee to share his wife with his partner. It looked as though Kelley, always a gambler, was taking advantage of his employer, but whatever the circumstances, Kelley left Dee to pursue his interests in alchemy. Popularly considered a sorcerer, Dee

ABOVE: HERMES TRISMEGISTUS, FATHER OF HERMETICA, LIVED FOR HUNDREDS OF YEARS AND ACQUIRED IMMENSE KNOWLEDGE.

petitioned King James I to clear his name, but the request was ignored. In 1608, Dee died penniless.

Soon afterwards and for the first time, Europe heard about the Rosicrucian Brotherhood. Through a series of pamphlets, its members introduced themselves to the Germany of 1614 as the possessors of spiritual secrets. With witch-burnings continuing apace, it is no surprise that the learned mind or minds behind the pamphlets chose to remain anonymous. However, historians have speculated as to whether the Rosicrucian Brotherhood extended beyond one man's productive mind. The Rosicrucian ideology of spiritual enlightenment did live on, however, and eventually emerged in the Freemasons and later in the Rosicrucian or 'Rosy Cross' orders.

Down the ages, the practitioner himself has always been the judge of the success of his own magic practices.

ELIPHAS LEVI

Down the ages, the practitioner has always been the judge of the success of his own magic practices. A key figure in the occult revival of the 19th century was Eliphas Levi. Born in Paris in 1810, Levi was destined for the priesthood until he abandoned theological college in favour of politics and writing. It is for his books, primarily *Dogma and Ritual of High Magic* and *The History of Magic,* that he is remembered.

In 1866 the English *Societas Rosicruciana* was founded by Robert Wentworth Little after apparently discovering a mysterious ancient text. By 1885 French Rosicrucianism was launched. Popular among passionate Parisian poets its short history was marked by spectacular rows, schisms and accusations of deadly psychic attacks.

ORDER OF THE GOLDEN DAWN

A direct descendant of English Rosicrucianism was the Hermetic Order of the Golden Dawn, a

ABOVE: YEATS WAS INTRIGUED BY HERMETICA AND BECAME A KEY FIGURE IN THE GOLDEN DAWN.

secret magical society founded by coroner Dr William Wyn Westcott, the eccentric Samuel Liddell MacGregor Mathers and retired doctor William Woodman.

The five magic rituals which were fundamental to the Golden Dawn were discovered on a dogged-eared manuscript by an elderly parson and presented to Westcott. A diligent student of Hermetica, Westcott translated the rituals and Mathers embellished them. It's difficult today to discern the authenticity of the original script. However, one of the flourishes inserted into it was certainly a lie.

An addition to the manuscript mentioned Fraulein Spengler of Stuttgart as a chief adept. She was a figment of somebody's fertile mind yet Westcott and Mathers pretended they had consulted with her and produced letters purporting to contain her wisdom and support. The aim was to show that Golden Dawn was the bona fide English branch of a long-standing European occult group. Its pedigree established, the non-existent Fraulein was duly killed off.

A complex system of grades, orders and temples was established. For good measure, the high-ranking Third Order existed only on the

astral plane. By 1888 with the hierarchy in place the Golden Dawn was ready to begin recruiting members. Disillusioned spiritualists, Freemasons and Rosicrucians were eager to join its ranks. Women were admitted alongside men. Among its members was Irish poet W. B. Yeats.

The exotically named temples were in London (Isis-Urania), Bradford (Horus No 5), Weston-Super-Mare (Osiris No 4) and, later, Edinburgh (Amen-Ra No 6). By the end of 1981 over 80 people had been initiated in the London temple alone to study occultist arts in the Outer Order.

THE SECOND ORDER

When they graduated to the Second Order members had to make their own magical instruments including a lotus wand, magic sword and further ceremonial wands, cups, daggers, pentacles and regalia which were then consecrated. Mathers constructed a highly demanding curriculum to stretch the capacity of the student magicians. It was a worthy attempt to establish a University of Hermetica. Without the power-crazed Mathers at its helm it might have endured, too.

Mathers, however, was stormy and dictatorial. He had already ousted Westcott in a fit of paranoia. At that crucial moment he chose to reveal that the Fraulein Spengler letters were

DID THE INCANTATIONS OF RITUAL MAGICK REALLY WORK OR WERE THE EFFECTS OF SPELLS IN FACT INDUCED BY DRUGS LIKE OPIUM?

forged. To the horror of its members, it was clear that the Golden Dawn was based on a lie. When Mathers insisted on the controversial Aleister Crowley joining the Golden Dawn, against his colleagues' wishes, there was uproar and Mathers was expelled in 1900. The Golden Dawn split in 1903, with those loyal to Mathers forming the Alpha et Omega Temple. Apart from the Golden Dawn, the major legacy bequeathed by Mathers to occultists was his book *Key of Solomon*.

The success of magic practice down the ages has been dependent on the word of the practitioner. If they believe themselves successful it could be because the obscure magic formulae they used have worked. Likewise, it could be an hallucination willed by the practitioner or a vision kicked up by the subconscious mind.

It's true too that many magic practices depend on habit-forming drugs. To the user, the incantations appear to have had spectacular success. In reality, the sights and sensations experienced after spells have been cast are due to the effects of drugs.

He went by the names of Prince Chioa Khan, the Master Therion, Frater Perdurabo, Count Svareff and Count Vladimar. To women he was a demon lover. To his mother he was 'the Beast'.

Aleister Crowley revelled in his reputation as mystic, magician, debaucher and diabolist. Most found him repulsive, but a few, testifying to his hypnotic gaze, thought him irresistible.

He was born on 12 October 1875 in Leamington Spa, Warwickshire – on the day that magician Eliphas Levi died. His parents were of the puritanical Plymouth Brethren. Suffocated by their religious fervour, even in his early years the young Edward Alexander Crowley sought to outrage.

A bizarre looking figure, Crowley swept around in a scarlet cloak and jewelled crown, or a turban and silks. His hair was waxed into a horn as he emulated the 'Great God Pan'. His front teeth were sharpened to points to give women a 'serpent's kiss', drawing blood as he did so.

In 1903 he married Rose Kelly, who believed herself to be a psychic. One day Rose fell into a trance and uttered the words, 'Horus is waiting for you'. Crowley knew nothing of the Egyptian god Horus until, soon afterwards, he visited the Cairo Museum. There on view was an image of the falcon-headed god, with the exhibit label 666.

ALEISTER CROWLEY (1875-1947)

AUTOBIOGRAPHICAL REVELATIONS

In his autobiography, Crowley admitted he was only 11 when he killed the family cat. Testing the 'nine lives' theory to its limits, he hanged, stabbed, slashed and smashed the head of the unfortunate creature. Then he burnt, drowned and threw it out of the window.

'I was genuinely sorry for the animal,' he said. 'I simply forced myself to carry out the experiment in the interest of pure science.'

He lost his virginity at 14 and thereafter maintained a voracious sexual appetite.

At Cambridge University, Crowley abandoned his degree studies and concentrated on writing poetry and studying the occult. He joined the Hermetic Order of the Golden Dawn, a short-lived but influential occult group which was founded in 1888 and attracted people like poet W. B. Yeats. He was known as Perdurabo, 'I will endure to the end'.

It was the number of the beast with which Crowley was identified – he took it as a sign.

That night Crowley invoked Horus. If Crowley is to be believed, Horus dispatched a spirit guide called Aiwass who dictated prophecies and teachings through Rose. Crowley transformed them into his shambling epic *The Book of the Law*. Key among its messages was, 'Do what thou wilt shall be the whole of the law'. It was *carte blanche* for Crowley and his followers to indulge themselves to the full.

ORGIES AND DRUG ABUSE

For four years Crowley lived in America until, in 1920, he moved to a hillside villa in Sicily, southern Italy, where he gained most of his notoriety. Crowley hoped the Cefalu villa, 'Abbaye de Theleme', would be a world centre for the study of the occult – but it was not to be.

Perverted rituals took place alongside sex orgies, animal sacrifices, self-mutilation and drug misuse. His followers included a number of 'Scarlet Women' who were thoroughly degraded by Crowley as they acted as his assistants in the practice of magic.

Revelations about the goings-on at Cefalu were made public in 1923 after the death of a 23-year-old Oxford undergraduate Raoul Loveday who believed he was cursed by the Egyptian high priestess Amon-Ra. Loveday died after sacrificing a live cat and drinking its blood. The dead man's wife, Betty May, loathed Crowley and was only too happy to inform on him.

In May 1923 Crowley and his entourage were expelled from Italy by a shocked Mussolini.

It seems Crowley's lust for sex began to overshadow his passion for magic. His writings about the supernatural were outweighed by the pornography that he churned out. In his book *Magick* he wrote about human sacrifice: 'A male child of perfect innocence and high intelligence is the most satisfactory and suitable victim.' It was a silly quip, but rumours linking Crowley with infanticide and cannibalism persisted.

Crowley died on 1 December 1947 in a boarding house in Hastings. Although he was an egomaniac who became hooked on heroin, he was nevertheless highly accomplished in the field of magic and an inspiration to many.

ABOVE: A PORTRAIT OF CROWLEY BELIES HIS REPUTATION AS 'THE BEAST'. BELOW: CROWLEY'S CEREMONIAL SEAL.

In 1951, following pressure from the spiritualist lobby, the laws against practising witchcraft in England were rescinded. The persecution of witches had, of course, long since subsided. The last witch was burned at the stake in England in 1684 and the final witch trial of Jane Wenham was in 1711.

With deregulation, it was time to come out and be counted. Leading the way was former civil servant Gerald Gardner, who became interested in the occult during a spell as a rubber planter in Malaysia. On a visit to England, he was apparently initiated into a coven in the New Forest by a witch called Old Dorothy Clutterbuck. Gardner was then 55 years old.

THE OLD RELIGION

Later, he wrote, 'I realised that I had stumbled on something interesting; but I was half-initiated before the word, Wica, which they used, hit me like a thunderbolt, and I knew where I was, and that the Old Religion still existed.' He used a single 'c' in Wicca.

Gardner seized the opportunity to incorporate all his unorthodox desires into a new manner of witchcraft. His blueprint for a revival of the 'Old Religion' included nudity, scourging and sexual intercourse. Gardner was himself a naturist. The theme was fun and frolics.

For assistance he turned to Aleister Crowley, 'the Beast', who had penned some ritual chants in the name of his pet religion, Thelema. They were drawn from Romany law, Gnostic writings, a smattering of Rudyard Kipling, bits of William Blake, William Butler Yeats and Doreen Valiente and became known as *The Book of the Shadows*. In 1954, Gardner published *Witchcraft Today*.

GERALD GARDNER (1884-1964)

The response to this book was phenomenal and the cult's influence spread, crossing the Atlantic to America. The object of Wiccan devotions was a Mother Goddess.

The Book of the Shadows includes the following section which is known as The Charge: 'Whenever ye have need of anything once in the month and better it be if the Moon is full, then shall ye assemble in some secret place and adore Me who am Queen of all Witcheries. There shall ye assemble, ye who are fain to learn all sorcery. I shall teach ye things unknown and ye shall be free

'I realised that I had stumbled on something interesting; but I was half-initiated before the word, 'Wica', which they used, hit me like a thunderbolt, and I knew where I was, and that the Old Religion still existed.'

from all slavery. As a sign that ye be really free ye shall be naked in your rites and ye shall dance, sing, feast, make music, make love – all in Praise of Me.'

Altogether Gardner pursued eight different ways of creating magical power: meditation, chants or spells, trance, incense with drugs or wine, dancing, controlling blood circulation, scourging and ritual sex. Although his sexual peccadilloes were at times extremely shocking his beliefs were sincere and his knowledge about magic immense.

THE MEANING OF WITCHCRAFT

In 1959 Gardner published *The Meaning of Witchcraft* which still holds significance for Gardnerians today. On Gardner's death in 1964, aged 80, the binding force was lost and his influence on witchcraft fractured. Monique Wilson, otherwise known as 'the Lady Olwen', was the main beneficiary of Gardner's will but sold off many significant items, including a witchcraft museum on the Isle of Man, to buy a café in Torremolinos in Spain.

Not surprisingly, the heyday of Gardnerian Wicca was in the sixties and seventies, when free love became gospel. Apart from those seriously interested in witchcraft, it attracted many voyeurs and sexual delinquents. It also appealed to those with dull lives and who felt they at last had a chance to take control of their lives. Witchcraft moved from its roots in rural areas into the cities and suburbia.

Gardnerian Wicca is faithful to the advice 'An' (if) it harm none, do what you will'. Different covens may add to or take out tracts from *The Book of Shadows* but it remains at the core of their activities. While Gardnerians admit to working 'skyclad' (naked) and have covens with balanced male to female ratios, there's still little debate about their rituals in the public arena, as they are sworn to secrecy.

NEW WITCHES, OLD WORDS

To distinguish themselves from old-style witches – generally portrayed as vicious hags – modern witches substituted the Old English word Wicca for witchcraft. Likewise, magick was adopted to set the art apart from modern-day conjuring.

A WICCAN WITCH STANDS BEHIND AN ARRAY OF RITUAL OBJECTS, INCLUDING A SKULL, INCENSE BURNER AND SHAMANIC TRUMPET.

CONTROVERSY SURROUNDED ALEX SANDERS AFTER HE EMERGED AS THE LEADING LIGHT OF WITCHCRAFT IN BRITAIN.

In the wake of Gerald Gardner came another great British Wicca enthusiast, Alex Sanders.

Born in a Manchester suburb, Sanders insisted he was initiated into the 'Old Religion' at the age of seven by his grandmother. She told him that he was the latest in a line of witches dating back to the 15th century. By nine he was playing a part in witchcraft ritual. Although he kept all this secret from school friends, he could not resist sharing the occasional prediction which came to him in visions. Later he said he was something of a playboy healer until his 31-year-old sister died. After that he undertook many purification rituals before discovering the true path of Wicca. That is the legend he used to promote himself. His detractors have a different story.

DETRACTORS AND CRITICS

They claim experienced Wiccan practitioner Patricia Crowther declined to intiate him in 1961. Later one of her ex-coven members carried out the ceremony.

Sanders says he was passed down the secrets of *The Book of Shadows* by Gardner himself. But, critics say that he purloined text from the version belonging to the witch who initiated him. They insist the differences between Gardnerian Wicca and the Alexandrian Wicca begun by Sanders arose when he misread or misheard the rituals.

Whatever the truth, Sanders went on to form his own coven with a few personal touches one of which was the use of the athame, a ceremonial knife symbolising fire, and another the wand symbolising air. He used other occult imagery.

ALEX SANDERS AND OTHER PRACTITIONERS

THE DEBATE ABOUT NUDITY AND ITS VALUE IN
MODERN WITCHCRAFT STILL CONTINUES.

As Gardnerian Wicca fragmented, the Alexandrian strain came to the fore. Its appeal was its informality and increasingly liberal attitudes. Nudity was an option rather than a requirement.

Sanders and his High Priestess Maxine Morris were prominent in the sixties, but after they split up in 1971 their influence waned.

Present-day witchcraft in America is based on the English and European styles. Many stateside witches are called Gardnerites. Raymond Buckland was a key exponent of Wicca in America.

WITCHCRAFT IN AMERICA

Buckland and his wife Rosemary settled in the New York suburb of Brentwood in the 1950s. He was introduced to witchcraft by Gerald Gardner himself and was given the name Robart, Rosemary being rechristened 'Lady Rowan'.

For several years the couple quietly built up a network of covens. Only when witchcraft was repeatedly attacked in the press did Raymond feel moved to become its spokesman. As a national figure he earned the media's respect by his scathing attacks on the cranks and poseurs that joined the Wiccan ranks. Eventually he quit his job with an airline company and began collecting relevant items for a museum on Bay Shore, Long Island.

He is among the many who advocate nudity for ritual ceremonies. To some it seems a flimsy pretext for lewd behaviour, but those who believe in it do so because nudity is a leveller and the sexual tension enhances the occasion.

America's most famous witch was Sybil Leek. Her credentials were spotless. She claims to trace hereditary Wicca back to the 12th century on her mother's side, while her father was from a family of eminent occultists. She was initiated in the south of France by an aunt on her father's side.

She came to America in 1964 after being a High Priestess in England. Her views on witchcraft were widely respected. 'Everyone is dedicated to witchcraft as the Old Religion, everyone has a flair for healing and we are all determined to use our powers for good and to deflect some of the evil which Black Magic tries to create throughout the world. If we can remain true to these basic ideals, so rooted in tradition, then we are doing our duty.'

In England she had courted publicity which continued in America. It earned her considerable sums. She even had her own radio show, a restaurant, 'The Cauldron', and a chauffeur-driven limousine. This new breed of witches who exchanged Wiccan wisdom for money were greeted with unease by other covert practitioners.

A CANDLE-LIT ALTAR BEARING KEY OBJECTS, INCLUDING THE ATHAME,
CHALICE AND GRIMOIRE — INTEGRAL ELEMENTS OF WITCH RITUAL.

MYSTICS AND SEERS

Man has been to the moon and a manned mission to Mars is promised. When it comes to probing space, science is making eager headway. However, mysteries of the mind are more difficult to fathom. Moreover, they do not attract the same excited response from most scientists.

For years people have accepted that space is the final frontier. However, perhaps the dark recesses of the mind that are in fact the most significant remaining barriers to human understanding.

CHAPTER SIX

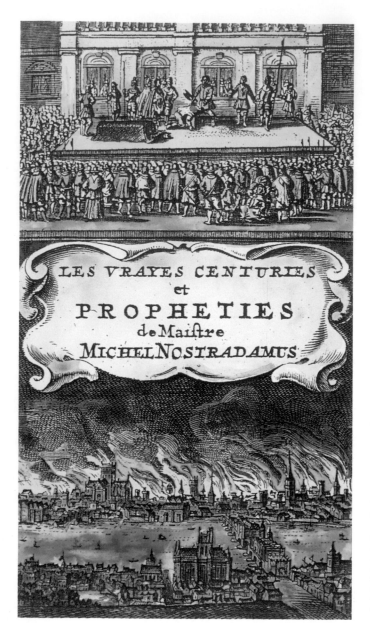

'A leader of Great Germanies who will come to give help which is only counterfeit. He will stretch the borders of Germany, and will cause France to be divided into two parts. Living fire and death hidden in globes will be loosed, horrible and terrible, by night the enemy will reduce cities to dust.'

So reads a prediction made by Nostradamus, the French seer, in the mid-16th century. With the advent of the Second World War, France was split into two following German occupation. Globe-shaped bombs reduced major cities to rubble.

Was Nostradamus a prophet without equal? Or were the predictions a lucky shot in the dark? For centuries scholars have pored over his obscure words in an effort to discover the truth.

A MAN OF HEALING

Nostradamus was born Michel de Nostradame on 14 December 1503 to a lawyer and his wife in St Remy de Provence, near Avignon in France. Having studied medicine, it was his healing skills that first brought his name to prominence. When southern France was ravaged by the plague, Nostradamus did not 'bleed' people but applied his own potions with which he had some success. He changed his name to Nostradamus, meaning 'Man from Our Lady'.

NOSTRADAMUS
(1503-1566)

ABOVE: THE TITLE PAGE OF THE 1668 EDITION OF THE *PROPHECIES OF NOSTRADAMUS* ILLUSTRATED WITH TWO PREDICTIONS – THE EXECUTION OF KING CHARLES I AND THE GREAT FIRE OF LONDON.

After being accused of heresy by the Inquisition, he lived a nomadic life and it was then that he felt the power of prophecy, although it wasn't until he settled in the town of Salon-en-Craux de Provence and married his second wife, Anne Ponsart Gemelle, that he documented the visions.

Alone at night in his study he used the power of scrying, or divination by concentration, using a bowl of water on a tripod as the focus of his attention. In his own words: 'The wand in the hand is placed in the middle of the tripod's legs.

Nostradamus used the power of scrying, or divination by the power of concentration, to make his prophecies.

With water he sprinkles both the hem of his garment and his foot. A voice, fear, he trembles in his robes. Divine splendour, the god sits nearby.'

Nostradamus knew he risked being branded a magician and heretic. Accordingly, his notes, written in Greek, French, Provencal and Latin as well as anagrams, were obscure. The verses he wrote are known as quatrains and there are 100 in each book or 'century'.

AN INSTANT SUCCESS

The code, together with the patronage of Catherine de Medici, wife of King Henri II, protected him from prosecution in an age of Catholic paranoia. The first book of prophecies published in 1555 was instantly successful. Its sequel did not appear until after his death on 2 July 1566, aged 62. His works were littered with prophecies, which extended to the year 3797 when he believed the world would end.

There are undoubtedly words of wisdom within Nostradamus's verses. In the 8th century he wrote: 'The blood of innocents, widow and virgin, with many evils committed by the Great Red One, holy images placed over burning candles, terrified by fear, none will be seen to move', deemed to refer to the Bolshevik revolution and the slaughter of the Russian royal family.

Those brave enough to investigate the prophecies must consider not only the implications of the language but the era and outlook of Nostradamus, a man who believed in the divine right of kings and planet cycles which have since altered.

One sobering quatrain reads: 'In the year 1999 and seven months there will come from the skies the Great King of Terror. He will bring back to life the great King of the Mongols. Before and after war reigns happily.'

This is the third 'anti-Christ', following in the footsteps of Napoleon and Hitler bringing terror to earth for 27 years. 'The unbelievers are dead, captive, exiled: with blood, human bodies, water and red hail covering the earth.' But after the prophecy of doom comes hope – for Nostradamus believed it was possible to alter the course of the future through awareness and action.

A MURAL OF NOSTRADAMUS REGALES THE SHOP FRONT AT THE ENTRANCE OF ST MICHAEL'S CHURCH, SALON, WHERE THE PROPHET LIVED.

LEFT: STALIN IGNORED MESSING'S WARNINGS ABOUT HITLER.
BELOW: CAROLE LOMBARD DIDN'T HEED THE ADVICE OF JEANE DIXON (BOTTOM RIGHT).

WOLF MESSING (1899-1972)

Wolf Messing knew it was the challenge of his life. Few people can resist inventing impossible tasks for psychics and Josef Stalin, the Russian dictator, was no exception: Messing was to use his incredible psychic powers to rob a bank. If he failed, Messing knew he was doomed.

Armed with the only tools he needed for the job, an empty attaché case and a blank piece of paper, Messing passed an unsuspecting Moscow bank clerk both items and willed him to fill the case with 100,000 roubles. To a man of Messing's abilities, it was a cinch. The bank clerk handed over the cash without a fuss. Clearly Messing had missed a lucrative vocation.

Relieved his task was over, Messing immediately handed back the cash. The clerk, on the other hand, was filled with terror at the realisation of his actions and suffered a heart attack.

STALIN WARNED
Messing's feat saved his skin. Fascinated, Stalin went on to have personal audiences with this incredible psychic and seer, ignoring to his even-

tual cost warnings given by Messing about Hitler's deadly intentions concerning Russia.

Messing was born on 10 September 1899, near Warsaw in Poland. Aged 11, he ran away from school and boarded a train from his Russian-dominated homeland, heading for Germany. A ticket collector hauled him out from his hiding place beneath the seat of the train. A fearful Messing handed him a blank piece of paper and willed him to believe it was a valid ticket.

'Our gazes crossed. How I desperately wanted him to accept that scrap of paper as a ticket!' Messing revealed years later.

'I mentally suggested to him, "It's a ticket, it's

a ticket, it's a ticket." The iron jaws of the ticket punch snapped. Handing the "ticket" back to me and smiling benevolently he asked me why I had been sleeping under the seat when I had a valid ticket. It was the first time my power of suggestion manifested itself.'

Messing went to Berlin, where he earned his living at public performances of his psychic abilities. Such was his reputation that, aged 17, he sat between two of the greatest men of the era – Albert Einstein and Sigmund Freud. The story goes that Freud thought up a command for Messing after he sank into a trance. On the silent order, Messing seized a pair of scissors and clipp-ed three hairs from Einstein's moustache. It was exactly as the mischievous Freud had intended. Both Einstein and Freud remained interested observers of parapsychology, although both stopped short of complete conviction.

Messing travelled the world, although based from 1922 in the newly independent Poland.

With the coming of Hitler and Second World War, Messing looked east to Moscow for salvation. But psychic performances were banned by Stalin, who first met Messing after his arrest for giving public performances.

Messing warned that Hitler would invade the USSR in June 1941. He was spot on. Happily he was later able to forecast the exact date of Hitler's demise and the Nazi surrender.

However, Messing was condemned to a life of concert hall appearances. He described his talents as an ability to see pictures in his mind rather than clairaudience. Although rarely tested, Soviet scientists discovered Messing's head and chest radiated more heat than other parts of his body.

Following a heart attack, Messing died on 8 November 1972 and was given a hero's burial.

MOTHER SHIPTON

One of Britain's most famous seers, Mother Shipton, lived in Yorkshire from 1488 until 1561, the wife of a carpenter. She foretold the defeat of the French at Agincourt, the reign of a maiden queen (Elizabeth I) and the beheading of a widowed one (Mary Queen of Scots). However, a poem she is credited with writing, which many believed to foretell the arrival of cars, submarines, radios and metal ships, is widely held to be a fake – although interestingly the hoax was perpetuated in the 19th century, when many of its predictions were still years ahead.

'Around the world, thoughts shall fly,
In the twinkling of an eye,
Under water men shall walk,
Shall ride, and sleep and even talk,
Carriages without horses shall go,
And accidents fill the world with woe,
In water, iron shall float,
As easily as a wooden boat.'

ANOTHER SEER, JEANE DIXON (LEFT), BECAME A CELEBRITY IN AMERICA THROUGH HER PSYCHIC ABILITIES. AS EARLY AS 1952, SHE CLAIMED A 'BLUE-EYED DEMOCRAT' WOULD ENTER THE WHITE HOUSE. SHE SAID HE WOULD BE THERE IN 1960 – AND THAT HIS LIFE WOULD END IN ASSASSINATION. HER PROPHECIES ABOUT JOHN F. KENNEDY WERE, OF COURSE, PROVED.

ACTRESS CAROLE LOMBARD, AT AN AUDIENCE WITH DIXON, WAS WARNED NOT TO TAKE A FLIGHT WITHIN THE FOLLOWING SIX WEEKS. NEVERTHELESS, LOMBARD INSISTED ON MAKING JUST SUCH A JOURNEY TO FULFIL HER COMMITMENTS. THREE DAYS AFTER SEEING DIXON, SHE WAS KILLED IN A PLANE CRASH. JEANE DIXON HERSELF DIED AGED 79 IN JANUARY 1997.

The tragedy of the *Titanic* is well known, the liner which sank on 14 April 1912 after being holed by an iceberg in the Atlantic with the loss of more than 1,500 lives.

PRECOGNITION AND PREMONITION

There is an astonishing parallel tale in the novel *Futility* written by Morgan Robertson 14 years earlier about a prestige ship by the name of *Titan* which was, like the *Titanic*, thought to be unsinkable. It also became the victim of a collision with an iceberg; both ships bore remarkably similar dimensions, exactly the same passenger capacity and neither vessel had a sufficient number of lifeboats.

The uncanny way that art mimicked life in the novel is familiar to students of the paranormal and was just one of a host of prophecies, premonitions and precognition linked to the *Titanic*. A woman who stood watching the feted departure of the *Titanic* from her home on the Isle of Wight was suddenly gripped with panic. 'It's going to sink. That ship is going to sink,' she shrieked at her bewildered husband. 'Do something. Are you so blind that you are going to let them drown? Save them! Save them!' It was four days before the scene she saw in her mind's eye became a reality in the north Atlantic.

IMMINENT DISASTER
At the same time psychic V. N. Turvey predicted to a friend that the ship would go under and that the catastrophe was imminent. Passenger Colin Macdonald cancelled his ticket on the *Titanic's* first venture out to sea, convinced that a disaster loomed. Banker J. Pierpont Morgan was among several who pulled out of the trip claiming that they were superstitious about going on a ship's maiden voyage. Before cancelling his passage, businessman J. Connon Middleton twice dreamt

THE BOOK THAT MIRRORED THE TRAGEDY OF THE *TITANIC*. *FUTILITY* WAS PUBLISHED 14 YEARS BEFORE THAT ILL-FATED MAIDEN VOYAGE, IT CONCERNED A LINER CALLED *TITAN*.

FUTILITY
OR
THE WRECK of THE TITAN

MORGAN ROBERTSON

The evidence for psychic warnings is compelling if not proven. Millions of people will confess to experiencing some form of extra-sensory perception, the tantalising sixth sense.

The evidence for a wave of mass psychic warnings is compelling although not proven. Millions of people around the world will confess to experiencing some form of extra-sensory perception, the tantalising sixth sense. An estimated 70 per cent of people have felt the effects of ESP, to a greater or lesser extent.

Strictly speaking, prophecy is divinely inspired, although the distinction between all forms of perceiving the future has become blurred. Premonition is a feeling of anxiety or depression, its cause is unknown. Those who have experienced premonitions, and there are many that do, are frequently unable to pinpoint the exact cause of their fears other than to say 'something bad is going to happen'.

ABERFAN PREMONITIONS

Before the Aberfan disaster in South Wales, which claimed the lives of 116 children and 28 adults when a coal slag landslide engulfed a school, there were more than 200 premonitions felt throughout the country. These included choking sensations, seeing black, billowing clouds and hearing the screams of children.

Afterwards three surveys reported on the extent of the prophetic senses and the result was the founding of the British Premonitions Bureau, intended to listen to the warnings from psychics and others. A like-minded body was established in America soon afterwards, the Central Premonitions Registry.

Precognition is the knowledge of an impending event and usually comes by way of visions, dreams or merely a sense of knowing. Usually it concerns a loved one, although not always. With this more specific form of ESP it is more likely a disaster will be identified and possibly averted.

BEFORE THE COAL SLAG LANDSLIDE ENGULFED THE SCHOOL IN THE WELSH VILLAGE OF ABERFAN IN 1966 THERE WAS A SPATE OF PREMONITIONS FELT NATIONWIDE.

of seeing a sinking ship with its passengers and crew floundering in the water.

Journalist W. T. Stead was aboard the *Titanic*. It was 20 years since he had penned a fictional story about an ocean liner which was crippled and sank after being breached by an iceberg. The story was part of his continuing campaign to press shipbuilders to include the necessary number of lifeboats on the increasingly large liners. He pursued the theme in a lecture given in 1910, passionately illustrating his point by depicting himself as a shipwreck victim stranded in icy waters, shouting for help before slipping beneath the waves. Unwittingly Stead had graphically described his own fate.

It's not unusual for children to have invisible friends. Most parents accept that the playmate, which may be christened and even have a place at the dinner table, is a figment of an over-active imagination. But could it be that some youngsters are playing with a spirit that they alone can see?

PSYCHIC CHILDREN

THE FOX CHILDREN

Children have played a significant role in the history of the paranormal. The very origins of mediumship and spiritualism lay with the Fox children of Hydesville, New York. The story of how devout Methodists John and Margaret Fox and their daughters Kate and Margaret were plagued by a phantom rapper who embarked on a coded communication with the children has often been told.

Neighbours and friends were called in to witness how the spirit answered questions, rapping out the alphabet with one knock for a, two for b, three for c and so forth. From these communications they learned that the spirit had been a pedlar who was murdered in the Foxes' house years before and still lay buried in the cellar. When the basement was eventually dug up human remains were found.

GLADYS OSBORNE LEONARD BEGAN HER ASTONISHING CAREER AS A PSYCHIC IN CHILDHOOD. BORN ON 28 MAY 1882 IN LYTHAM, LANCASHIRE. LEONARD REVEALED HER GIFT AT AN EARLY AGE FOLLOWING A BEREAVEMENT. SHE SPOKE ABOUT 'HAPPY VALLEYS', A PARADISE INHABITED BY BEAUTIFUL PEOPLE IN FLOWING GARMENTS. HORRIFIED, HER FAMILY TRIED TO SUPPRESS HER VISIONS AND URGED HER NEVER TO DISCUSS WITH OTHERS WHAT SHE SAW. THE VISIONS STOPPED OCCURRING YET LEONARD REMAINED INTRIGUED AND FINALLY BECAME A MEDIUM WITH A SPIRIT GUIDE CALLED FEDA WHO WAS, ALLEGEDLY, HER GREAT-GREAT-GRANDMOTHER.

It seemed that the pedlar was joined by many other lost souls with messages of their own to impart. When Kate and Margaret moved to live with another sister, Leah, the noises followed them. The Fox sisters were told by the unseen spirits, 'You have been chosen to go before the world to convince the sceptical of the great truth of immortality.'

The sisters themselves and the meetings they held were subject to scrutiny, but observers remained baffled. Spiritualism was born and it spread rapidly across the Western world. Even a confession by Margaret Fox in her adult life that she and her sister achieved the knocking sounds merely by cracking their knee and toe joints failed to curtail the fervour. Her declaration that the phenomenon was 'all fraud, hypocrisy and delusion' has been countered by the claim that she was an old, ailing, alcohol-dependent widow who was jealous of the fame and fortunes of her more successful sister Leah.

There have been many impressive examples of how children have been 'in tune' with spirit messages. Nicklas Mason, of Shifnal, Shropshire, was only three when his grandfather died in 1987. But he insisted the man he loved had become his 'guard' and would talk to him in empty corners. His parents Rosanne and Terence put the behaviour down to childish games until their car – which had once belonged to Rosanne's father – was stolen.

Soon afterwards Nicklas told them not to worry, that the car would be recovered. He said it was near a place where there were two bridges that you could go under and over. There were shops too, he added, a church and a place where the family had been for picnics.

'The next morning the police phoned – they had found the car,' explained Rosanne. 'It had been abandoned on a slip road to a dual carriageway with two road bridges. It was also near a shopping centre where we'd been to have picnics and close to a church which I had joined since my father died.'

ON-COMING CAR WARNING

Lesley Skeels was a 13-year-old schoolgirl when she was flashed a warning message. She and a friend were about to cross the road outside their school in Egham, Surrey, when she suddenly knew an on-coming car was putting them in danger.

As the car pulled on to the road about 200 yards away she told her friend Sylvia Hedges, 'That car is going to knock you over.' When the car stopped near them Sylvia decided to cross – only to find the driver starting up once more and heading straight for her. Sylvia was bruised and shaken in the collision, but otherwise unhurt. 'I didn't hear a voice telling me that the car was going to run into her. A message ran through my body saying it,' said Lesley.

LEFT: GLADYS OSBORNE LEONARD SAW STRANGE VISIONS AS A CHILD.
BELOW: WERE THE FOX CHILDREN MAKING CRACKS WITH THEIR KNEE JOINTS TO IMPERSONATE SPIRIT ACTIVITY?

PSYCHIC SLEUTHS

As she stepped into the bungalow, Nancy Myers was felled by 73 stabs wounds. She believed she was doomed, yet moments later she was recovering in the yard. Although she was emotionally exhausted, there wasn't a single wound on her. Nancy Myers, a psychic detective, was suffering the fate of a 73-year-old murder victim in Wilmington, Delaware.

A policeman had taken her to the old lady's home on a pretext when a blinding flash had taken Nancy into the mind of the victim during her death throes. Despite her agonies, Nancy was able to reveal two important clues to the policeman with her. There was insufficient evidence to bring about a conviction. Still, it had proven to be a valuable lesson for Nancy. 'I learnt to put myself next to the victim, instead of inside them,' she admitted.

Psychic sleuths have been around for many years. In 1827 Maria Martin was killed by her lover William Corder at a barn in Polstead, Suffolk. Her family believed Maria was living in London with Corder until her mother dreamt of the murder three times. The barn was searched, Maria's body found and Corder was hanged.

VARIABLE SUCCESS RATES

Although hundreds of psychics have been used by police, their success rate has been variable. Successful psychics receive wide publicity. Yet more than 19,000 tips from people claiming to be psychic were given to police in Atlanta, Georgia, investigating a string of child murders. None proved influential on the case.

There's considerable evidence to show that psychics have certainly lent invaluable assistance in the past. And plenty of policemen, at a dead end during an investigation, have turned to psychics for help. Police use psychics to flesh out information they already have and provide new leads. It remains impossible to present psychically drawn evidence in court.

Psychics called in by police have different ways of operating. By handling an object or garment once close to the crime victim, some psychics are able to detect an aura or vibration which will yield information. The technique is known as psychometry and was developed in the middle of the 19th century by an American physiologist, Joseph R. Buchanan. Other options include hypnosis, automatic writing, channelling through spirits and even dowsing to locate bodies, murder weapons etc.

MULTIPLE MURDER

Dr Maximilien Langsner was able to clear up a multiple murder on behalf of Canadian police by reading thoughts. Austrian Dr Langsner was called in after a woman, her son and two workers were found dead on 9 July 1928 on a farm in Manville, Alberta. The remaining son, Vernon Booher, claimed he had found the bodies after returning home. Police discovered that the murder weapon belonged to neighbour Charles Stephenson, although he claimed it had been stolen a week previously.

When he attended the inquest, Langsner read the mind of Vernon Booher – and realised the 'grieving' son was responsible for the killings. He was able to lead police to the dumped rifle used by Booher and stolen from Stephenson. Langsner was even able to pinpoint a witness who had seen Booher slip out of church the previous week in order to steal the rifle.

For the motive, Langsner said that Vernon had wished to marry a girl in the locality, but his mother had strongly disapproved. A quarrel broke out and ended in violence and Booher killed everyone there to eliminate possible witnesses. Langsner learned all of this by sitting outside Booher's cell for an hour. Booher was hanged on 29 April 1929.

SEVERAL PSYCHICS WERE HAUNTED BY THE IDENTITY OF THE YORKSHIRE RIPPER, THE MAN WHO KILLED 13 WOMEN DURING A REIGN OF TERROR THAT LASTED SEVERAL YEARS. NELLA JONES COULD SEE A VISION OF THE KILLER INCHES FROM HER FACE. SHE COULD SMELL THE ODOUR OF HIS BREATH AND SEE SHINY BEADS OF SWEAT ON HIS BROW. ACCURATELY SHE PREDICTED THAT HIS FINAL VICTIM WOULD HAVE THE INITIALS J. H. (IT WAS JACQUELINE HALL). THERE WERE A HOST OF OTHER CLUES WHICH SHE LEARNED, INCLUDING HIS JOB AND THE TOWN HE CAME FROM, BUT NONE WHICH COULD CONCLUSIVELY PROVE HIS IDENTITY. TO HER RELIEF SHE SAW IN A VISION CLOSE TO CHRISTMAS 1980 THAT THE RIPPER WOULD SOON BE CAUGHT. LORRY DRIVER PETER SUTCLIFFE WAS ARRESTED ON 3 JANUARY 1981, WHEN MUCH OF WHAT NELLA JONES KNEW ABOUT THE RIPPER FITTED INTO PLACE LIKE A JIGSAW PUZZLE.

ABOVE LEFT: MEDIUMS LIKE ROBERT JONES, WHO DIED IN 1930, WOULD BE THE CRIME-BUSTERS OF THE FUTURE, ACCORDING TO AN OPTIMISTIC SIR ARTHUR CONAN DOYLE.
RIGHT: PSYCHIC SLEUTH GERALD CROISET POINTED POLICE TO THE BODY OF A MURDERED BOY IN A DUTCH CANAL.

In a darkened room a small group of expectant people link hands in silence. All eyes turn to the presiding medium. The low lights flicker and the closed curtains rustle as her wavering voice splinters the night. 'Is there anybody there?'

MEDIUMS

It's the traditional picture of mediumship painted by sceptics who think the table only levitates with a jerk of her knees, and the rapping which purports to be communicating spirits is in fact the heel of her shoe.

Investigators have found difficulty explaining away all the stunts that occur at seances. Although most stop short of admitting a new-found belief, there are cynics who have left seances utterly convinced in life-after-death having received a highly personal and relevant message from a medium.

Mediums can be physical, on these occasions their seances will be peppered by inexplicable noises, levitation of objects or the movement of items around the room; or mental – the elements of mental mediumship include clairvoyance or 'clear seeing', clairaudience, automatic writing or automatic speech.

'THE OTHER SIDE'

To channel communication from 'the other side', mediums have spirit guides and it is this that distinguishes them from psychics. Mental mediums may sink into a trance and assume the voice, facial expressions and gestures of their spirit guides. Some reach an altered state of consciousness via hypnotism.

In the past, famous mediums have discovered their extraordinary powers during childhood or following an illness or trauma. The talent of Gordon Higginson was recognised in his boyhood by his mother, also a medium, while Dutch clairvoyant Peter Hurkos knew nothing of psychic experience until, aged 32, he fell from some scaffolding and was knocked unconscious.

Keith Charles, a British police officer, had rare moments of insight as a child, but only discovered his gift when he spent long hours on official duty outside No 10 Downing Street, home of the British Prime Minister. When tourists approached him, he would find himself asking questions

SEANCES BECAME POPULAR PARLOUR PASTIMES IN VICTORIAN ENGLAND. SOME EFFECTS WERE STUNTS WHILE OTHERS WERE NOT EASILY EXPLAINED AWAY.

such as, 'Have you a sister called Susan?' or 'Were you born in the north-east?' He was unnervingly accurate.

FAKES AND FRAUDS

When spiritualism was in its ascendancy during the latter part of the 19th century, the number of practising mediums mushroomed and the search for frauds intensified. In the autumn of 1876, American medium Henry Slade and his assistant were convicted under the *Vagrancy Act* of 'unlawfully using subtle craft, means and devices to deceive and impose upon certain of Her Majesty's subjects'.

Slade's speciality was automatic writing on a slate held beneath a table with a pencil on top. In addition, hands used to appear and furniture would move during seances. In Britain he was rigorously tested twice and passed with flying colours before coming to the attention of archsceptic Professor E. Ray Lankester.

During a seance, Lankester snatched the slate from under the table before the spirit began to write to expose a message that was already in place. Although he could not explain them, Lankester insisted Slade's exploits were no more than conjuring tricks. After a riotous trial, Slade was sentenced to three months' hard labour.

FURIOUS HOUDINI

Escapologist and conjurer Harry Houdini was a life-long sceptic, although he longed to believe in the power of mediums in order to contact his beloved dead mother.

A shared obsession with the afterlife brought him into contact with Sir Arthur Conan Doyle, creator of master rationalist Sherlock Holmes. Like many, Sir Arthur was convinced in the value of seances following the death of his son in the First World War. Lady Doyle was herself a medium and she persuaded Houdini to attend a seance and attempt to contact his mother.

BE PREPARED . . .
IF YOU GO TO A SEANCE YOU MAY EXPERIENCE:
WHISPERED, APPARENTLY DISEMBODIED VOICES; ICY BLASTS OF AIR; THE TOUCH OF INVISIBLE HANDS; THE APPEARANCE OF ECTOPLASM, A WHITE SUBSTANCE EXUDING FROM THE BODILY ORIFICES OF MEDIUMS AND MOULDED INTO IMAGES LIKE CLAY BY THE SPIRITS; SPARKS OF LIGHT IN THE AIR; OBJECTS APPEARING IN THE ROOM (APPORTS); RAPPING SOUNDS; LEVITATION OF TABLES ETC; THE PLAYING OF MUSICAL INSTRUMENTS.

Apparently possessed by the spirit of the dead woman, Lady Doyle made the sign of the cross and wrote a message to Houdini.

The magician was furious. He wrote afterwards: 'Lady Doyle claimed that the spirit of my dear mother had control over her hand – but my mother could not write English.'

Not only couldn't she write English, but Houdini's mother was a Jewess and most unlikely to make the sign of the cross. The seance had also taken place on her birthday, 17 June, although the spirit had apparently failed to mention this during contact with Lady Doyle. Houdini refused to speak to Sir Arthur again.

THE CRASH OF AIRSHIP R101 IN FRANCE WAS FORETOLD BY EILEEN GARRETT.

DANIEL DUNGLAS HOME

Sometimes the amazing feats of mediums will prompt even the most cool-headed observer to concede that they are in possession of some extraordinary powers.

Few could top the antics of 19th century medium Daniel Dunglas Home. Before three independent witnesses, he once floated head first out of an open window some 40 ft above the ground and returned feet first through the window of an adjoining room some 7 ft 6 in away.

At seances, Home levitated along with the table, while unseen hands tugged at the clothes of sitters. Objects flew through the air and musical instruments burst into tune. Home insisted on having seances in well-lit rooms to enable observers to see that there were 'no strings'.

Once Home stretched his body to reach a height of 6 ft 6 in, some 11 inches more than his normal size. He also shrank to a height of 5 ft.

MEETING WITH THE CZAR

Home was born in Edinburgh on 20 March 1833, the son of a psychic mother. At the age of nine the family moved to Connecticut, where Home continued to experience the visions he had known as a small boy. His first levitation occurred at 19 years of age, and then randomly until he learned to control the phenomenon. Although he was world famous and had seances with the doomed Czar Nicholas II, Home spent his life in poverty.

CZAR NICHOLAS II (1868–1918) WAS INTRIGUED BY MEDIUMS AND MYSTICISM AND INVITED THEM TO HOLD SEANCES AT HIS PALACE.

The supernatural gifts came via the spirit guide Bryan, according to Home. Until his death in 1886 Home was widely investigated and no evidence of trickery was ever turned up.

One psychic researcher of the era who verified Home's activities was Sir William Crookes, the man who discovered thallium and a pioneer of electricity. Crookes was widely discredited when he championed medium Florence Cook.

Cook, born in 1856, began seances as a teenager, claiming her spirit guide was buccaneer's daughter Katie King. Cook went behind a curtain during the seance where she was tied to a chair, the knots sealed with wax.

DANIEL DUNGLAS HOME (1833–1886) WAS ONE OF THE MOST
FAMOUS PHYSICAL MEDIUMS TO EVER LIVE. BUT DESPITE HIS
REPUTATION HE DEPENDED ON PATRONAGE AND REMAINED POOR.

THE APPEARANCES OF KATIE KING

Thereafter Katie King appeared in a blaze of light
to the sitters. In 1880 Sir George Sitwell seized the
spirit and pulled down the curtain screening
Cook from the sitters to find the chair empty.
Allies of Cook were always among the sitters to
deflect the curious and the cynical. However,
Crookes was convinced of Cook's abilities.

Despite her reputation as a hoaxer, Cook had
loyal supporters who claimed some of the sights
they had seen at her seances could not be faked.

Some mediums have warmly welcomed investigation. The British medium Leslie Flint has
connected with some extremely famous spirits,
such as Oscar Wilde, Queen Victoria, Winston
Churchill and Gandhi.

Flint said, 'I think I must be the most tested
medium the country has ever produced. I have
been boxed up, tied up, sealed up, gagged, bound
and held, and still the voices have come.'

EILEEN GARRETT

Eileen Garrett, born in County Meath, Ireland,
in 1893, was a mental medium working in
America and England. A notable success was
her ignored warnings of the R101 airship disaster in 1930.

A crewman, Flight Lieutenant Carmichael
Irwin, who died in the crash, gave Garrett details
about the disaster long before the inquiry. The
technical data she gave in a trance was far beyond
the limits of her knowledge.

Experts later suggested that there was nothing
which came from Garrett that was new or relevant. Some suggested that she picked up the mind
waves of a journalist absorbed in the R101 story
who was attending the same seance. Garrett herself never tried to explain away the information
channelled through her, nor did she take money
for seances.

Garrett was eager to promote the investigation of psychic occurrences and took it upon
herself to found the Parapsychology Foundation
in 1951. Her control spirit was generally Uvani,
an Oriental, although a Persian physician by the
name of Abdul Latif also aided her. Nevertheless,
their contributions puzzled her. She concluded
that her powers were not supernatural, but were
drawn from her inner self.

EILEEN GARRETT IN THE CONTROL OF HER SPIRIT
GUIDE ABDUL LATIF.

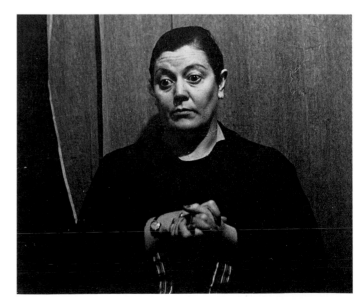

URI GELLER
(1946-)

Uri Geller earned himself a worldwide reputation for his amazing spoon-and-fork-bending abilities. Just a rub of the metal was enough to transform the strength of the solid implements into dangling limpness. Thereafter the phenomenon of fork-bending was christened 'the Geller effect'.

Uri Geller was born in Tel Aviv, Israel, in 1946. His psychic abilities kicked in from the age of five, after he received an electric shock from his mother's sewing machine. He practised his new-found abilities by reading his mother's mind and speeding up the hands on his watch. While he was eating a bowl of soup one day, he was surprised to find the spoon wilting in his hand.

URI GELLER HAS AMAZED THE WORLD WITH HIS SPOON-BENDING ABILITIES. AT THE RUB OF A FINGER METAL TURNS FLOPPY.

GELLER SHOOTS TO STARDOM
In 1969, Geller became a performer after a spell in the Israeli army. He was featured on a show hosted by David Dimbleby and the gateway to international stardom opened.

Two years later, Geller was taken to the Stanford Research Institute in California, America, where he underwent a series of highly publicised tests. Geller acquitted himself well. In one of the examinations a die was thrown out of Geller's view and it was his task to identify the number it revealed. The results found that Geller had given the correct number an astonishing eight out of eight times. Shown a series of metal containers, Geller was then asked to say which were empty. On 12 occasions out of 14 he was right.

Three years later British mathematician John Taylor conducted more experiments. Now Geller bent cutlery even when they were protected in plastic tubes.

The study of his spoon-bending abilities was inconclusive, but even if the researchers failed to pinpoint his specific paranormal abilities they could not prove him a fake.

Throughout the seventies, Geller was a travelling performer, convincing sceptics around the globe that he was endowed with an awesome talent. But just as he won fans, so he attracted critics. Magicians proved they could manage the same effect by sleight of hand. David Berglas, a leading magician and a one-time head of the British Committee for Scientific Investigation of Claims of the Paranormal, viewed it like this.

'If [Geller] is a genuine psychic and genuinely does what he claims to by the methods he claims to use, then he is the only person in the world who can do it. He is the only one to have demonstrated [his powers] consistently. He is a phenomenon and we must respect that. If, on the other hand, he is a magician, or trickster or a con-man he is also phenomenal – the best there has ever been. So whichever way you want to look at him, we must respect him as one or the other.'

GELLER WITHDRAWS FROM THE LIMELIGHT

Suddenly Geller withdrew from the limelight. He admits the large amounts of money he received after growing up in poverty turned his head. He flew private jets, mingled with the rich and famous and lived lavishly. In a magazine interview he described the day that changed his life.

'It was in Geneva and my wife said, "Look at my Gucci suitcases. Just stand there for five minutes and look at them." There were 15 Gucci suitcases. And she said to me, "Now what are you trying to prove and to who?"'

AT LEAST ONE CYNIC HAS BECOME A BELIEVER, THANKS TO GELLER'S ABILITIES. WHEN WILLIAM SCANLON-MURPHY WAS SEARCHING FOR THE WRECK OF BRITAIN'S FIRST SUBMARINE, THE *RESURGAM*, HE ASKED GELLER FOR HELP. THE PSYCHIC LOOKED AT A CHART AND MARKED THE SPOT WITH HIS INITIALS WHERE THE WRECK LAY.

SCANLON-MURPHY SAID, 'I'M SCEPTICAL ABOUT PEOPLE LIKE URI GELLER AND I ADMIT I ASKED HIM OUT OF SHEER DEVILMENT. AFTER HE POINTED TO THE MAP I IGNORED WHAT HE SAID BECAUSE IT WAS ABOUT 15 MILES WEST FROM THE SPOT WHERE WE WERE LOOKING AND WHERE (ACCORDING TO THE LOG) THE SUB WENT DOWN. I JUST SHOVED IT IN MY MOTHER'S ATTIC.'

AFTER WEEKS OF LOOKING AND AT A COST OF MORE THAN £1 MILLION, SCANLON-MURPHY GAVE UP. IT WAS ONLY WHEN A FISHING BOAT SNAGGED ITS NETS IN LIVERPOOL BAY DID A DIVER DISCOVER THE *RESURGAM*, 71 FT DOWN ON THE SEA BED. A SATELLITE READING PLACED THE SUBMARINE JUST 5 M AWAY FROM GELLER'S LONG-FORGOTTEN MARK.

SAID SCANLON-MURPHY: 'I DON'T KNOW HOW HE DID IT, OR IF IT WAS JUST PURE CHANCE, BUT HE WAS SPOT ON.'

MIRACULOUS BODY AND UNKNOWN MIND

Volumes have been written about incredible occurrences which are irresistibly fascinating to mankind. So far nobody has provided the answers which believers and sceptics alike are seeking.

Clearly, the problems presented to science by peculiar phenomena are immense. Scientists have plumbed the depths of our minds, our souls and the universe in the quest for fresh facts. It has become patently obvious that what is known to us is only the tip of the iceberg. Presented with the weight of unproved evidence, it is probable that most hearts accept that there is more in life than we will ever know – while many minds cannot.

CHAPTER SEVEN

Nobody knows why we fall in love, what gives rise to the imagination or fashions the contents of the human subconscious. Given the limited amount that we do know about the workings of our bodies, it is not inconceivable that illness can be diagnosed and cured by the power of positive thought.

HEALING

MIRACULOUS CURES

The twin arenas of faith and psychic healing are fraught with difficulties. Believers quote the numerous examples of people who have been miraculously cured without so much as a scalpel or drug. Cancer patients go on to be disease-free after healing.

An unknown number of people are persuaded to bypass modern medicine yet, due to its fringe nature, no research has been done in discovering how long-lasting the effects of spiritual healing actually are.

Belief in faith healing of the kind illustrated by Jesus in the New Testament has enjoyed a revival in the past century, first with the interest in spiritualism and then with the rise of evangelism.

There has long been faith in and testament to miracles in the Christian Church. The shrine at Lourdes in France was established after a peasant girl, Bernadette, saw 18 visions of the Virgin there in 1858. Then came claims of miraculous cures taking place at the very spot where Bernadette saw the vision, which have continued to the present day.

The faithful who gather at Lourdes do not rely on a single cure. It is their strong beliefs brought

MARY BAKER EDDY (1821–1910) FOUNDED THE CHRISTIAN SCIENCE CHURCH AFTER DISCOVERING THE POWER OF SELF-HELP IN HEALING.

sharply into focus there which help them to achieve their ends.

THE CHURCH OF CHRISTIAN SCIENCE

At the end of the 19th century, Mary Baker Eddy, from New Hampshire, was near death from internal injuries after a fall on an icy pavement. She turned to the Bible and read in Matthew 9:1–18 how Jesus told an invalid to 'take up your bed and go home'. Convinced that illness could be overcome from within, Eddy recovered and went on to found the Christian Science Church in 1875. It adopted her philosophy that unity with God was the key to healing.

Although Eddy rejected charges that she was an occultist, she did, however, believe that psychic forces could be used for harm and her paranoia and controversial character gave the Church a dubious reputation. Today Christian Scientists refrain from using regular medicines and medical

Not all faith healers demand a belief in their God. The latest term for the practice is energy healing.

services, choosing instead an intense spiritual discipline as the way forward.

EDGAR CAYCE (1877–1945)

One of the most remarkable healers of the century, Edgar Cayce, was also a confirmed Christian. Cayce, born in 1877 in Kentucky, played with invisible spirits when he was a child. Aged 13, he saw a vision of a woman. 'Tell me what you would like most of all so that I may give it to you,' she asked. Cayce replied that he wanted to help the sick.

His first success was when he was a schoolboy, following a knock on the base of his spine by a ball. Later that day Cayce suffered a bout of uncharacteristic aggression. Soon afterwards he went to sleep and it was then, with his eyes tight shut, that he told his parents that he was in shock and needed a poultice. They did as they were asked and the very next day Cayce was back to normal, remembering nothing of the previous day's incidents.

This ability to heal came to light again in 1898 when, under self-induced hypnosis, Cayce identified the problem causing his troublesome throat ailment and the treatment required to cure it. It launched a career of psychic healing which lasted until his death in 1945.

Although the Association for Research and Enlightenment was established to study Cayce's work, he himself was generally distrustful of scientific testing. This stemmed from the time when he sank into a trance before an audience of sceptics. One stuck pins in his hand, another inserted a hat pin through his cheek while a third cut off part of a finger nail. While Cayce did not react during the trance, he was in agony when he came out of it.

Cayce worked by relaxing into an unconscious state. In this state he answered questions put to him by his aides and spoke of himself in the third person. He saw the human body as a whole; one malfunctioning part and the natural equilibrium was sent haywire. The patient needed faith in the power of God before the curative compounds could be effective. His favourite phrase was: 'Mind is the builder'.

Cayce achieved some phenomenal successes, sometimes in person but frequently by letter, and he gave about 30,000 readings. There were reports of some wholesale cures from delighted clients, although on at least two occasions he read for people who had already died. Sceptics found it surprising that he had not divined their passing in his altered state.

Cayce always remained true to his Christian doctrine. He disliked taking money for readings and, until 1923, he carried out his psychic work in tandem with his day job as a photographer. His concern for sick people moved him to work until he was exhausted. Consequently any accusations of fraud left him horrified.

Benjamin Franklin (1706–1790), a philosopher and statesman was extremely impressed by the demonstrations of psychic healing that he witnessed in 1784.

MAGNETISM AND HYPNOSIS

The root causes of hypnosis still defy logical explanation, yet the initiator of hypnotism was in no doubt what was behind its powers – Franz Anton Mesmer described the phenomenon as animal magnetism.

ANIMAL MAGNETISM.

Viennese-born Mesmer believed an invisible magnetic fluid linked man, animals, earth and the planets. While the effect of planetary influence on everyday life was not new when he qualified as a physician in 1765, the results Mesmer achieved were astonishing. He not only alleviated symptoms, but in doing so sent people into a trance. This was, he assumed, a by-product of the healing process and had no long-term effects.

To alleviate the pain of his patients, Mesmer used magnets. Later he abandoned the use of these when he discovered that he could achieve the same results with his pointed finger. Gradually he was able to render a cure with the laying on of hands. Mesmer decided his own

body was magnetic, which is why he called it 'animal' magnetism. His methods were too radical for the higher medical circles of Austria and Mesmer went to France.

MAGNETIC SIDE-EFFECTS

There he favoured an oak tub, or baquet, inside which were iron filings and ground glass. When it was filled with water it was deemed to be 'magnetised'. Rods protruded from the baquet which patients could grasp hold of, or apply to diseased body parts. An amazing side-effect of Mesmer's cure emerged: those in a trance-like state could report on events around them even though their eyes were shut. Some visualised what was going on elsewhere – and statements made in a trance proved correct.

Mesmer's work ultimately won the backing of the ill-fated French Queen Marie Antoinette. Under her influence the king established the Franklin Commission in 1784 to investigate. Notables such as Benjamin Franklin, who was then the US ambassador to France, astronomer Jean-Sylvain Bailly and Dr Joseph Guillotin, inventor of the unfortunate device which bears his name, were extremely impressed. They saw for themselves how patients were sleepy, yet entirely under the control of the hypnotist. 'It was

ABOVE: MESMER WAS ALWAYS EAGER TO DEMONSTRATE ASTONISHING FEATS OF MAGNETISM.

impossible not to recognise, in these effects, an extraordinary influence acting upon patients,' the commission decided.

However, the commission went on to dismiss that magnetism, or even electricity, had any meaningful role, declaring that the patient's imagination played the biggest role. The commission was undoubtedly suspicious of Mesmer's increasingly theatrical approach to work. Debate continued to rage in France about animal magnetism, but its progress was impeded with the onset of the Revolution. Mesmer escaped by moving to Switzerland. He died in relative obscurity in 1815, but gave his name to the business of hypnosis – mesmerising.

MEDICAL ACCEPTANCE OF HYPNOSIS

The practice flourished fitfully for the next two centuries and in 1843 the term hypnotism was coined by Manchester surgeon John Braid. Later Freud and Jung both adopted hypnotic techniques and discarded them, Freud because he found it difficult, whilst Jung thought suggestion played the greatest part in establishing a trance.

Today, hypnotism is used as a bona fide medical option. It can be induced as an anaesthetic in minor operations or as a treatment for migraines, allergies and even in obstetrics.

It is not always necessary for the patient to enter a trance for treatment. Like Cayce, healers often need to alter their consciousness before embarking on diagnosis. To do this some choose meditation in the same way as shamans.

PSYCHIC SURGERY

An altogether less attractive facet of healing is psychic surgery. A practitioner uses either his bare hands, or perhaps some domestic implements, to operate on a patient (or victim) having psychically diagnosed the problem. Perhaps there were some genuine operations of this kind. However, the scope for charlatans to cash in on this gruesome practice is enormous.

The audience is amazed to see spurting blood, human tissue, cancerous tumours or kidney stones brought forth from the body. After the operation the patient gets up without after-effects or scars and is allegedly disease-free. The healer displays the internal organ which was allegedly

MESMER BELIEVED THAT THE MAGNETISM THAT LINKED ALL EARTHLY THINGS WAS THE KEY TO HYPNOTISM. THIS 1900 POSTER SHOWS ITS POPULARITY AS A PIECE OF THEATRE.

the cause of the problem. All too often these body parts are no more than props supplied by the healers, or their aides, from a local butcher. Jim Jones, the self-styled messiah who perished with his disciples at Jonestown, Guyana, after an orchestrated mass suicide, used this technique.

To the patient who visits a healer and leaves with an unchanged condition, the stock response of believers is that he did not have sufficient faith. True, the attitude of the patient is crucial to the result, but the healer could also be at fault. After all, even the psychically gifted can have off days.

All students of physics know that nothing travels faster than light – unless you believe in telepathy. For telepathically-dispatched messages frequently reach their destination before the event to which they refer has even happened. Can information really be sent at such fantastic speed?

This is just one question mark over extra-sensory perception. Parapsychologists, despite many years of trying, have never come up with satisfactory evidence to support their case that ESP actually exists.

EXTRA-SENSORY PERCEPTION

TELEPATHIC COMMUNICATION

ESP is the basis of telepathy, remote vision, precognition and clairvoyance. It's the elusive 'sixth sense' which many claim to have experienced. There's much testimony in its favour, notably between loved ones at a time of crisis. To tribal people it is an accepted method of communication. Smoke signals between villages did not in themselves contain words or symbols; their purpose was to alert the shaman or medicine man of an incoming telepathic message; yet there's virtually no substantive information about ESP.

Scientist Professor Pouchet challenged psychical researchers to produce proof as long ago as 1893: 'Find it for us, good people, show it us and your name shall be greater in immortality than that of Newton.'

JOSEPH BANKS RHINE

Many have sought answers, particularly Joseph Banks Rhine, a First World War veteran and botany student who became intrigued by parapsychology after listening to a Sir Arthur Conan Doyle lecture. On hearing that British physicist

J. B. RHINE ATTEMPTED TO ESTABLISH PROOF THAT ESP AND ASSOCIATED PHENOMENA ACTUALLY EXISTED. HIS EXPERIMENTS WERE FOUND WANTING BY SCEPTICS.

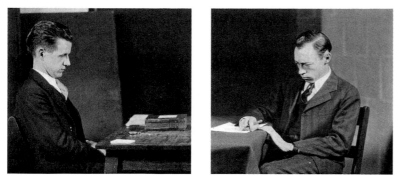

Sir Oliver Lodge believed in life after death, Rhine decided this was an increasingly reputable science which deserved thorough investigation.

He won a place at the newly created department of psychology at Duke University, North Carolina. Rhine knew psychic occurrences 'happen and are gone, leaving nothing but memory, none of the hard reality of a meteorite or a fossil'.

PSYCHIC TESTING

Colleague Karl Zener created for Rhine a pack of 25 cards comprising an equal number of five different designs – a plus sign, square, star, circle and wavy lines. Rhine asked test subjects to guess the motif on each card before it was turned up. Chance decreed they would get about five right.

Adam J. Linzmayer, in 1931, astonished Rhine with nine correct guesses in a row. In 1932 Hubert E. Pearce displayed a similar talent or knowledge, with an average of 10 correct guesses in every 25. In 1934 Rhine collated his work in a small book, simply entitled *Extra Sensory Perception*.

Criticism began only when Rhine's work was closely scrutinised, generally the same set of objections arose with parapsychological research, foremost that it is open to fraud. Rhine himself had no interest in forging results. However, he sacked his protégé Walter Levy when the latter was discovered manipulating research results.

CONVINCING THE SCEPTICS

It was difficult to introduce the correct controls for valid research. Who's to say that the test subject is correctly reading the hidden card – or telepathically poaching information from the examiner's head? Could he have a fantastic memory, enabling him to predict results from the last shuffle? Did the examiner inadvertently give the game away with body language?

Statistics are a major factor in ESP research. Rhine was striving to prove that his gifted subjects consistently scored higher than average against chance. It took three years for the American Institute of Mathematical Statistics to declare that Rhine's calculations were sound. And Rhine, in common with other parapsychologists, was never able to replicate his experiments. His 'guinea pigs' were subject to the usual human weaknesses of tiredness, boredom and 'off days'.

Rhine was among the first to admit that ESP can be inaccurate. It is notoriously vague, so that when intuitive people receive warnings about major disasters, there's insufficient information to prevent loss of life.

INIGO SWANN

Some examples of telepathy give food for thought: Inigo Swann was able to reproduce drawings and patterns accurately before ever seeing them. Swann felt an inner-self travel from his body to sneak a peak at the pictures. Alternative theories are that he clairvoyantly saw the pictures or read the mind of whoever chose the picture in the first place.

For those who believe in the powers of ESP there's been speculation that it is caused by undiscovered airwaves, an unfathomable dimension or unusual behaviour by antimatter. If it could be controlled and channelled, the potential for ESP is boundless, as a Scottish theologian, Henry Drummond, realised.

In 1894 he claimed that telepathy was 'theoretically the next stage in the evolution of language'. It was like electricity, he said, and would one day be widely used.

'It affords a rational basis for prayer and inspiration and gives us a distant glimpse of the possibility of communion without language, not only between men of various races and tongues, but between every sentient creature, which if not attainable here may await us all in that future state when we shall "know even as we are known".'

PSYCHOKINESIS

Every gambler dreams of being able to direct the skittish roulette ball into a particular slot with nothing more than a moment's concentration. In theory it is possible. Those who have mastered mind over matter, or psychokinesis (PK), as it is nowadays known, would be able to determine the movements of a roulette ball. As casinos are still gleefully opening their doors across the globe and depriving punters of large amounts of hard-earned cash, we can safely assume the art has yet to be comprehensively learned.

EMPIRICAL EVIDENCE

PK, like ESP, still leaves scientists at a loss. The term comes from the Greek words psyche, meaning 'breath', 'life' or 'soul', and kinein, 'to move'.

Professor J. B. Rhine devoted years to proving the existence of PK, without discernible success. At first he worked with a gambler who was convinced that he could influence the fall of a die. While initial results showed the gambler capable of scoring well against chance, the trials were abandoned when the 'human' factor played its part. The gambler grew weary of endless dice throwing and his scores markedly dropped.

The dice-throwing experiments had far to go, with specially designed shakers introduced to negate any hidden talents on the part of the thrower. Later automatic dice throwers were brought in to further isolate the subject of the experiments from the dice.

Rhine proved, at least to himself, that PK was an extension of ESP. It probably played its part in psychic healing, he decided, and was diminished by tiredness, despondency and drugs.

SEANCES AND MEDIUMS

Rhine largely avoided the twilight world of seances where PK was potentially at work. If mediums were genuinely producing apports, manifestations and levitations, then it was presumably thanks to the power of PK. However, it was notoriously difficult for anyone to carry out properly controlled experiments on people who preferred to work in the dark or behind closed curtains. There were very few mediums who were keen on being investigated, Eileen J. Garrett being the notable exception.

One of the most widely reported phenomena at seances was that of table-turning. The table on which sitters were resting would suddenly buck or even take flight. Clearly, by the use of levers and threads, it was easily possible to achieve such an illusion, although many of the sitters at the table would insist that the phenomenon happened without any human help. And PK could also be the rogue responsible for troublesome poltergeist activity.

> *'It is shocking but true that we know the atom today better than we know the mind that knows the atom.'*

MIND BENDING POWER

The study of PK was assisted more recently by the emergence of two astonishing new talents. One of these was Nina Kulagina who revealed a remarkable ability to move solid objects through willpower alone.

Dr Zdenek Rejdak, a Czechoslovakian philosopher, witnessed some of the exhibitions that Nina put on for researchers. In these she sent compass needles swinging crazily and moved matches into patterns.

'She even moved a whole pile of about 20 matches at once. I put my gold ring on the table afterwards; its movements were the quickest of all the objects used…I then selected some glass and china objects weighing up to 200 g (7 oz) from a sideboard. Kulagina made them move as well.'

To the delight of the examiners watching her she worked in full light and 'to order' rather than illustrating set pieces.

Afterwards Kulagina was on the point of collapse with only a faint, flickering pulse.

In a further test lasting 30 minutes, during which she separated the yolk and white of an egg cracked into a saline solution, Kulagina lost about 1 kg (2 lb) in weight. An electroencephalograph (EEG), which measures brain waves, showed that she was emotionally disturbed while she worked while her heart beat was no longer rhythmic. The electrostatic field around Nina increased when she worked, acting like the vibrations of magnetic waves.

Dr Genady Sergeyev, who supervised the tests, concluded: 'They cause the object she focuses on, even if it is something non-magnetic, to act as if magnetised. It causes the object to be attracted to her or repelled by her.'

IF GAMBLERS COULD ONLY MASTER PSYCHOKINESIS' ART OF MIND OVER MATTER THEY WOULD CLEAN UP IN CASINOS.

URI GELLER

Another of the most noted practitioners of PK is Uri Geller. While he has his critics, it is by any standard fascinating that clocks and watches go haywire in the homes of numerous viewers whenever he performs on TV. Clearly, somebody's mind is at work!

PK – invisible, intangible and scientifically unproven – still stretches the understanding of investigators. For the moment this unknown quantity looks like staying that way.

Before his death in 1980, Rhine summed it up like this: 'It is shocking but true that we know the atom today better than we know the mind that knows the atom.'

Of all paranormal phenomena, teleportation is among the most difficult on which to gather evidence. Whereas parapsychology researchers can often point to photographs or film in support of a claimed supernatural occurrence, reports of teleportation tend to lack any hard evidence. Producing the occasional object said to have materialised out of time and space is hardly enough to sway the sceptics.

'BILL HELP ALICE'

But in the early 1990s, Bill Harrison, a psychic healer in Blackford, Somerset, England, began to experience an unprecedented level of random teleport activity. The first objects, known as apports, were small pieces of metalware such as candlesticks, a brass tap and some miniature scales. These were followed by other metal items.

Within three years, Mr Harrison estimates he acquired some 4,500 coins (including foreign currency), 900 keys and 16 cannonballs, followed by more unusual objects. He says many were covered in a fine, gold-coloured dust. Others had blackened edges as if they had been subjected to heat.

TELEPORTATION

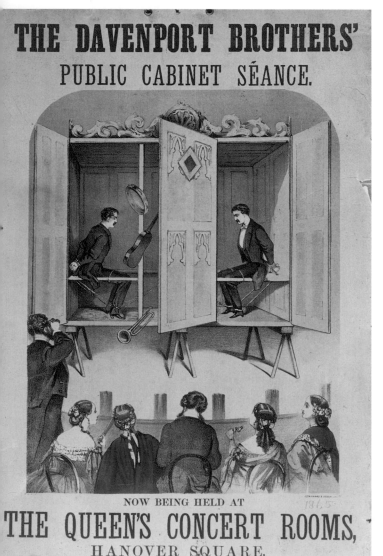

THE DAVENPORT BROTHERS'
PUBLIC CABINET SÉANCE.

NOW BEING HELD AT

THE QUEEN'S CONCERT ROOMS,
HANOVER SQUARE.

There were few signs of any consistent link, although on one occasion he received a huge key with his name on. Bizarrely, there was also a 19th century copy of *Alice's Adventures in Wonderland*. Inside was a message: 'Bill Help Alice'.

CHRISTMAS PAST

By Christmas 1996, arrivals included a tiny sterling silver cross, a lock of blonde hair, a snail shell, a broken ring, a brass pendant shaped like a flower, a feather, and a postcard of First World War soldiers dated 6 July 1919 and franked 'Liverpool'. There was also what appeared to be wafer-thin, curled-up photographs, blackened at the edges, showing a museum information board with portraits of two passengers who died on the *Titanic* – a father and daughter from Ilfracombe, Devon, called Robert and Alice Phillips.

Mr Harrison, a former fireman at Bristol airport, says items often turn up on his roof, or in his kitchen near the back door. He cannot explain why they come to him, apart from the fact that he is a practising psychic specialising in healing and the removal of spirits from buildings.

THE DAVENPORT BROTHERS, FAMOUS PSYCHICS OF THE DAY, ADVERTISE THEIR SHOW IN 1865.

'My only theory is that these items have been lost at some time and are now, for whatever reason, being returned to me,' he said. 'I never know when they are coming, or where they will appear, and I certainly haven't a clue what will appear. I know there are lots of people who think I am completely mad. But I have absolutely nothing to gain from this.'

HUMAN TRANSPORTATION

Sometimes people are inexplicably transported. In 1593 soldiers in the plaza before the Grand Palace, Mexico City, were joined by a further soldier, in a different uniform. He explained that he was ordered to guard the Governor's Palace in Manila – half-way round the world in the Philippines. The Governor had been murdered the night before and the city was in unrest, he added.

As puzzled as his interrogators, the stranger said: 'I now see this is not the Governor's Palace, so evidently I am not in Manila. But here I am and this is a palace and so I am doing my duty as nearly as is possible.'

He was jailed and released two months later, when a ship from the Philippines arrived with news that the Governor there had been killed on the night the soldier had said. After returning home the mystery man was never heard of again.

VANISHMENT

There are those who are not so lucky and disappear completely. An old cripple named Owen

Parfitt vanished from outside his home in 1769. He was sitting at the door of his isolated cottage in Somerset, unable to move because he had been paralysed by a stroke. His cousin went into the house for one minute, re-emerging to find Parfitt's rug on the chair, but Parfitt himself gone. He had vanished into thin air.

The most famous 'vanishment' of all time was that of British diplomat Benjamin Bathurst in 1809. On his return journey to Hamburg following a mission to the Austrian court, Bathurst stopped for dinner at an inn at the town of Perleberg. After the meal, he and his companion returned to their waiting coach. The friend watched as Bathurst walked towards the front of the coach to examine the horses – and disappeared, never to be seen again.

Some theorise that time may 'slip', enabling events and distance to be telescoped together. Others believe that the universe may contain strange cosmic whirlpools which draw people irresistibly into them and move them at will to anywhere on the planet. Or possibly that these whirlpools whisk them away into another dimension altogether. Typically of paranormal stories, the proof is perplexingly vague.

Can a seven-year-old boy living in Swansea, South Wales, really be the reincarnation of one of British history's most tragic figures? His mother thinks so. For years she has listened to young Scott Knill's burblings about a time in history about which he could otherwise know nothing.

PAST LIVES

GREAT SCOTT

'I never dressed myself. I had maids and wore a long dress with puffy sleeves. I had pearls all over it and around my neck,' he revealed to his family. 'The corset hurt as they had laced it up so tight. My dress was stiff and my petticoats itchy.'

Curious talk for a lad of an age to show more interest in bicycles and computers than the costumes of middle history.

'I believe him,' admitted Helen Knill. 'It's been going on so long there can be no other explanation. I saw a picture of the young Mary and it was just like Scott.'

How can it ever be satisfactorily proved? It is usually children who recall past existence, the theory being that psychological immaturity presents fewer barriers to the subconscious.

REINCARNATION

One of the earliest cases of spontaneous past-life recall occurred in Japan in 1824, when nine-year-old Katsugoro told his sister that he was the son of a farmer in another village in a previous incarnation. In fact his past life ended in 1810 with smallpox, just five years before the present one had commenced.

He even remembered the period between death and rebirth. The description he gave of his former village and family was sufficiently detailed to convince investigators of the day.

There are four ways in which memories of a past life manifest themselves in children: the most usual is through idle chat. A child might mention an unknown location or unfamiliar name and insist on its validity. The next benchmark is when children recognise places or people that they have not previously known. They may display personality traits or even skills which were also evident in their past selves. Finally, they might have birthmarks or other physical traits in common.

Sceptics believe telepathy, inherited memory or forgotten memories are to blame.

Still, the case of Shanti Deva gives food for thought. In 1935 she told her parents that she had once lived in a place called Muttra. Her name was Ludgi, a mother of three who died in childbirth. Her family were reluctant to believe her – until they discovered there was indeed a place called Muttra where a woman, Ludgi, had died in labour. On visiting Muttra for the first time, Shanti lapsed into the local dialect and recognised her (former) husband and two older children.

PAST LIVES RECALLED

In adults, a trauma, such as a head injury, has been known to start past-life memories. However, hypnosis is the prime catalyst and the process is called regression. The most famous hypnotically induced past-life experience is that of a Colorado housewife who revealed details of her existence as Bridey Murphy in 19th century Ireland.

Hypnotist Morey Bernstein was convinced it was a clear case of reincarnation. Unfortunately, he failed to check the facts before publishing a book on the subject. It was quickly established that there was not only no Bridey Murphy born on 20 December 1798 as the woman had claimed, but also no record of her death. Her Irish accent was convincing enough as was her grasp of old-Irish slang, but she failed to pronounce the name Sean correctly. There were other gaps too – along with some truths, including the name of her local grocery store, a description of the Antrim coastline and an account of a trip from Belfast to Cork.

When investigators discovered the housewife was the daughter of two part-Irish parents and had lived with them until the age of three when

In 1824 a Japanese boy, Kastugoro, recounted the five-year period between death and rebirth. His description of the village where he had lived and the family he once belonged to was sufficiently detailed to convince investigators of the day.

she was adopted by an uncle, they believed buried memories were behind her amazing tales.

SCIENTIFIC EXAMINATION

Psychologist Helen Wambach was persuaded in the late 1960s that there was a case for reincarnation after a ten-year survey of past-life recalls on 1,088 subjects under hypnosis. With the exception of only 11 people, the descriptions given of the minutiae of past lives, including kitchen utensils, footwear and clothing, were accurate. She found that most of the lives described were lower class, accurately mirroring the population trends. Unnervingly, she found that 49.4 per cent of past lives were female and 50.6 per cent were male, which reflects the biological balance.

It is difficult to check facts, however, and few accounts of past lives bear scientific scrutiny.

SYLVESTER STALLONE BELIEVES HE HAS LIVED FOUR TIMES, ONCE AS A NOBLEMAN GUILLOTINED IN THE FRENCH REVOLUTION.

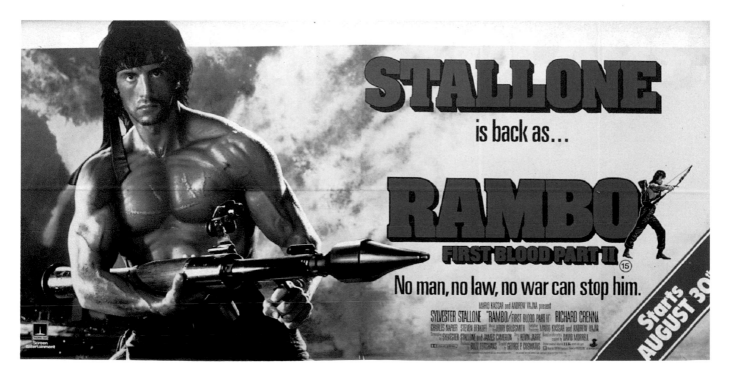

OUT-OF-BODY EXPERIENCES

Two-year-old Inigo Swann lay anaesthetised on a table in a hospital room about to undergo a tonsillectomy. None of the attending medical staff noticed anything unusual about Swann. From his perspective, however, something was radically awry.

ASTRAL PROJECTION

In the operating theatre, Swann found himself floating about 1 m (3 ft) above his own body. He watched as the surgeon's scalpel pierced his skin. He saw a nurse collect his tonsils in a glass jar and hide them beneath a pile of tissues on a table.

When he came round the child demanded to see the tonsils. The nurse insisted they had been thrown away, but he pointed to the exact spot that they were hidden; neither he nor the assembled adults could explain why. Swann had known an out-of-body experience (OBE), also called astral projection and exteriorisation. Some people consider it to be the stuff of dreams, or the result of too much prescribed drug-taking. Swann went on

to become a noted psychic and wrote about the incredible journey he took as a young child. Yet psychic ability is not a prerequisite for undergoing OBEs and they are not considered to be in the realms of the paranormal.

About 20 per cent of the population experience this phenomenon, usually when young. The subject is so mainstream that Oxford University awarded its first doctorate for work on OBEs in 1993 to Charles McCreery, a research officer at the Institute of Psychophysical Research.

McCreery researched two groups of people, 200 of whom had never had an OBE and 406 who had. He quizzed them to establish levels of hypomania – the ability to experience heightened excitement – to discover that the OBE group scored significantly higher.

Dr McCreery was able to describe those most likely to have OBEs: 'The people who did not score highly tended to be placid and not to have OBEs. The ones at the top had the big mood swings. They were the worriers, the creators, the ones most likely to suffer bouts of depression.'

When people age, their nervous systems stabilise, which is why OBEs occur mostly in young, passionate people.

ASTRAL TRAVELLERS

Some find the experience terrifying. Melvyn Bragg suffered from OBEs as a teenager, although it was some 30 years before he discussed them publicly, in his novel *The Maid of Buttermere*.

'It happens to me usually when I am alone and may be associated with fear of solitude or with that greatest fear of all . . . death.' Something unknown escaped his body and 'hovers above it looking back on this vacated thing of flesh, bone, blood, breath, water, matter.'

The main fear is that the unknown part which flees the body may never be reunited presumably resulting in death. It's a comfort to some to believe both bits are linked by a silver cord, although reports of the cord are not uniform in all OBEs.

Some OBEs are not so frightening. Melanie Benton, 34, said of her unexpected OBE: 'One moment I was hurrying along, the next I was high in the air gazing down on myself and people below. As I stopped at the kerb and looked both ways before crossing the road, I noticed that the parting in my hair was not even at the top of my head, giving the appearance of a tiny bald spot. This created a shock of indignation and within a flash I found myself walking along again, inside myself this time.'

THREE STAGES OF ASTRAL PROJECTION FROM 1929. FIRST THE ASTRAL BODY LEAVES THE PHYSICAL BODY, IT SLOWLY ASCENDS THEN BECOMES UPRIGHT BEFORE BEGINNING ITS JOURNEY.

ASTRAL JOURNEYS

Some OBE travellers claim to move at the speed of thought and pass through walls and doors like ghosts. Sometimes they are seen and recognised by people, sometimes they are invisible to others. One theory, proposed by OBE veteran Robert A. Monroe, is that these journeys leave the earth's plane and enter the infinite and strange astral plane or may even travel to a parallel universe.

Those with a special interest in OBEs may induce them through meditation and there are enabling exercises to practise.

A bible for the astral traveller is *The Projection of the Astral Body* published in 1929 by Sylvan Muldoon and Hereward Carrington. Muldoon began spontaneous OBEs at the age of 12 and they only diminished when his general health improved. He thought that dreams of flying and falling were somehow linked to astral travel.

OBEs are not the same as Near Death Experiences (NDEs). It's believed that the sensations reported by those who pull back from the brink of death are caused entirely by chemical changes in the brain. The cause of OBEs remains a mystery. To the doubters it is clearly 'all in the mind', as one expert puts it, 'the ego's denial of the inevitable death of the physical body'.

Dr McCreery wants to take the trauma out of OBEs. His advice to the reluctant astral traveller is to stay calm and seek an immediate distraction.

'Try not to worry, if possible adopt the attitude of a detached observer. Persuade yourself this is a neutral and interesting experience.'

'They turned round and faced the enemy, expecting nothing but instant death, when, to their wonder they saw, between them and the enemy, a whole troop of angels. The German horses turned round terrified and regularly stampeded.'

ANGELS

VISION AT MONS

Weary British soldiers, beaten back from the Belgian border at the start of First World War, had no place to hide. With the Kaiser's army closing in on them, the British Expeditionary Force found themselves in a boggy field at Mons, where they looked doomed to make their last stand.

The Tommys were not short on valour, but the German troops were fresh and superior in number and it seemed nothing would stop them. Preparing to face their doom, some soldiers seized the moment to utter a heartfelt prayer. Suddenly, a heavenly host surged down from the sky in the narrowing gap between the two forces.

British troops stared in awe as the Germans were thrown into disarray, their horses rearing and shying. Soon the retreating forces gathered their senses once more and capitalised on this heaven-sent opportunity to regroup and escape.

DIVINE INTERVENTION

To students of the paranormal, it's a familiar legend. for years it was dismissed as a heartwarming hoax. The story of the vision at Mons was the subject of a short story written by Arthur Machen, published in the *London Evening Standard* on 29 September 1914. It was this rather than bona fide accounts from the front line which was peddled as 'right is on our side' propganda by the British government to a public desperate to believe that such a fantastic story could be true.

Yet investigator Kevin McClure believes the urge to dismiss the story has overridden some vital facts. In his book, *Visions of Bowmen and Angels* he reassesses the evidence and finds sufficient to indicate that something occurred that day which saved the lives of countless British troops.

Communications were, of course, much slower. It was six months after the publication of Machen's tale that *Light*, a paranormal journal of the day, printed a military officer's account:

'It took the form of a strange cloud interposed between the Germans and the British …[and] had

AT HOME THE WAITING FAMILIES OF SOLDIERS WERE DELIGHTED TO HEAR THAT ANGELS INTERVENED ON THE BRITISH SIDE.

featuring St George and the bowmen of Agincourt, followed the model of Machen's fictional story, while the other, describing an indistinct cloud, formed part of veterans' accounts. In the latter there is no mention of angels being armed or harming the Germans, in keeping with the traditional view of angels. 'Neither the events nor their effects bear any resemblance to Machen's work of fiction,' McClure declares.

It is also possible that Machen's tale unwittingly reflected events at Mons in the same way that Morgan Robertson's book, *Futility*, about the liner *Titan* predicted the *Titanic* disaster.

HEAVENLY MESSENGERS

Angel fever swept America in the 1990s and reports of heavenly messengers who saved the day came in thick and fast. The angels in question were not cherubic harp-players but everyday good Samaritans mysteriously vanishing after averting a disaster. Some accounts were remarkable.

Ann Cannady was stricken with cancer when she opened the door of her Miami home to an unexpected caller. On her step was a black man standing about 6 ft 6 inches (2 metres) with piercing blue eyes. His name, he told her, was Thomas and he had been sent by God. He held up his right hand and from it came a burning white light. Before he went he said her cancer had gone. Although the incident lasted only a matter of moments the disease had inexplicably disappeared.

Chantal Lakey was certain that angels in a mist cushioned her plunge from a cliff overlooking the Pacific Ocean in Oregon. The fall had killed her boyfriend and her perch on the cliff face was so remote she had to be rescued by helicopter.

A voice behind Shari Peterson told her to fasten her seat belt during a 747 flight from Denver, Colorado, to New Zealand. Amazingly, when she looked around there was no one there. But within a minute a short circuit opened the cargo door and the decompression sucked out the passengers sitting around her. She would have died if she hadn't obeyed the disembodied voice.

the effect of protecting the British against the overwhelming hordes of the enemy.'

CHINESE WHISPERS

A parish magazine published details heard from the daughter of a canon describing one man's experiences: 'They turned round and faced the enemy, expecting nothing but instant death, when, to their wonder they saw, between them and the enemy, a whole troop of angels.

'The German horses turned round terrified and regularly stampeded.'

The Roman Catholic newspaper, the *Universe*, told of an officer at Mons who saw a line of bowmen protecting the British. Later a German prisoner asked him the identity of the officer on a great white horse who led the charge. The officer deduced that this must have been St George.

As the influence of what had gone before seeped deep into the national psyche it was difficult to determine which were genuine. An investigation by the Society for Psychical Research at the time located few credible witnesses.

McClure points out that there were two accounts circulating about the incident. One,

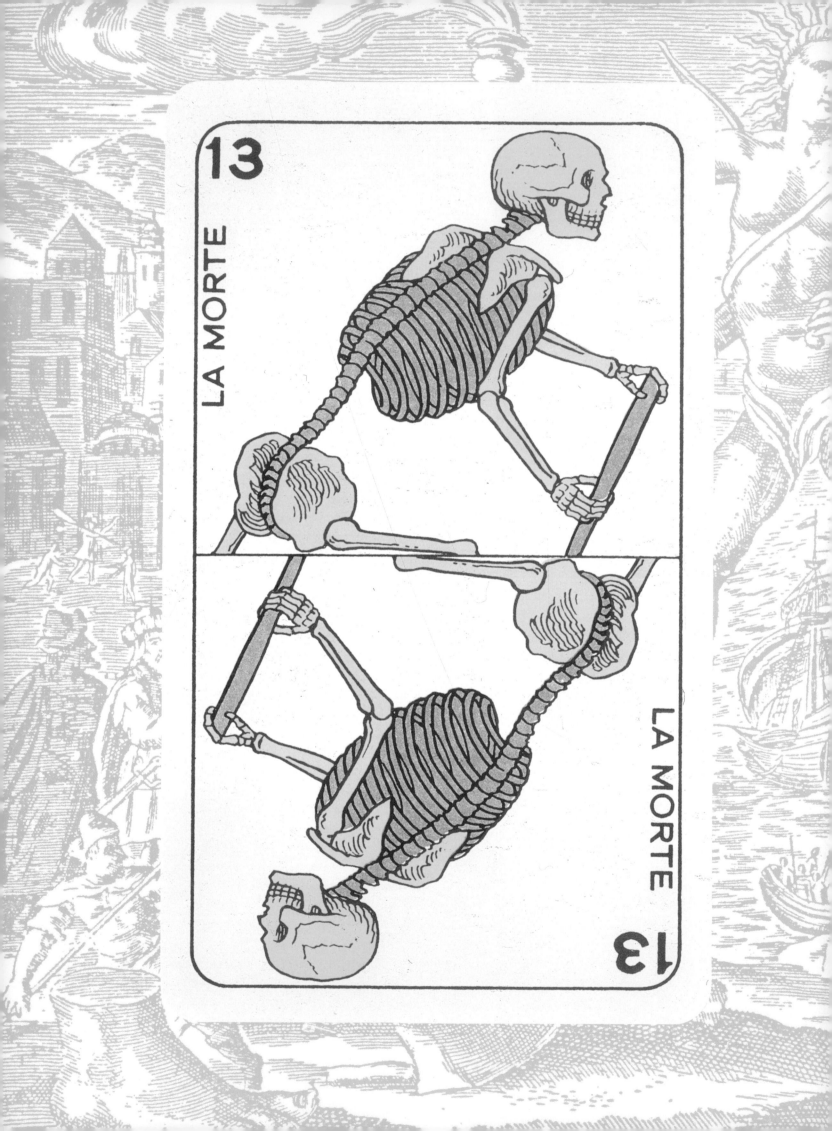

DIVINATIONS

It is impossible for man to know his future – with that knowledge comes infinite wisdom, but the allure has dominated mankind throughout history.
Early attempts at augury were grisly affairs. An animal, or even a human, was killed and the entrails torn out. The death throes, coupled with subtle marks on the liver, heart and other organs, and the spread of the intestines, gave pointers to the future. Today the choices are more palatable, ranging from horoscopes, runes or tea leaves and incorporating an awesome variety in between.

CHAPTER EIGHT

Few can resist looking at the tabloid horoscopes, although it is ridiculous to suggest that a twelfth of the population will be cutting an important business deal, while a similarly sized chunk are expecting a nice surprise – horoscopes of this kind are several planets short of a constellation and have devalued a complex and fascinating art.

ASTROLOGY

THE CIRCUS OF ANIMALS

Everyone knows the zodiac sign under which they were born. It is only one layer of information which an astrologer takes into account. The position of the sun, moon and planets is important, as is the interaction of opposing celestial forces; in short, horoscopes are just a guide.

Astrology is probably as old as mankind. The Babylonians are credited with formalising the zodiac in about 3000 B.C., although the term, meaning 'circus of animals', was not adopted until the time of the Greeks. The most potent criticism of astrology is that the heavens have shifted since those days but the zodiac has not.

DEMONIC PRACTICE OR LEGITIMATE ART?

Yet astrology influenced all the ancient civilisations. By A.D. 200, the most important book in the history of Western astrology had been written by Ptolemy, mathematician, astronomer and geographer, who lived in Alexandria, Egypt. His words are still influential today; but within 150 years, astrology was condemned by the Church as a 'demonic' practice and it wasn't until the Middle Ages that the art regained its credibility.

It took another knock in the 16th century when the findings of Copernicus, Galileo and, later, Newton, were adopted as physical law. Until then the planets were thought to be revolving around earth, but when it was firmly established that the earth was actually spinning around the sun, the old beliefs were questioned.

Still astrology survived and its popularity today is as great as it has ever been. Disregarding the horoscopes of the popular press, consider the work of the astrologer compiling your birth chart, officially called natal astrology.

ABOVE: THE STUDY OF THE STARS FOR HOROSCOPES IS SO PRECISE THAT SOME OBSERVERS CAN SEE THE OUTLINE OF THE THREE MAGI IN THE CONSTELLATIONS.

'The stars above us govern our condition.' *Shakespeare*

ZODIAC SIGNS

The zodiac, which is the sky split into 12 equal 30-degree divisions, contains the 12 familiar signs of Aquarius, Pisces, Aries, Taurus, Gemini, Cancer, Leo, Virgo, Libra, Scorpio, Sagittarius and Capricorn. Your birthdate puts you firmly into one of these 'sun' signs. But the astrologer needs to know the exact time and place of your birth to find out the precise position of the planets. He or she will calculate the sidereal time, that is the true time, as the 24-hour clock takes about four minutes longer than the time it takes for the earth to revolve once.

There is the ascending planet to consider, the one peeping over the eastern horizon at the moment of birth, and the mid-heaven sign overhead. That's before looking at the positions of the sun, moon and other planets and their significance. In addition there's a second 12-section dimension, the 'houses', to be applied. Clearly, the astrologers who do their work properly draw up a highly individual, if not unique, chart. Jung paraphrased their philosophy when he wrote, 'Whatever is born, or done, in this moment of time, has the qualities of this moment in time.'

THE SCIENTIFIC FRATERNITY

Science has no query with the nuts and bolts of astrology – it's difficult to fault something so exact. However, the interpretation laid against the position of stars pushes the credulity of scientists to its limits.

Yet research has come up with some surprising results. Those with similar planetary positions at birth appear to favour particular professions. For example, scientists are likely to be born with Saturn in ascendancy while soldiers and athletes have Mars in that same influential spot. And astrologers given limited personal details 'blind' have been able to match the identities of the people involved, scoring better than 100:1 against chance. One Czechoslovakian astrologer, Eugen Jonas, used the stars to predict the sex of babies and achieved a 98 per cent accuracy rate. He also advised on the right times for intercourse to conceive the chosen sex.

FAMOUS CONVERTS

Comic Peter Sellers was a convert to astrology. 'The simple rules of astrology definitely work out in real life,' he claimed. Pop giants the Beatles sought the advice of an astrologer when they set up the Apple recording company. Hitler was convinced in the veracity of astrology and employed star-gazers during his war campaign. This, of course, does little to enhance the reputation of astrology, but there's nevertheless a sound argument to prove the words of Shakespeare, 'the stars above us govern our condition'.

Lyall Watson, author of *Supernature*, concludes: 'There are some mystical things about astrology, but there is nothing supernatural about the way it works. Man is affected by his environment according to clearly defined physical forces and his life, like all others, becomes organised by natural and universal laws. To believe otherwise is tantamount to assuming that the *Encyclopaedia Britannica* was thrown together by an explosion in a printing works.'

By 1661 THE THEORIES OF COPERNICUS, THAT THE PLANETS REVOLVED AROUND THE SUN, HAD GAINED CREDENCE ALTHOUGH NOT ALL THE SIGNIFICANT STARS WERE AT THAT TIME RECOGNISED.

Can the future really be told at the turn of a card? Tarot practitioners believe that it can, and insist that each person is drawn to various cards in different combinations, giving a cosmically significant result.

TAROT

EARLY TAROT

The origins of the Tarot are obscure. Probably the close relation of playing cards, which were in circulation by the 14th century, the Tarot is far more evocative and exotic.

Today the earliest example of cards which may have been Tarot are in the Bibliothèque Nationale of Paris and are thought to be the work of painter Jacquemin Gringonneur who made them to amuse the unstable French king, Charles the Well-Beloved. Tarot cards were certainly made in the early 15th century for the Visconti and Visconti-Sforza families of Milan.

There are many Romantic stories that surround the Tarot's inception. In the 16th century, French Egyptologist Antoine Court de Gebelin declared that Tarot cards were key pieces of Egyptian wisdom drawn from the mystical and mythical *Book of Thoth*.

Later, fellow Frenchman Eliphas Levi stated that the Tarot symbols were representative of the Cabalah, the Hebrew occult belief. While there are some likenesses, the truth of his statement seems doubtful. Other theories have it that Tarot was created in the East, perhaps China or India, and travelled west with Romanies.

TAROT ICONS

In the past Tarot cards were used by way of entertainment, as a game. Nowadays, they are exclusively for divination.

The composition of the Tarot pack varies, but in general it can be divided into two parts: there is the 'Greater Arcana', or major trumps, numbering 22 cards, and the 'Lesser Arcana', or minor trumps, a further 56 cards.

The major trumps are symbols which have a correct running order. With some variances, they are The Fool, The Juggler, The Female Pope, The Empress, The Emperor, The Pope, The Lovers, The Chariot, Justice, The Hermit, The Wheel of Fortune, Strength, The Hanged Man, Death, Temperance, The Devil, The Falling Tower,

CUTTING AND DEALING THE DECK OF CARDS WAS SEEN AS A VITAL PROCEDURE IN READING THE TAROT.

The unstable French King, Charles the Well-Beloved was amused by the Tarot cards of the painter Jacquemin Gringonneur.

The Star, The Moon, The Sun, The Day of Judgement and The World.

From the card titles it is easy to see a medieval influence. Each has a different meaning, although the exact relevance is dependent on the order and placing of the card in a spread during a reading.

It is this first section of the pack which is so strongly suggestive of the Cabalah, in which 22 is a particularly significant number. There are 22 letters in the Hebrew alphabet and 22 paths on the Tree of Life, so the number represents the universe in its entirety.

DEALING THE TAROT

The minor trumps reflect the four suits of regular playing cards: Cups (Hearts); Swords (Spades); Wands (Clubs); and Pentacles (Diamonds). In Tarot packs there is, however, an additional card: between the Jack and Queen comes a Knight.

Once again the placing of each card is key, for example, while the King of Swords indicates a powerful man, that same card placed upside-down means treachery and betrayal.

A spread dominated by Cups is said to indicate happiness, a majority of Wands indicates change, if there are mainly Pentacles then the future holds wealth, while Swords are thought to bring bad luck.

There are a number of different ways to deal the Tarot – some choose to have five piles of seven mirroring the pattern of the cabbalistic tree of life, the rest being left in a pile for later reference; or a reader will turn up the first ten cards if they are seeking specific advice.

INTERPRETING THE CARDS

The Tarot is not meant to provide a definitive answer, rather the cards reflect the energies relevant at the time and the direction they may take. To successfully read Tarot cards takes time, patience and intuition.

JUDGEMENT AND THE WORLD – TWO CARDS TAKEN FROM THE TAROT PACK DESIGNED IN 1910 BY PAMELA COLMAN SMITH AND ARTHUR EDWARD WAITE. HOWEVER, REGULAR PLAYING CARDS CAN ALSO BE USED FOR PREDICTION.

Amateurs may well choose to read ordinary playing cards instead of the Tarot. If a genuine psychic ability exists, then it is likely to reveal itself in all manner of card decks. Once again, every card in each of the four suits holds a different meaning, depending on the combination in which it appears.

Generally speaking, the Ace of Diamonds next to the Ace of Spades means a railway journey; two black Aces together implies unexpected news; the Ace of Diamonds next to the 10 of Hearts indicates a betrothal, while the Queen of Spades next to the 10 of Spades tells the subject to beware of fire.

Once again there are various patterns in which the cards should be laid. However, each reading should begin with the sitter shuffling the deck and then cutting the cards with the left hand, towards the left. All the while the sitter should concentrate on his hopes, dreams and problems. This concentration will reveal itself in the cards which will be dealt and interpreted by the reader.

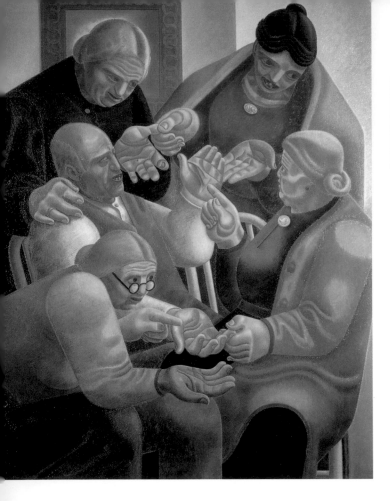

A large hand (relative to the size of the body) usually belongs to someone skilled at detailed work, while a small hand may belong to someone more intuitively led.

PALMISTRY

It comes as no surprise to know that the finger and palm prints of every one of us are different. Hand prints are often left at the scene of a crime, as every good policeman knows. And they are so specific that the identifying lines and contours can be matched exactly to just one person.

The awakening of modern forensic science to this fact came as joyful justification to palmists, who had for years asserted the individuality of each hand. Their contention is that the lumps, bumps and lines on each hand vary wildly, not to mention the length and shape of fingers. A competent interpretation of all this material, they claim, will give an accurate character reading and could even reveal predictions for the future.

THE BEGINNINGS OF CHIROMANCY

Palm reading, also known as chiromancy, chirology or chirosophy, has a very colourful history stretching back 3,000 years. From its inception, in China or India, the skill travelled westwards and was particularly popular in the Middle Ages.

Supporters of palmistry quoted the Bible to further enhance its reputation. 'He sealeth up the hand of every man; that all men may know his work.' (Job 27:7) 'Length of days in her right hand, and in her left hand riches and honour.' (Proverbs 3:16)

However, the Church frowned upon it. Still, it was a palmist, Marie-Anne Le Normand, who told Napoleon he would marry a beautiful woman, father two sons and earn 'sufficient glory to make him the most illustrious of all Frenchmen'.

Eventually the art waned and became mere entertainment, although it retained public esteem in Eastern countries. Only in the 20th century has it regained credibility.

That each hand is one of a kind is a fact. Whether a reader can accurately determine its contents on sight is a matter for debate.

Most schoolchildren are aware of the lines of the hand and their potential significance, but there's much more to reading palms than the etched lines on the hand.

PALM READING

Amateur psychologists say that people who 'talk with their hands' are usually of a certain type. Bitten nails and crunching knuckles implies nervousness, while people pointing fingers are aggressive. Those twisting their rings show a confusion of ideas and holding your thumbs inwards, next to the palm, means you are being secretive.

The hand used for writing is read for current personality and prediction. The other shows the past and predispositions.

When the palm is presented for perusal, further simple deductions can be made about the person on the end of it. An open hand with splayed fingers reveals a love of life, closed fingers indicate distrust while fingers set unevenly into the palm indicate an unpredictable life.

A large hand (relative to the size of the body) usually belongs to someone skilled at detailed work, while a small hand may belong to someone more intuitively led. Likewise the shape of the fingers and nails is telltale. There are four primary finger shapes: square (practical, conventional), pointed (sensitive), round (sympathetic, inconsistent) and spatulate (energetic, adventurous). Each finger has a planetary name, the index finger being Jupiter, the middle finger Saturn, the third or ring finger is known as the Sun while the little finger belongs to Mercury. Thumb size, shape and flexibility are equally crucial. A palmist will also take into account the smoothness of the hand and its sweatiness.

Already, it is clear to see the palmist has plenty of clues before surveying the landscape of the hand and deciphering its lines.

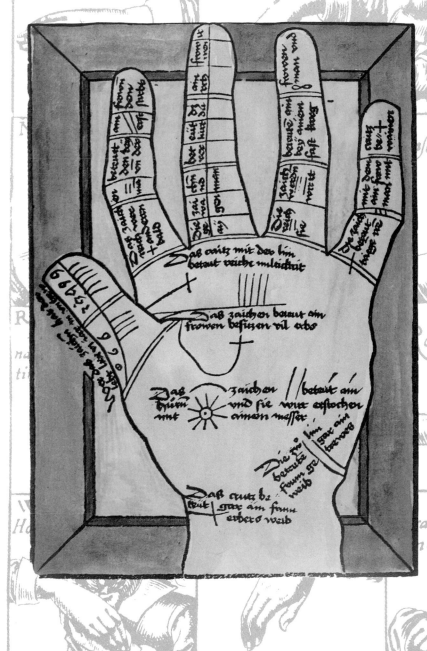

HEAVENLY HANDS

Once again, the lumps on the hand have celestial names. The Mount of Venus is the pad below the thumb; a raised Mount of Venus denotes a capacity for love and affection. Conversely a flat Mount does not point to an unloving soul, but to someone driven by the mental and spiritual instead of the physical. The opposite 'cheek' is called the Mount of the Moon which is linked to travel, imagination and emotions of the heart. There are three Mounts of Mars across the centre of the palm, beneath pads which correspond to the fingers and share their names.

The lines on the palm include the four principles of head, heart, life and fate in addition to the sun, Mercury, marriage and widowhood lines, the wrist wrinkles and the rings of the family.

Carl Jung was one of those who was swayed by the validity of palmistry. He wrote: 'The global concept of modern biology, based on data from an amount of observations and research, in no way rules out the possibility that hands – whose form and function are so closely allied to the psyche – prove clear and therefore easily interpretable evidence of psychic characteristics, which is to say the human character.'

EVEN IN 1475, WHEN THE EARLIEST BOOK ON THE SUBJECT APPEARED, PALMISTRY WAS IMMENSELY DETAILED AND A DEMANDING ART.

A shiny mirror, a still lake, a witch's cauldron, a polished thumbnail – even a bowlful of blood – down the centuries all have been used in the ancient art of scrying, a solution to the whereabouts of lost objects, the identity of villains and events of the future.

Scrying is taken from the old English word 'descry' – to discern or dimly make out. The reflecting object used by the scryer is called a speculum.

SCRYING

CRYSTALLOMANCY

This practice has existed for centuries, initially by using water as a viewing point. The magic of ancient Persia made use of the early glass mirrors, and this established the art of crystallomancy, or catoptromancy as it is sometimes called. Since then bizarre objects, such as a sheep's shoulder blade, have been used, as well as the embers of a fire or the blade of a sword.

Of course, scryers do not literally see into the future just by peering into a glassy object. Their speculum is merely the trigger to the necessary clairvoyance. Relaxed and dreamy, the scryer will watch the speculum cloud over and, out of the murky depths, emerge shapes and colours. Only with psychic skill and practice will sharply focused images appear.

The 14th century Islamic writer Abd al-Rahman ibn Muhammad ibn Khaldun described the process of scrying: 'The diviner looks fixedly at the surface until it disappears and a fog-like curtain interposes itself between his eyes and the mirror. On this curtain the shapes that he desires to see form themselves.'

It is for the scryer to interpret the outlines which become apparent. In some countries, it is traditional for fortune-tellers to use young virgins to study the speculum, relaying what they see to an older, wiser fortune-teller. That's because the young are reputedly better endowed with spiritual powers, while the old have the wisdom of interpretation.

PROFITEERS SAW THE PUBLIC'S DESIRE FOR PREDICTION AS A QUICK ROOT TO RICHES.

ECCLESIASTIC DISAPPROVAL

Like many other methods of divination, scrying was outlawed by the Church, although its attraction remained very potent. In the 5th century, Bishop Sophronius drew the Church's anger when he took to scrying in an attempt to discover the name of a thief.

In 1467, William Byg was accused of heresy on account of his devotion to scrying. His punishment was surprisingly lenient – he was compelled to walk around the Cathedral Church of York with a lighted torch in one hand and his books in the other, wearing a placard which branded him a soothsayer and invoker of spirits. At the end of his procession he had to burn the books.

Still the practice flourished throughout the centuries, perhaps reaching its zenith when Nostradamus used a bowl of water set on a brass tripod to summon up his amazing prophecies. As the poor relation of other forms of divination, scrying sank into becoming a sideshow spectacle in the 19th century.

JOHN MELVILLE

Following a revival of interest, a handbook for scryers was published in 1920 by John Melville which gave helpful hints to the aspiring amateur.

In *Crystal Gazing and the Wonders of Clairvoyance* he wrote, 'The crystal should be about 4 cm (1.5 in) in diameter or at least the size of a small orange. It should be enclosed in a frame of ivory, ebony or boxwood, highly polished, or stood upon a glass or crystal pedestal.'

Melville gave the details of the mystic names which should be engraved on the north, south-east and west sides of the frame in raised gold letters. He gave these as Tetragrammaton, Agla, Emmanuel and Adonay. The pedestal should bear the name Saday, while candlesticks suggested for the ritual of scrying should be inscribed with the names Elohim and Elohe.

'No crystal or mirror should be handled by other than the owner, because such handling mixes the magnetism and tends to destroy their sensitiveness,' he warns.

'Others may look into them but should not touch them . . . If the surface becomes dirty or soiled, it may be cleaned with fine soapsuds, rinsed well, washed with alcohol or vinegar and water, and then polished with soft velvet or a chamois leather …

'The magnetism with which the surface of the mirror of crystal becomes charged collects (from the face of the crystal) and from the universal ether, the brain being as it were switched on to the universe, the crystal being the medium.'

THE READER CONCENTRATES ON HIS CRYSTAL BALL SO HE CAN SEE THE FUTURE IN HIS MIND'S EYE.

BALL WATCHING

The 17th century antiquary, John Aubrey, pondered on the power of suggestion and its possible links to scrying after the following incident. 'When Sir Marmaduke Langdale was in Italy, he went to one of those magi, who did shew him a glass, where he saw himself kneeling before a crucifix; he was then a Protestant; afterwards he became a Roman Catholick.'

Many people say that the success of scrying is due to thought-transference or mind-reading. Gazing at a crystal ball has also been interpreted as a form of automatism, with the subconscious mind transferring messages to the conscious self.

NUMEROLOGY

Numerology appears a lightweight and frothy aspect of divination, little more than a parlour game and strictly for amateurs. Critics have good cause to be sceptical of its powers as there are plenty of grey areas.

NUMEROLOGISTS

Briefly, numerologists work on the premise that each letter of the alphabet coincides with a number. The sum of the numbers comprising each name are added together to reach a number between one and nine. This figure corresponds to a personality type.

The first dilemma facing the numerologists is which number grid to use. Most commonly employed is that relevant to the Western alphabet, as follows:

```
1 2 3 4 5 6 7 8 9
A B C D E F G H I
J K L M N O P Q R
S T U V W X Y Z
```

However, there is an alternative based on the Hebrew alphabet which has only 22 letters, all of which have a numerical equivalent.

```
1 2 3 4 5 6 7 8
A B C D E U O F
I K G M H V Z P
Q R L T N W
J S X
Y
```

The first contradiction becomes apparent. If we use Sam as an example, he would be personality type 6 by the first grid (1 + 1 + 4) but personality type 8 (3 + 1 + 4) in the second. Already it seems numerology is fatally flawed.

Then comes the choice of name. Most of us have a first, middle and surname. Sometimes the first name is shortened. Occasionally the middle name is dropped. After marriage, a woman's surname might change completely. It is likely that each choice available would offer a different score. So which name should we choose for the purposes of numerology?

Experts say it is the one you are known by. Nicholas Charles Smith would add up the numbers in Nick Smith only, while Susan Catherine Dixon would have the sum of numbers in Sue Dixon only. Of course, if you disliked the analysis provided by one sum of letters then you could simply throw in an initial or two to come up with a completely different picture.

The naming of children by parents appears to be random. Can the personality of a child really be influenced by its name when it is named after its father, a popular film star or long-dead pet?

ABOVE: A SCENE FROM DANTE'S INFERNO. NUMBERS PLAY A VITAL PART IN THE TALE WITH TWENTY-FOUR CIRCLES OF HELL, TWO TERRACES AND SEVEN CORNICES OF MOUNT PURGATORY.

YOUR NUMBER'S UP

To occultists there is no such thing as chance and the chosen name is relevant to that child alone.

Other important numbers are the sum of vowels which reveal the heart number or inner self. Likewise the sum of consonants comprises the personality number or outer self. The birth number, a total of the day, month and full year of birth added together to establish a single digit, give you an abiding number which will have a life-long significance. Hopefully, all numbers will harmonise to provide a broad picture. Conflicting numbers indicate trouble spots. An outline of the qualities associated with numbers is as follows:

One: Powerful, dominating, self-sufficient, well-organised, quick-tempered

Two: Docile, intuitive, gentle, diplomatic, conciliatory

Three: Energetic, proud, versatile, attractive, creative

Four: Solid, uninspired, capable, industrious, traditional

Five: Nervy, risk-taker, resourceful, erratic, adventurous

Six: Well-balanced, domesticated, loyal, hard-working, gossipy

Seven: Reserved, scholarly, mystical, superior, reflective

Eight: Materialistic, tough, persistent, cautious, eccentric

Nine: Visionary, romantic, impulsive, unorthodox, humanitarian

If, at first glance, numerology seems a bit of a slapdash method of divination, consider its deeper meaning.

PYTHAGORAS

The man behind numerology was Pythagoras, the Greek philosopher born 600 B.C. He moved to Crotone in Italy to found a religious group which included in its doctrines silent contemplation and vegetarianism.

He discovered that musical intervals could all be expressed in the numbers 1 to 4. Those numbers added together came to 10. Pythagoras went on to express the universe in terms of numbers and number patterns. His reasoning has been satisfyingly sound and difficult to undermine.

PYTHAGORAS AND METAPHYSICS

Pythagoras was not alone in believing that numbers were fundamental to life. The Jewish belief describes numbers and letters as the building blocks which God used to create the universe. The incidence in the numbers from 1 to 10 appearing in varied interpretations of life is immense, claim Pythagorean students, who believe in both maths and metaphysics. They point to there being one God; two opposites; three parts of the Holy Trinity; four ingredients to life (fire, water, earth and air), as well as four seasons; five senses; six points on a pentagram, the symbol of natural balance; seven musical notes, days in a week and wonders of the world; eight paths of Buddhism and, on its side, the mathematical symbol of infinity; nine is the time of human gestation in months and the sum of any multiplication of nine can be added together to make nine once more (for example, $3 \times 9 = 27$; $2 + 7 = 9$).

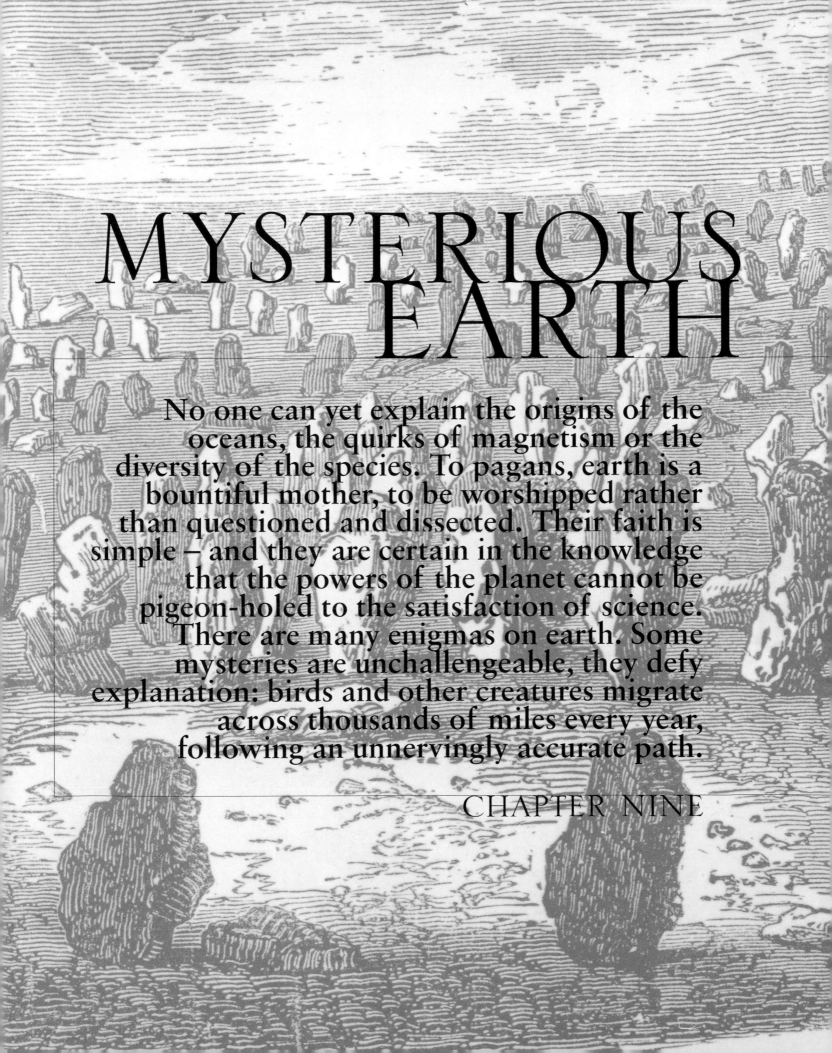

MYSTERIOUS EARTH

No one can yet explain the origins of the oceans, the quirks of magnetism or the diversity of the species. To pagans, earth is a bountiful mother, to be worshipped rather than questioned and dissected. Their faith is simple – and they are certain in the knowledge that the powers of the planet cannot be pigeon-holed to the satisfaction of science. There are many enigmas on earth. Some mysteries are unchallengeable, they defy explanation: birds and other creatures migrate across thousands of miles every year, following an unnervingly accurate path.

CHAPTER NINE

There are eccentric Englishmen who prowl around fields under cover of darkness creating elaborate patterns in the sprouting corn. Using garden rollers, planks of wood, pivots, mats and bare feet and hands, they manufacture circles and swirls which transform an ordinary corn field into a work of art. Just why they do so is difficult to fathom.

CROP CIRCLES

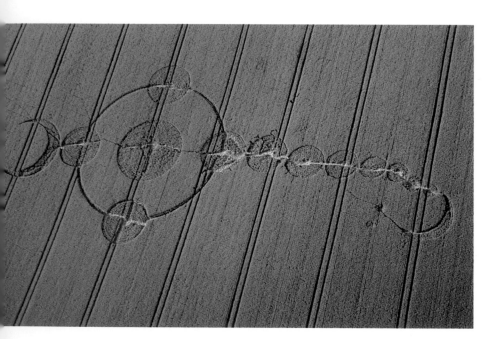

COMPLEX WORKS, LIKE THIS IN A FIELD SOUTH OF AVEBURY, WILTSHIRE, IN 1994, ARE BREATH-TAKING BUT THEIR SIGNIFICANCE IS UNKNOWN.

At first the cause of the arable artwork, which appeared at the end of the 1970s, was a mystery. Some of the explanations offered at the time included mating animals, hedgehogs driven by dementia and aliens' attempts to communicate with earth. World-wide attention was focused on the fields of a clutch of counties which became peppered with circles.

CROP-CIRCLE INVESTIGATORS

In 1988, consultant meteorologist Dr. Terence Meaden, of the Tornado and Storm Research Organisation, announced that wind energy was a key factor. Crop circles appeared on one side of hills which buffeted gusts in whirlwinds that in turn flattened the corn.

Another investigator, Colin Andrews, confidently declared that Unidentified Flying Objects, hoaxers, whirlwinds and helicopters had all been ruled out by his team. The blame, he said, lay with the hole in the ozone layer which was wreaking atmospheric havoc.

Andrews, a local authority electrical expert, said: 'We now believe that the shifts in the earth's electromagnetic conditions caused by the ozone hole may be responsible.

'One of the circles that appeared recently in Hampshire amazed us even more than the others because the flattened crops grew back in a dartboard formation. There were seven concentric rings of crops, with a series of perfect spokes going out from the centre.'

He was even convinced that the molecular structure of the affected corn was changing, persuading him that 'some form of higher intelligence' was behind the circles.

Apparently not. In the early 1990s there were claims by pranksters that they were responsible for the numerous crop circles which had appeared in many of England's southern counties. More than 1,000 circles, between 10 ft (3 m) and more than 200 ft (60 m) in diameter, had been discovered in the 1980s.

FOOLING THE CEREALOGISTS

Chief hoaxers were Doug Bower and Dave Chorley. Artists, UFO enthusiasts and inveterate jokers, they teamed up and began creating crop circles in the mid-1970s. To achieve the patterns they used a 'stalk-stomper', a wooden step on a piece of rope which they could hold in each hand, placing the wood under one foot. However, as their works of art became more sophisticated, so did their equipment, which extended to sighting devices and side-bars. To their intense satisfaction, many of the circles they had made were described by experts – otherwise known as cerealogists – as genuine phenomena.

A CHARMING PATTERN FROM THE MARLBOROUGH DOWNS WHICH CAN ONLY BE PROPERLY APPRECIATED FROM THE AIR.

The fact that circles had been cropping up sporadically in England for the past 300 years did not sway the sceptics. Fairies were then blamed for the formations.

In 1686, Robert Plot, Professor of Chemistry at Oxford University, was perplexed by the appearance of such circles. He believed rutting deer or rampant cattle a more likely explanation than 'the little people' – although he did not rule fairies out completely, admitting 'they may indeed occasion such circles'.

WEATHER OR NOT?

Like some of his latter-day counterparts, Professor Plot blamed the weather. 'They must be the effects of lightning exploded from the clouds most times in a circular manner.'

Yet there are still more alternative explanations for the circles which have appeared in America, Australia and Japan. Professor Yoshihiko Ohtsuki from Tokyo's Waseda University said in 1991, 'The circles are caused by an elastic plasma which is a very strong form of ionized air.

'In an experiment…we created a plasma fireball which, if it touched a plate covered in aluminium powder, created beautiful circles and rings, just like the ones seen in fields.'

Given that the fields were covered by corn and not aluminium, it is not clear how fundamental this research will prove to be. Perhaps the last word goes to a couple who claim they were in a field during a crop circle's mysterious creation.

Gary and Vivienne Tomlinson, of Guildford, Surrey, were walking in a Hampshire field when the action happened.

Vivienne said: 'There was a tremendous noise. We looked up to see if it was caused by a helicopter but there was nothing. We felt a strong wind pushing us from the side and above. It was forcing down on our heads – yet incredibly my husband's hair was standing on end. Then the whirling air seemed to branch into two and zigzag off into the distance. We could still see it like a light mist or fog, shimmering as it moved. As it disappeared we were left standing in a corn circle with the corn flattened all around us.'

ICE RINGS

ANOTHER CIRCULAR CURIOSITY WHICH HAS RECENTLY COME TO NOTICE IS THE ICE DISC. ACCORDING TO THE *FORTEAN TIMES*, THE PUBLICATION ESTABLISHED TO PURSUE THE WORK OF UNIVERSE OBSERVER CHARLES FORT, RINGS OF ICE WERE RECORDED AS LONG AGO AS 1900. BUT IT WAS ONLY AT THE END OF 1986 WHEN CLAS SVAHN, A UFO WATCHER FROM SWEDEN, DISCOVERED AN ICE RING 165 FT (50 M) IN DIAMETER THAT SERIOUS STUDY BEGAN. ICE RINGS WERE SUBSEQUENTLY SPOTTED IN RUSSIA AND AMERICA, SOME OF THEM FIXED, SOME REVOLVING. IT'S POSSIBLE, BUT NOT PROBABLE, THAT THEY ARE THE WORK OF HOAXERS. NO ONE HAS YET EXPLAINED HOW THEY WERE CREATED.

Imagine life in Britain circa 4000 B.C. with no cities, towns or villages, fields or hedgerows. There were, of course, no roads.
But there's a theory which says the ancient Briton had well-worn straight routes criss-crossing the countryside by which to travel – leys, derived from the Saxon word meaning 'meadow'.

LEY LINES

ALFRED WATKINS

Alfred Watkins started the debate on the existence of leys with a pamphlet in 1922. His work, *The Old Straight Track*, published in 1925, outlined evidence leading to fascinating deductions.

He realised that churches, crossroads, burial mounds, megaliths, holy wells and other significant sites were built on straight lines, sometimes with several miles between each landmark. On the horizon, another stone or peak continued the ley, although the ultimate destination is a mystery. Watkins thought that leys were mapped out between 4000 B.C. and 2000 B.C. and were used for trade, religious or astronomical purposes.

Watkins lyrically described a ley as: '. . . a fairy chain stretched from mountain peak to mountain peak, as far as the eye could reach, and paid out until it touched the high places of the earth at a number of ridges, banks and knowls. Then visualise a mound, circular earthwork or clump of trees planted on these high points, and in low points in the valley other mounds ringed round with water to be seen from a distance.

A LEY LINE SCYTHING THROUGH THE ENGLISH COUNTRYSIDE TAKES A STRAIGHT ROUTE.

Then great standing stones brought to mark the way at intervals, and on a bank leading up to a mountain ridge or down to a ford the track cut deep so as to form a guiding notch on the skyline as you come up.'

LEY HUNTING

Ley hunting, fashionable after the thoughts of beer salesman Watkins came out in print, became resurgent in the sixties and seventies. Watkins himself gave tips on marking a ley. Much can be achieved on an Ordnance Survey map with a scale of 1 mile : 1 inch. Spread out, with the aid of a T-square, protractor, compass and pins, the map will throw up a pattern. But, warns Watkins, it is still essential to tramp around the area. That's when you will identify stones or mounds not marked on maps. Other clues may come in place

names or field gates, which are rarely moved. 'Three points alone do not prove a ley,' says Watkins, 'four being the minimum.'

Critics of the Watkins thesis say that landmarks seen by him as significant may have been established hundreds of years apart. He also used both secular and religious sites for his purposes. Are the leys nothing more than a coincidence?

THE NAZCA LINES

Some suggest that leys are navigational aids for UFOs. Those convinced by the validity of leys claim an energy force flows along them which drew prehistoric man to them. Intersections of ley lines are considered particularly potent and mystical. Stonehenge is at such a junction of leys.

Watkins was not alone in his investigations. Probes into the alignment of key points had gone ahead independently at the end of the 19th century in both America and Germany.

South America showed the most impressive evidence for the existence of leys. The Nazca lines in Peru are desert tracks which stretch without deviation for up to 6 miles (9 km). And there are similar lines in Bolivia, the longest of which stretches for 20 miles (32 km). They are known as *taki'is*, which according to local Aymaran Indians means 'straight lines of holy places'. Infrared measuring equipment proved that the paths were astonishingly straight, but left researchers clueless as to how they were defined and why.

In 1936, sixteen-year-old Stephen Jenkins was exploring on Loe Bar, a junction of four leys and the point near which King Arthur was said to have died. To his shock a host of horsemen in medieval garb appeared. Yet as he stepped forward, they vanished. Bizarrely, 38 years after this, both Stephen and his wife saw the vision once more from the exact same spot. Again, it disappeared when they stepped to one side.

Five leys come together at Chanctonbury Ring on England's south coast, the site of a Saxon fort. On 25 August 1974, William Lincoln and three friends went there at night to experience the power of the place. Without warning, Lincoln was lifted 5 ft (1.5 m) into the air and held there for 30 seconds. Nobody saw anything lift him, although a tape recorder captured his cries for help.

of the dowsing tool is all that's needed. Little wonder that dowsing is known in America as 'water-witching'.

The Nobel prize-winning Charles Richet, a French physiologist, challenged the rationalists: 'It is a fact we must accept. Don't experiment to find out whether it is so. It is so! Go ahead and develop it!'

ANYONE CAN DOWSE

It is easy to understand why so many people have their doubts. Most self-respecting dowsers start by dangling a pendulum over a map to glean hints of the location they need before getting out into the field. So does the power emanate from the person instead of the land? Here the dowsing skill apparently overlaps the gift of remote viewing. Yet it is widely held that everyone has the ability to dowse. It simply takes time and sensitivity.

Historically people used V-shaped hazel twigs to dowse, although cherry, dogwood or hawthorn are equally viable. Today two L-rods – one side measuring about 12 in (30 cm) and the other about 5 in (12 cm) – are commonly used, made out of a variety of materials, even wire coat-hangers. Many dowsers believe the tools don't matter. They are there only to amplify the responses inside the dowser.

DOWSING

Converts know dowsing to be an inexplicable earth mystery. Sceptics declare the astonishing success rate as nothing more than coincidence.

DESPERATELY SEEKING… ANYTHING

Even adept dowsers cannot explain the power by which he or she is able to detect water, oil and other hidden things. Yet top-class dowsers have frequently proved themselves by pinpointing the exact whereabouts of whatever they are seeking, be it a faulty engine part, a lost gem or even a dead body. If it's water that is being sought, they can tell not only where, but how deep and how much. Simply an imperceptible and involuntary twitch

JACK LIVINGSTONE

There are outstanding dowsers who achieve fantastically accurate results and there are those who are only pedestrian. The fallibility of those less able to achieve success inspires the continuing hostility of the scientific world.

The ability of dowser Jack Livingstone in America is breathtaking. During the drought of 1976–1977, his neighbourhood of Pine Grove in

LEFT: 16TH CENTURY DOWSERS USING RODS TO DISCOVER SILVER.
RIGHT: A WATER-DETECTING DOWSER.

California had as much water as it wanted, thanks to the well sunk in 1965 to the specifications he laid down. Repeatedly, Livingstone has been proved correct not only in locating the well, but also by the quantity and quality of the water.

A good dowser will come up with water even when geologists and hydrologists declare there is none in the area. Dowsers have long felt that water surges up to the earth's surface through secret veins – in addition to the channels accepted by scientists.

Two-thirds of the earth's surface is covered by water, but it comprises three-quarters of the human body. Perhaps the performance of today's dowsers echoes the abilities of ancient man who had to 'tune in' to the whereabouts of fresh water for his very survival. Aborigines in Australia are famed for their ability to discover new sources of water, and judge its volume, too.

BLACK STREAMS

One theory of dowsers on the outer fringes of medical practice is that hidden 'black' streams could be responsible for arthritis or even cancer. Once he became convinced of his abilities at dowsing, Dr Herbert Douglas, of Arlington, Vermont, discovered apparently malign water sources beneath the beds, chairs and couches of 25 arthritis sufferers in 1965.

ELEPHANTS

NOT SURPRISINGLY, MAN IS NOT ALONE IN DIVINING WATER SOURCES. ELEPHANTS HAVE BEEN KNOWN TO WANDER FAR AND WIDE TO QUENCH THEIR THIRST. ONCE THEY COME UPON THEIR CHOSEN SPOT – WHICH APPEARS TO THE HUMAN EYE MUCH LIKE THE NEXT – THEY DRILL HOLES WITH THEIR TRUNKS UNTIL THEY FIND THE WATER THEY NEED. GENERALLY, BABY ELEPHANTS HAVE FIRST DRINK, FOLLOWED BY MOTHERS AND THEN THE MALES. IN INDIA, OBSERVERS HAVE NOTED ELEPHANTS ALLOWING OTHER PARCHED ANIMALS TO DRINK AT THE NEWLY CREATED WATER HOLE BEFORE THEY DO THEMSELVES. AFRICAN ELEPHANTS USE CHEWED BARK TO SEAL THEIR WATER HOLES.

'At first I felt it to be coincidental,' he admitted. 'It was too crazy to believe. But I repeated the test around these beds in 55 consecutive cases. Each time, without a single exception, there were intersections of dowsing reaction lines, presumably caused by underground veins of water and generally underneath that part of the bed where the person usually lay.'

When the patients moved their beds to a spot entirely dry beneath the earth's crust their condition improved markedly.

Dowsing is gaining respectability – police forces, surveyors and even oil companies call on the services of dowsers. The question 'why' is never asked – the results speak for themselves.

Surely the greatest bequest to us left by prehistoric Europeans is the breathtaking array of henges, standing stones and stone circles, which have fascinated and perplexed subsequent generations.

In Ireland there is the stone jungle at Loch Roag in Donegal. In England the mighty Stone-henge dominates, Scotland is peppered with beautifully preserved ancient stones while in France the impressive stone row complex at Carnac thrills today's visitors.

Some 50,000 megaliths are to be found in Western Europe and North Africa. While some have crumbled, been struck by lightning or removed by farmers, there are plenty more which still exist to excite the imagination. Yet their exact purpose remains shrouded in mystery.

HENGES

Henges, circular in shape, date from the Neolithic and Bronze Age periods. The smallest are about 30 ft (9 m) in diameter, while the largest measure a staggering 1,500 ft (450 m). There is generally a bank on the outside and an internal ditch, usually insignificant, although the ditch at Avebury in Wiltshire, where there is a famous crop of stones, is a mighty 70 ft (21 m) wide and 30 ft (9 m) deep.

One type of henge has a single entrance, whilst others have two or more. In some excavated sites, the settings for circular timber posts have been uncovered and there were pits, cairns and monoliths on some sites too.

Standing stones were single, paired or in long lines, called stone rows. Sometimes these stones appear to have been the markers for boundaries, while others seem to have been linked to some nearby burial mounds. At the foot of some standing stones tools, weapons and even bones have been unearthed.

THE BOULDERS OF STONEHENGE HAVE BEEN PERPLEXING HISTORIANS FOR CENTURIES. LATEST RESEARCH SAYS IT TOOK MORE THAN 2,000 YEARS TO COMPLETE.

RELIGIOUS SACRIFICE

Stone circles were built from the later Neolithic period and there's no evidence that any were erected after 1200 B.C.; it seems likely that they were used for religious rites. Whenever prehistoric stone circles are discussed, there is inevitably speculation about the use of sacrifice by religious leaders of the day.

One circle on the moor at Curragh in Co. Kildare, Ireland, has a central grave within which the remains of a young woman was discovered. The position of the skeleton suggests that the unfortunate lady was buried alive as the head was probably upright, one hand and one leg were pressed against the side of the grave and the legs were spread apart. A few miles away from this site, although thought to be unconnected, is the Punchestown standing stone which, at 21 ft (6.5 m), is the tallest in Ireland.

STANDING STONES

ASTROLOGICAL IMPORTANCE

Recent research points to the amazing accuracy with which some of the rock arrangements align with moon, sun and stars. It's difficult to prove the case conclusively since many stones in the complex constructions have fallen down or been removed. Also, the positions of the planets have changed in the 4,000 years since their erection.

Archaeologist Ann Lynch's research in southwest Ireland shows conclusive links to astronomical alignments. Of the 37 short stone rows she plotted, 23 showed significant alignments to the solstices and/or the major extremes of the moon.

But this does not necessarily imply that Neolithic or Bronze Age astronomers had an advanced scientific understanding. These were people who spent much of their lives staring at the night sky when the movements of the sun, moon, stars and planets would have evoked far more general interest among the population than they do today. The stone rows may simply have been an aid to observation, and therefore to the timing of rituals and festivals.

STONEHENGE

Of all the prehistoric sites of Western Europe, Stonehenge still inspires the most discussion.

Despite study over three centuries, it is still not known who built this vast arena, or why.

Stonehenge looms out of the windswept reaches of Salisbury Plain, about 80 miles (135 km) west of London. It consists of two concentric rings enclosing a stone horseshoe and various isolated stones with such lurid titles as Altar Stone, Slaughter Stone and Hele Stone.

It's known that Stonehenge was built in various stages between 3500 B.C. and 1100 B.C. Once completed it had 30 upright stones bridged by 30 enormous lintels forming an unbroken ring about 100 ft (36 m) in diameter. The circle and the horseshoe had 'doorways', the highest measuring nearly 30 ft (9 m).

The first phase was a circular embankment around wooden poles and several upright stones.

Two rows of the bluestones, a type of sandstone, were then put up. Some are now missing, but an estimated 80 slabs weighing 26 tons a piece comprised the spectacular circle. The source of the bluestone has been pinpointed to Preselli in Wales, 130 miles away. It was probably transported before the wheel was invented and erected by hefty levers without the benefit of pulleys.

The doorways came next and finally the boulders were rearranged on the site, with sophisticated mortise-and-tenon joints fixing the lintels to the uprights. One of the world's colossal pieces of engineering had been completed entirely by hand, without mechanical assistance.

POPULAR MYTH

Such was the splendour of Stonehenge that for centuries its construction was put down to Merlin's magic. Contemporary suggestions for its use include a power source for aliens, a solar temple, and a trading market and racetrack.

The most enduring explanation for its creation has been as a lunar observatory. In 1965 Gerald S. Hawkins discovered 165 significant alignments between the stones and the night sky. His investigation was reinforced by Professor Alexander Thom in 1973, who saw new patterns in the way the henge was built, discovered the megalithic yard, a length of 2.72 ft (0.83 m) which was used throughout prehistoric Europe, and the astronomical importance of the stones in relation to burial mounds and earthworks in the vicinity.

STRANGE RAINS

The cool of the evening on 17 May 1966 suddenly turned to an ominous chill. Ruth Harnett would hardly have noticed the dip in temperature as she hurried to bring shopping in from her van if she had not stopped suddenly at the sound of a thud.

To her astonishment, a fish measuring about 4 in (10 cm) was lying on the roof of the vehicle. Seconds later another hit the van's bonnet. Ruth scanned the neighbourhood expecting to see the disappearing heels of some prank-pulling children. But there were none.

When three more fish fell to earth, she realised they were coming from the sky and alerted husband David who was inside the house at Hatfield in Hertfordshire. 'As he came out, I looked up again which was a big mistake. I was bombarded with fish and one hit me in the face.' A further twenty or so fish rained down before the curious shower stopped.

The fish seemed fresh. On closer inspection they turned out to be young roach, rudd or dab, their combined weight was less than 4 lb (2 kg).

Bizarrely, falls of fishes – rare as they are – were not unknown to Ruth's family. 'I remember as a child my father telling me that his father was caught in a shower of fishes and frogs near Welwyn Garden City, just 7 miles (11 km) away, about 60 years ago,' she said. *Raining cats, dogs, frogs . . . Quite how creatures depart from their natural habitat, are sucked up into the sky and then cascade back down to earth is, not surprisingly, a mystery.*

One of the first recorded events occurred in A.D. 200 when a rain of frogs hit Sardinia. Since then some weird weather has been noted.

IT RAINED 'CATS, DOGS AND PITCHFORKS', ACCORDING TO THE OLD SAYING.

• In 1578 a shower of yellow mice fell in Bergen, Sweden, a number of them swimming ashore from the sea where they landed.

• In February 1861 bucketsful of fish fell in Singapore following an earthquake.

• Tiny frogs were found in the blocks of ice which fell on Iowa during a snowstorm in June 1882.

• After a heavy thunderstorm in Worcester in May 1881, periwinkles, some of them still alive, were discovered scattered on the streets.

• In Brignoles, France, thousands of small toads fell during a freak storm in September 1973.

Snakes, rats, worms, insects, larvae and even dead ducks have reportedly fallen to earth. One London woman described a storm. 'We first thought they were hailstones until we saw they were all tiny frogs and were jumping about. The brim of my husband's hat was full of them while the storm lasted. They were everywhere.'

Typically in frog-falls, the creatures are small, between tadpole and full-grown frog. No pond contents accompany them, so the commonly-held opinion, that they were whipped up in a whirlwind, seems doubtful. Ancient records claim that one fish-fall in Greece lasted for three days, far too long for a powerful wind to hold out.

CHARLES FORT

Such happenings fascinated American journalist Charles Fort, who devoted his life to collecting notes about the phenomena which science could not explain. Although he carefully marshalled his evidence into four books – *Book of the Damned, New Lands, Lo! and Wild Talents* – he resisted the temptation to offer explanations. About falls of fishes, he would only say they come from 'somewhere aloft. Whether it's the planet Genesistrine, or the moon, or a vast amorphous region super-jacent to this earth or an island in the Super Sargasso Sea should perhaps be left to the researches of other super – or extra-geographers.'

He was likewise absorbed by the occurrence of ice blocks tumbling to earth. With today's busy skies it is all to easy to say that chunks of ice that whistle through the air are from aircraft.

Of course, modern aircraft have sophisticated de-icing equipment as substantial ice formation could cause crashes, and some notable falling ice blocks occurred before the days of flying. In the reign of Charlemagne, an ice block measuring 16 x 11 x 17 ft (5 x 3.5 x 5 m) was allegedly witnessed. At Ord in Scotland in 1849, a 19 ft (6 m) wide block was reported.

In Timbersville, Virginia, an ice block the size of a basketball crashed through the roof of a family home on 7 March 1976. The noise was so loud that neighbours rushed out of their homes to find out what had happened. They were just in time to see an almost identical ice block fall on the ground less than 165 ft (50 m) away.

A SHOWER OF FROGS MADE FRONT PAGE NEWS FOR *FATE* MAGAZINE IN MAY 1958.

THE DAY IT RAINED FROGS

FATE MAGAZINE

PDC

UFO Solution – The Gravity Drive? –MAX MILLER

May 1958   35c

The Mystic Religion Of Zoroaster

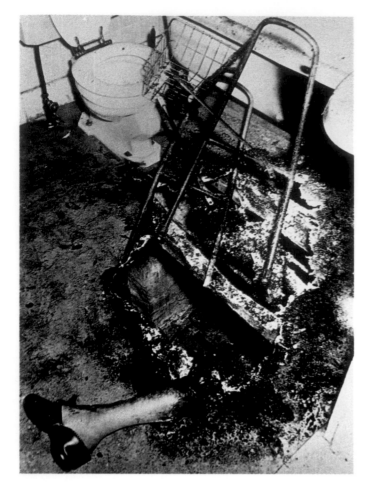

THE ODDEST THING

Yet there have been strange deaths which fall into neither category, like that of Dr John Irving Bentley, who died at his home in Pennsylvania in 1966. All that remained of him was the lower part of his right leg and a pile of ashes.

There was no trace of petrol, and, while that part of one limb was recognisable, there were no other blackened body parts which one would expect of a victim in a regular fire. The flesh, tissues and bones of the 92-year-old had been reduced to a sooty powder.

So just what had ignited this frail human body? Was this sudden and shocking death proof of the phenomenon of spontaneous human combustion in which people are engulfed in a conflagration which has no apparent cause? Coroner John Dec was at a loss to explain what

SPONTANEOUS HUMAN COMBUSTION

It's hard to set a human body ablaze. Those who do so intentionally use liberal amounts of highly inflammable fuel. Accidental fires claim lives by charring the body or through asphyxiation.

had happened. Later he maintained the death of Dr Bentley was 'the oddest thing you ever saw'.

The reality of spontaneous human combustion is disputed by scientists who believe that a spark from a cigarette or hearth is always responsible for unexpected fire deaths. However, there are marked differences between deaths ascribed to SHC and those ascribed to house fires.

INCONCLUSIVE EVIDENCE

Investigators have been intrigued by the comprehensive way in which bodies have been consumed by fire. Even corpses committed to the soaring temperatures of local crematoria are not burned away to ashes. There are fragments of bones which survive the heat and undergo a further reducing process. In those cases marked out as SHC, the remains defy normal physical laws in that they are little more than dust.

Curiously, deaths put down as SHC are notable for the lack of damage caused to clothing and other surroundings. In the case of Dr Bentley, the paint on the bath close to where he died was black but not blistered, despite the obvious intensity of the fire. Other possible SHC victims have been found reduced to ashes while their clothes have survived virtually unscathed.

The evidence, though compelling, is still not sufficient to entice scientists into areas of speculation. Dr Gavin Thurston, a London coroner, went out on a limb when he wrote in the *Medico-Legal Journal* in 1961, 'There are undisputed instances where the body has burned in its own substance, without external fuel, and in which there has been a remarkable absence of damage to surrounding inflammable objects.'

NATURAL OR SUPERNATURAL PHENOMENON

Jenny Randles, author of twenty books on the paranormal, insists: 'Spontaneous Human Combustion is obviously a genuine phenomenon. It is probably a natural – rather than supernatural – energy dormant in our midst. Just because we can't explain it doesn't mean that it doesn't happen. SHC may be triggered by forces that are just as puzzling for us as electricity was to Leonardo da Vinci.'

Her book *The Unexplained* outlines some possible causes of SHC. 'Theories about SHC include the notion that electrical fields inside the human body can short-circuit, that atomic chain reactions can generate phenomenal internal heat, and that a deadly cocktail of chemicals can form in the gut as a result of Western society's poor dietary habits. The last may explain why SHC seems almost non-existent in animals and why there are few, if any, cases recorded outside the more developed nations.'

Peter Hough, co-author with Jenny Randles of the book *Spontaneous Human Combustion*, says, 'It is possible that the answer lies somewhere on the fringes of physics, in little-understood phenomena like ball-lightning, electromagnetic force-fields or electrostatic energy.'

MIND-OVER-MATTER

Another cause suggested by researchers is a deadly mind-over-matter syndrome in which loneliness, illness or some similar emotional affliction leads to a negative state of mind.

This has a tangible effect, with phosphogens, including Vitamin B10, building up in the muscle tissue. (Phosphogen, a compound like nitroglycerin, is extremely combustible in certain circumstances.) Electricity generated by intense sunspots, magnetic storms or even electric energies produced in some unknown geographical blip then triggers the combustion.

A report by investigator Livingston Gearhart, published in the journal *Pursuit* in 1975, showed that a significant number of SHC events coincided with local peaks in the earth's magnetism.

While the exact cause of these personal infernos may not be understood, one fact remains a certainty. The victims' deaths, although swift, are hideously unsavoury, as they suffocate on the fumes emitted from their blazing bodies.

A SOLDIER'S FIERY DEATH IN SCOTLAND IN 1888 WAS THOUGHT TO BE A CASE OF SHC.

THE BLUE FLAME

One of the most graphic descriptions of a suspected case of spontaneous human combustion comes from Jack Stacey, the leader of a Fire Brigade team who were called to a derelict house in Lambeth, south London, on 13 September 1967. The blaze they were to extinguish was consuming the body of a tramp named Bailey.

'There was a 4-inch [10 cm] slit in his abdomen from which was issuing, at force, a blue flame which was beginning to burn the wooden stair. We extinguished the flames by playing a hose into the abdominal cavity,' said Stacey.

'Bailey was alive when he started burning and must have been in terrible pain. His teeth were sunk into the mahogany newel post of the staircase. I had to prise his jaws apart with a metal bar to release the body.'

A pathologist concluded that Bailey's death was 'a result of asphyxia due to inhalation of fire fumes'. Although Bailey was a known drunk, he was not a smoker. All the power to his house had been turned off.

SHC IN HISTORY

Cases of spontaneous human combustion were reported in ancient Egypt when 'the heavens consumed their own'. Later, in medieval Italy, a countess was 'reduced to a blackened mass of greasy ashes'. In Victorian days, with the strange death of Krook in his novel Bleak House, Charles Dickens described the phenomenon.

HENRY THOMAS

On 6 January 1980, John Heymer, a Scenes-of-Crime officer with Gwent CID, was called to a house fire in Ebbw Vale to find the lower legs of Henry Thomas, aged 73. The rest of his body had been reduced to a pile of ash.

Heymer was perplexed. Even the fiercest fires that he had previously encountered left more evidence than this. The blaze must have been ferocious. Yet at the same time the carpet and rug where the victim burned were not even scorched beyond the limits of the body. He deduced that the man's body contained no less than 12 gallons (45 litres) of water. Surely blazing clothes must have been the cause of the tragedy.

However, a pathologist's report concluded that 'the centre of the fire was the body itself'. It had started in the abdomen – while the victim was still alive – and moved outwards. After retiring from the police force, Heymer launched a study into recent cases of SHC.

He became convinced that the 'candle effect', when the human body becomes like a wick after an externally sparked blaze – frequently said to be the real cause of SHC – was a red herring. He decided that, in the five cases he investigated, 'the burning was fierce and gas-fuelled'.

MRS MARY REESER

One of the best-documented cases of SHC is that of 67-year-old Mrs Mary Reeser, who died in her apartment in St Petersburg, Florida.

When her landlady entered the apartment with the help of two workmen, they felt fierce heat. To their horror, they stumbled on the remains of Mrs Reeser.

THE DEATH OF MARY REESER IN 1951 IN FLORIDA WAS WIDELY ASCRIBED TO SHC. WHILE HER ARMCHAIR WAS DESTROYED A NEWSPAPER NEARBY ESCAPED FROM THE INFERNO.

The heat had shrunk her skull to the size of a baseball; her left foot was intact, but burned off at the ankle; on the foot, untouched by fire, was a satin carpet slipper. It seemed Mrs Reeser was in her armchair when the fire started and that was now completely destroyed. But a newspaper lay near the body, entirely unscorched.

An inquest was told that the temperature of the blaze reached over 2,500°F, yet the fire had not extended by more than inches from the body.

Renowned forensic anthropologist Dr Wilton Krogman, of the University of Pennsylvania School of Medicine, reported: 'I regard it as the most amazing thing I have ever seen. As I review it, the short hairs on my neck bristle with vague fear. Were I living in the Middle Ages, I would mutter something about black magic.'

BURNING ISSUES

On 8 January 1988, Southampton firemen were called to the terraced home of 86-year-old Alfred Ashton and entered a room 'filled with smoke and radiating intense heat'.

All that was left of Alfred was a blackened skull and his lower legs. The rest of him had been reduced to ashes, which had fallen through the hole in the wooden floor on which he had been incinerated.

On 2 February 1980, the ashes of Annie Webb, 75, were found in her home in Newport, Gwent.

There only remained a blackened skull, lower legs and one arm, still with its recent hospital name tag attached. There was slight damage to a plastic tablecloth that was inches away from her body. Apart from this everything in the room had remained unscathed.

In 1938, Phyllis Newcombe, aged 22, was leaving a dance hall at Chelmsford, Essex, when blue flames suddenly engulfed her body.

In vain, her fiancé Henry McAusland tried to beat out the flames and badly burned his hands. He and other witnesses told an inquest that Phyllis was reduced to a pile of ashes within a matter of minutes. The coroner reported, 'In all my experience I have never come across anything as remarkable as this.'

ALARMING CASE OF SPONTANEOUS COMBUSTION.

"Oh! Law! There's Pa's boots—but where's Pa?"

A MONTH BEFORE D-DAY IN WORLD WAR II THE DAILY TELEGRAPH CROSSWORD FEATURED FIVE CODEWORDS KEY TO THE INVASION. THE COMPILER WAS QUIZZED BUT NOT CHARGED.

A divorcée returned to her home town of Fleet in Hampshire and one day met a man in a pub. To her surprise she discovered he was living in the house where she grew up. Not only that, his two cats bore the same names as her childhood pets, a rabbit and a guinea pig, the names being Whiskey and Ginger. Deciding that fate was playing its hand, they married.

SYNCHRONICITY

We have Carl Jung to thank for making sense of the myriad coincidences that occur. A mystic by inclination, he determined that some coincidences were connected so meaningfully that the statistical probability of their occurring was tiny. The coincidences were therefore predestined or

COINCIDENCE

You are thinking about a long-lost friend and the telephone rings. That same friend was, for no apparent reason, thinking about you and is calling on impulse. It is strange, but it happens.

MEANINGFUL COINCIDENCE

The word is synchronicity, the principle of 'meaningful coincidences'. In Eastern civilisations, synchronicity has long been accepted as a factor of everyday life, a spiritual phenomenon which may defy explanation, but nevertheless exists. However, sceptical Westerners are tempted to discount it as nothing more than mere chance.

Most people experience coincidence to a lesser or greater degree. Imagine the surprise of motorcyclist Frederick Chance in 1969 after a collision with a car when he discovered the driver was . . . Frederick Chance.

'meant'. He quoted the example of a patient who noticed a strange gathering of birds around the window of the bedroom where her grandmother had recently died. The patient dismissed it as a chance occurrence. She was left in wonder, however, when the same phenomenon happened on the death of her mother.

Jung first used the term 'synchronicity' in 1930 and went on to link it with Extra Sensory Perception, and even the power of horoscopes.

There have been numerous examples of people driven to make contact with a loved one shortly before their sudden death. For those who believe in the forces of synchronicity, this is an example of the subconscious merging into the conscious mind, prompted by some invisible and unfelt wave of communication.

DALLAS 1963

One of the most powerful examples of coincidence occurred with the assassination of US

President John F. Kennedy. Lincoln's secretary was called John and Kennedy's secretary was called Lincoln. Kennedy was elected President 100 years after Lincoln. His killer, Lee Harvey Oswald, was born a century after Lincoln's killer, John Wilkes Booth. Both Presidents were killed by bullets in the back of the head, with their wives sitting beside them. Neither assassin lived to stand trial. Both Kennedy and Lincoln were succeeded by southerners named Johnson who were also born 100 years apart. And both confessed to having psychic warnings about their impending deaths.

RONALD OPUS

An astonishing coincidence claimed the life of Ronald Opus, who suffered a more bizarre end than most. On 23 March 1994 Mr Opus decided to end his life by plunging from the top of a ten-storey building. A suicide note confirmed his intentions – so how did he die from a bullet wound in the head? The President of the American Association for Forensic Science, Don Harper Mills, told an annual awards dinner the following amazing sequence of events.

In the split second that Mr Opus sailed past the window of the ninth storey, a shotgun blast rang out. The gun was fired by an elderly man during a domestic row. Although he was threatening his wife, the bullets crashed through the window and hit the unfortunate Mr Opus.

The case was further complicated by a safety net strung out at the eighth floor on behalf of some window cleaners. That meant that the dive from the roof would not have been fatal, although Mr Opus had not known it. He would have been saved and would have lived. Investigators were looking at a case of murder.

However, the elderly man and his wife swore the gun was never normally loaded. In the course of their fiery relationship it was not unusual for the husband to wield the weapon while it was empty. He had no intention of killing his wife – and certainly did not mean to shoot the body as it passed his window. It was accidental death. But the story had another twist.

Weeks before, a witness saw the couple's son loading the gun with live ammunition in the hope that his father would shoot his mother. The son hated her because she had cut off his financial support, but he grew increasingly depressed at the failure of his plot to achieve a quick result. So he climbed to the top of the ten-storey building and jumped off. The son was, of course, Ronald Opus. He was killed by the gun he had loaded. The verdict was suicide.

ABRAHAM LINCOLN SAW HIS DEATH IN A DREAM BUT FAILED TO SAVE HIMSELF FROM THE ASSASSIN'S BULLET.

GLOSSARY

Absent Healing: Spiritual or psychic healing which happens at a distance. The 'patient' may not even know it is happening at all.

Acupuncture: Chinese healing involving a series of needles being inserted under the skin. Mysteriously, the location of the needles may have nothing to do with the whereabouts of the illness.

Akasha: A Hindu or Bhuddist term meaning 'life principle' or 'space of the universe'. Every event that's ever happened in life, including emotions and ideas, is held on Akashic Record, on the astral plane, according to some faiths.

Animal psi: Potential paranormal abilities of pets, including clairvoyance, telepathy and precognition.
Also known as Anpsi.

Ankh: Ancient Egyptian symbol of life, now used as a lucky charm.

Aura: Supposed energy field around living things displaying itself as multi-coloured lights, only visible to those with 'second sight'. Haloes are deemed to be auras although their existence has never been proven. Also called 'the human rainbow'.

Automatic writing: Words penned by mediums in a trance. Sometimes complex and beyond the understanding of the writer in a usual state of consciousness, the words are thought by some to be dictated by spirits. However, a more popular theory is that they come from the writer's subconscious, either telepathically received or buried information.

Blavatsky, Madame Helena Petrovna (1831-1891): Russian-born psychic who travelled the world, giving displays of mediumship, levitation, clairvoyance, clairaudience and clairsentience. To promote her Hermetic beliefs she helped to found the Theosophical Society which became most famous for its headquarters in India. Tainted by a fraud scandal, she retired to Germany to write. Her death on 8 May is still commemorated by Theosophists as White Lotus Day.

Cabbalah: The mystic beliefs of ancient Judaism. Also known as Kabbalah.

Cagliostro, Count Alessandro (1743-1795): Occultist, magician, healer and psychic from an unknown background in Sicily. He studied the Cabbalah and alchemy with the Order of the Knights of Malta before heading to London where he joined the Freemasons. He held seances - for which he never took money - and astounded audiences by his apparent rapport with the spirit world. He moved to Paris where he allegedly predicted a violent end for the doomed King Louis XVI, adding that the queen, Marie Antoinette, would become 'prematurely wrinkled through sorrow'. In the ensuing revolution both proved correct. He was disgraced in a theft accusation and moved to Rome where he was arrested by the Inquisition. After being tortured he and his wife were jailed where both perished.

Chakras: In yoga the points on the body through which vital energies are channelled. Although invisible to the naked eye they can be detected clairvoyantly.

Channelling: Apparent contact with higher beings, deities, spirits, angels or the dead through a trance medium.

Cheiro (1866-1936): Born William John Warner, he discovered his palm-reading talents as a child. Following a trip to Eygpt, he carried the severed hand of an Eygptian princess everywhere with him. A premonition revealed to him that the word 'cheir' was Greek for hand and that's how his strange nick-name came into being. Based first in London and later in America his clients included Oscar Wilde, Czar Nicholas II, King Edward VII, King Leopold II of Belgium, Rasputin and Herbert Kitchener. In 1927 he published a book of world predictions which included the onset of World War II, the return of the Jews to Palestine and the spread of communism. When a bid to become a Hollywood scriptwriter failed Cheiro ran a school of metaphysics until his death.

Clairaudience: Perception of sounds inaudible to normal human ears.

Clairsentience: From the French for 'clear sensing', it's the sensory detection of psychic information.

Clairvoyance: From the French for 'clear seeing', it refers to both internal and external visions and images.

Gerard Croiset (1909-80): Dutch clairvoyant widely used by international police forces to locate missing people and things.

Déjà vu: Sensation of familiarity in unknown places which is thought by some to indicate the memory of a past life surfacing. Another theory is that the subconscious mind has absorbed the relevant information fractionally more quickly than the conscious mind and is replaying it.

Dreams: Usually forgotten, powerful and recalled dreams are sometimes clairvoyant, telepathic or shared although no one can explain why. In lucid dreams the subject is aware that he or she is asleep.

Ectoplasm: Unknown white substance which appears to pour from bodily orifices during a seance. Spoiled by bright light, it has never been scientifically studied and is the reason given for the necessity of dim lighting while mediums are at work.

Fetish: An Item supposedly representing dead spirits on earth, linking humans to the world of the supernatural .

Findhorn: Spiritual community in the northern reaches of Scotland begun by Peter and Eileen Caddy and friend Dorothy Maclean who believe they were spiritually guided there. Despite adverse weather the garden produced mighty vegetables thanks to, they claim, spiritual advice on horticulture.

Fortune, Dion (1890-1946): Welsh-born, adept in ritual magic, she changed her name from Violet Mary Firth after being inspired by her family motto 'Deo, non Fortuna', meaning 'By God, not by chance'. Believing she had suffered psychic attack by a mean-minded work colleague, she suffered a nervous breakdown and turned to psychology to discover more about the mind. The lure of magic remained extremely powerful and, after a spell with the Golden Dawn, she began her own order, the Fraternity of the Inner Light, and later the Chalice Orchard Club. In later years, her magical powers declined. Critics believe this was because she imparted secrets in her books.

Freemasonary: Exclusively male society with spiritual development and fraternal charity at the core of its principles.

Ganzfield Stimulation: Restricted sensory deprivation used to encourage the reception of esp.

Glossolalia: The ability to speak in unknown tongues which usually manifests itself during charismatic Christian worship.

Gnosticism: Christian religion which flourished in the second century A.D. centring on knowledge rather than faith.

Gurdjieff, Georgei Ivanovitch (1877-1949): Influential if obscure teacher of mystic philosophy in which he encouraged 'man the machine' to search for an immortal soul.

Hermetica: Mystical wisdom as laid down by the mythical Hermes Trismegistus.

Hex: German word for witchcraft which in modern terms refers to cursing.

Huna: Philosophy of the Hawaiian people driven to virtual extinction by Christian missionaries.

Hurkos, Peter (1911-1988): Professional psychic who joined police on the hunts for the Boston Strangler and the Sharon Tate murders.

'I AM' Religious Activity: Movement founded by Guy Ballard and his wife Edna following an alleged meeting with Ascended Master Saint Germain on Mt Shasta in California.

Illuminati: Term for adepts in cults who had received the light of knowledge from higher authorities.

Incubus: A demon which mates with sleeping women.

Joan of Arc (1412-1431): French saint inspired by voices and visions to victory over the English. She was eventually captured by the English and, under interrogation, said she could see, hear and even embrace the saints that were guiding her. Although charges of witchcraft were dropped she was condemned as a heretic, not least for wearing men's clothes. She saved her skin by recanting. When she was caught again in men's clothes she was burned at the stake. In 1920 she was canonised.

Karma: The belief that misdemeanours or good deeds executed in past and present lives effect everyday living, i.e. you reap what you sow.

Knight, Judy Z (1946-): Successful psychic from Seattle who channels the wisdom of Ramtha, a Crp-Magnon man dating back some 35,000 years.

Krafft, Karl Ernst (1900-1945): Swiss astrologer employed by Hitler during World War II to construe the works of Nostradamus for propaganda purposes. It proved a knife-edge existence and Krafft was arrested twice by the Gestapo, spending two years in a concentration camp before his death in transit to Buchewald.

Lemuria: Supposedly a continent which stretched between Africa and Asia, the home of a telepathic race of giants who died when violent volcanic activity sent the land mass to the bottom of the ocean.

Gladys Osborne Leonard (1882-1968): Medium plagued in childhood by visions who as a member of the Spiritualist movement had the spirit control of Feda, allegedly the Hindu wife of Leonard's great-great-grandfather.

Lodge, Sir Oliver: Founder member of the Society for Psychical Research (SPR) set up in 1882. The American branch (ASPR) was founded in 1885.

Mandala: Carefully drawn circular diagram representing the cosmos which, duly consecrated, becomes a focus for occult power.

Mantra: Magic formula expressed in words or sounds. Like manadalas, it is usually linked to the Hindu and Buddhist religions.

Mu: Lost continent in the Pacific.

Near-death experience: The term for people who come close to dying but return to life, to recount mystical and often uniform sensations. Scientists speculate it may be caused by chemical changes in the brain. Fewer than three per cent of NDEs are unpleasant and many who embark on the journey to death are reluctant to return.

New Age: Broad adjective for seekers of spiritual alternatives, it includes mystics, psychologists, parapsychologists, ecologists, occultists and herbalists. It has replaced the Sixties equivalent of 'Age of Aquarius', which refers to the new astrological era that earth is entering.

Obeah: Form of magic practised secretly in the Caribbean. Its practitioners are believed to have supernatural powers.

Paracelsus (1493-1541): Swiss doctor, philosopher and sorcerer who won his reputation for the unorthodox treatments he offered patients and the lack of regard he had for accepted medical practise. Paracelsus consulted alchemists, magicians and 'old wives' as often as he delved into medical textbooks, with varying results.

Parapsychology: The study of mental phenomena that falls outside the boundaries of modern psychology.

Paroptic Vision: Another term for eyeless sight.

Piper, Leonora E. (1857-1950): Boston housewife who stumbled on her psychic skills when she visited a medium. Afterwards she gave hundreds of sittings and frequently produced impressive personal information through her spirit controls. Although she was frequently investigated she was never found to be fraudulent. Later in her career she concentrated on automatic writing.

Planchette: Ancestor of the Ouija board, used for automatic writing and drawing.

Price, Harry (1881-1948): Ghostbuster who won acclaim for exposing fraudulent mediums. However, he emerged as a questionable character himself after his conduct in the investigation of Borley Rectory, once considered the most haunted house in England. He was at best naive in the treatment of psychic evidence.

Retrocognition: Looking into the past using the powers of clairvoyance or clairsentience.

Runes: Letters and symbols of northern Europe thought to contain magical power.

Sheep/goat effect: Name given to the proven phenomena that believers (sheep) score consistently higher against chance in psi tests while the scores for sceptics (goats) are consistently lower.

Spiritism: Allan Kardec's philosophy that illnesses can be treated with advice from spirit guides. Also that certain afflictions were carried over from a past life.

Spiritualism: Religious movement advocating direct communication with the spirit world, popularly launched by the Fox sisters after 1848.

Succubus: Female demon which mates with sleeping males.

Swedenborg, Emanuel (1688-1772): Swedish scientist who laid foundations of spiritual and mystic beliefs which remained valid for centuries after his death.

Theosophy: A philosophy of spiritual enhancement, borrowing from Hinduism and Neoplatism, built on the teachings of wise Masters who, through reincarnation, live for centuries in their Tibetan hideouts. After being psychically contacted by Master Morya in 1951 Blavatsky formed the Theosophical Society to promote it.

Thoughtography: Paranormal photography in which images are made on photographic film through thought process.

Transcendental Meditation: Personally taught meditation system which aims to reach transcendental consciousness, pioneered by the Maharishi Mahesh Yogi.

Twins: Remarkable likenesses have been found between twins, not only in appearance, which have indicated paranormally close links. Thirty-two-year-old twins who died in separate wards in a state mental hospital in North Carolina in one night in April 1962 revealed not only telepathic communication but also mind over matter. They had protested vehemently about being split. Twins have provided convincing proof of their bonds by leading mirror lives even after being separated at birth.

INDEX

ACKNOWLEDGEMENTS

The publisher would like to thank the following sources for their kind permission to reproduce the photographs in this book.

AKG London: 62, 113, 141, 142, 143 background; /Manchester City Art Gallery 173 top

Bridgeman Art Library: /Biblioteca Madicca-Laurenziana, Florence 29 bottom; /British Library, London 19, 29 top left, 165; /British Museum, London 33 bottom, 164; /City of Bristol Museum and Art Gallery 162; /Derby Museum and Art Gallery 109 background; /Fitzwilliam Museum, University of Cambridge 24; /Herbert Art Gallery and Museum, Coventry 67 bottom right; /Leningrad Museum of Anthropology and Ethography 98; /The Louvre, Paris / Peter Willi 18; /Philip Mould, Historical Portraits Ltd 72, 77; /Museo Lazaro Galdiano, Madrid / Index 16; /National Museum of American Art, Smithsonian Institute/ Permlet Art Resource 32, 79; /Osterreichische Nationalbibliothek, Vienna 155 top left; /Phillips, Fine Art Auctioneers, London 20 bottom left, 46; /The Arthur Rackham picture is reproduced with the kind permission of his family 73 bottom; /Private Collection 7, 25 bottom left, 74, 82, 87, 106, 110, 112 background, 148, 156, 172, 178, 185; /Museo di san Marco Dell'Angelico, Florence 68; /Smithsonian Institution, Washington, DC 55 bottom; /Stapleton Collection 23 background, 34, 111 bottom; /Biblioteca Apostolica, Vaticana 33 top; /Chateaux de Versailles, France / Lauros-Giraudon 55 top; /Villa Isogna, Val D'Aosta / Giraudon 28

Camera Press: /Walter E.Bennett 125 bottom

Corbis-Bettmann: 118, 124 bottom

E.T. Archive: 76 top, 86 background, 154, 167 top; /British Library, London 166; /Imperial War Museum, London 184; /Chateau de Maintenant 41 top; /Musee de Versailles, France 54

Mary Evans Picture Library: 8 /9, 12, 13 bottom left, 14 bottom left, 44 background, 47, 51 top, 52 background, 52 top right, 75, 78, 81, 92, 96, 100, 101, 107, 108 left, 112 top left, 126 bottom left, 129, 130, 132, 133, 134, 138, 140, 143 top right, 145, 152, 153, 183 bottom; /Harry Price 115; /Manfred Cassirer 146; /Sigmund Freud Copyrights 109 top left; /Society of Psychical Research 80 top left, 135 top,left,135 bottom, 144

Fortean Picture Library: 2 /3, 6, 44 bottom right, 67 background, 91 bottom, 119 top, 120 /121 background, 125 background, 128, 179 bottom right, 181, 182; /Clas Svahn 171 bottom; /Ken Webster 84; /Klaus Aarsleff 86; /Larry E. Arnold 180; /Raymond Buckland 21 top right

Fotomas Index, London: 10 background, 10 top left, 11 top left, 14 background, 25 top right, 37 background, 39, 40, 43, 45, 93 background, 104, 139 background, 149, 160, 163 background, 169 background, 177 bottom background

Ronald Grant Archive: /AIP 76 bottom; /MGM/UA 83; /Sunset Productions 89 top; /Walt Disney Company 11 bottom right, 91 top

Getty Images: 20 top right,173 bottom

Image Bank: /Derik Murray 80 background

Charles Walker Collection/Images Colour Library: 1 background, 4 /5, 8 left, 13 top right, 17 top right, 22, 27, 30, 31 bottom, 36, 41 bottom, 42, 49 background, 51 bottom, 60 bottom, 66, 70/71 background, 73 top, 85, 88, 89 background, 90, 97, 99, 103, 114, 116, 117, 119 bottom, 120, 122, 123, 155 background, 158, 159, 161, 163 bottom left, 168, 170, 171 top, 174, 175, 177 top, 179 background, 183 top

Image Select: 35, 60 top, 105, 111 top, 126 background

MSI: 57

Peter Newark's Pictures: 124 top

Pat Hodgson Library: 15, 17 background, 21 bottom left, 38, 49, 157 background, 167

Rex Features: 26, 48, 53, 56, 58, 59, 61, 65; /Brendon Beirne 102; /Chris Capstick 137 top; /Clive Dixon 151; /Dalmas 131; /David McEnery 127; /Globe Photos Inc. 64; /Patrick Barth 95; /Robert Judges 136; /SIPA Press 69, 150; /The Times 147; /Charles Best / Uri Geller Enterprises 137 bottom

Tony Stone Images: 31 top, 50, /Michael Dunning 63, /Robert Hallman 176, /Robert van der Hils 94